New Perspectives on
Historical Writing

WITHDRAWN

Books are to be returned on or before

D0300153

WITHDRAWN

New Perspectives on
Historical Writing

Edited by Peter Burke

LIVERPOOL JOHN MOORES UNIVERSITY
Aldham Roberts L.R.C.
TEL. 051 231 3701/3634

Polity Press

Copyright © this collection, Polity Press 1991
Chapters 1 and 11 © Peter Burke; chapter 2 © Jim Sharpe; chapter 3 © Joan Scott;
chapter 4 © Henk Wesseling; chapter 5 © Giovanni Levi; Chapter 6 © Gwyn
Prins; chapter 7 © Australian Journal of French Studies 1986; chapter 8
© Ivan Gaskell; chapter 9 © Richard Tuck; chapter 10 © Roy Porter

First published 1991 by Polity Press
in association with Blackwell Publishers
First published in paperback 1992

Editorial office:
Polity Press, 65 Bridge Street,
Cambridge CB2 1UR, UK

Marketing and production:
Blackwell Publishers
108 Cowley Road, Oxford OX4 1JF, UK

All rights reserved. Except for the quotation
of short passages for the purposes of criticism
and review, no part of this publication may be
reproduced, stored in a retrieval system, or
transmitted, in any form or by any means,
electronic, mechanical, photocopying, recording or
otherwise, without the prior permission of the
publisher.

Except in the United States of America, this book
is sold subject to the condition that it shall
not, by way of trade or otherwise, be lent,
re-sold, hired out, or otherwise circulated without
the publisher's prior consent in any form of
binding or cover other than that in which it is
published and without a similar condition
including this condition being imposed on the
subsequent purchaser.

ISBN 0–7456–0501–X
ISBN 0–7456–1082–X

British Library Cataloguing in Publication Data
A CIP catalogue record for this book is available from
the British Library.

Typeset in 10 on 12pt Times
by Hope Services (Abingdon) Ltd.
Printed in Great Britain by
T. J. Press (Padstow) Ltd, Padstow, Cornwall

Printed on acid-free paper

Contents

Contributors

Peter Burke is Reader in Cultural History, University of Cambridge, and Fellow of Emmanuel College.

Jim Sharpe is Senior Lecturer in History, University of York.

Joan Scott is Professor of Social Science at the Institute for Advanced Study, Princeton.

Henk Wesseling is Professor of History, University of Leiden, and Director of the Institute for the History of European Expansion.

Giovanni Levi is Professor of History, University of Venice.

Gwyn Prins is Director of Studies in History and Fellow of Emmanuel College.

Robert Darnton is Professor of History, Princeton University.

Ivan Gaskell is Margaret S. Winthrop Curator of Paintings at the Harvard University Art Museums.

Richard Tuck is Lecturer in History, University of Cambridge and Fellow of Jesus College.

Roy Porter is Senior Lecturer in the History of Medicine, The Wellcome Institute, London.

1

Overture: the New History, its Past and its Future

Peter Burke

In the last generation or so the universe of historians has been expanding at a dizzying rate.[1] National history, which was dominant in the nineteenth century, now has to compete for attention with world history and with local history (once left to antiquarians and amateurs). There are many new fields, often supported by specialized journals. Social history, for example, became independent of economic history only to fragment, like some new nation, into historical demography, labour history, urban history, rural history, and so on.

Again, economic history has split into old and new. The new economic history of the 1950s and 1960s (now middle-aged, if not older) is too well-known to need discussion here.[2] There has also been a shift among economic historians from a concern with production to a concern with consumption, a shift which makes it increasingly difficult to separate economic from social and cultural history. The history of management is a new interest, but one which blurs if it does not dissolve the boundaries between economic and administrative history. Another specialization, the history of advertising, straddles economic history and the history of communication. Today, the very identity of economic history is threatened by a takeover bid from a youthful but ambitious enterprise, the history of the environment, sometimes known as eco-history.

Political history too is divided, not only into the so-called high and low schools, but also between historians concerned with centres of government and those interested in politics at the grassroots. The territory of the political has expanded, in the sense that historians (following theorists such as Michel Foucault) are increasingly inclined to discuss the struggle for power at the level of the factory, the school, or even the family. The price of such expansion, however, is a kind of identity crisis. If politics is everywhere, is there any need for political history?[3] A similar problem faces cultural historians, as they turn away from a narrow but precise definition of culture in terms of art, literature, music etc, towards a more anthropological definition of the field.

In this expanding and fragmenting universe, there is an increasing need for orientation. What is the so-called new history? How new is it? Is it a temporary fashion or a long-term trend? Will it – or should it – replace traditional history, or can the rivals coexist in peace?

It is to answer these questions that the present volume has been designed. A comprehensive survey of the varieties of contemporary history would have left no space for more than a superficial discussion. For this reason the decision was taken to concentrate attention on a few relatively recent movements.[4] The essays on these movements are concerned with much the same fundamental problems, at least implicitly. It may be useful to confront these problems at the start, and to place them in the context of long-term changes in the writing of history.

What is the New History?

The phrase 'the new history' is best known in France. *La nouvelle histoire* is the title of a collection of essays edited by the distinguished French medievalist Jacques Le Goff. Le Goff has also helped edit a massive three-volume collection of essays, concerned with 'new problems', 'new approaches' and 'new objects'.[5] In these cases it is clear what the new history is: it is a history 'made in France', the country of *la nouvelle vague* and *le nouveau roman*, not to mention *la nouvelle cuisine*. More exactly, it is the history associated with the so-called *école des Annales*, grouped around the journal *Annales: économies, sociétés, civilisations*.

What is this *nouvelle histoire*? A positive definition is not easy; the movement is united only in what it opposes, and the pages which follow will demonstrate the variety of the new approaches. It is therefore difficult to offer more than a vague description, characterizing the new history as total history (*histoire totale*) or as structural history. Hence there may be a case for imitating medieval theologians faced with the problem of defining God, and opting for a *via negativa*, in other words for defining the new history in terms of what it is not, of what its practitioners oppose.

The new history is history written in deliberate reaction against the traditional 'paradigm', that useful if imprecise term put into circulation by the American historian of science Thomas Kuhn.[6] It will be convenient to describe this traditional paradigm as 'Rankean history', after the great German historian Leopold von Ranke (1795–1886), although he was less confined by it than his followers were. (Just as Marx was not a Marxist, Ranke was not a Rankean). We might also call this paradigm the common-sense view of history, not to praise it but to make the point that it has often – too often – been assumed to be *the* way of doing history, rather than being perceived as one among various possible approaches to the past. For the sake of simplicity and clarity, the contrast between old and new history might be summed up in seven points.

1. According to the traditional paradigm, history is essentially concerned with politics. In the confident Victorian phrase of Sir John Seeley, Regius Professor of History at Cambridge, 'History is past politics: politics is present history.' Politics was assumed to be essentially concerned with the state; in other words it was national and international rather than local. However, it did include the history of the Church as an institution and also what the military theorist Karl von Clausewitz defined as 'the continuation of policies by other means', that is, war. Although other kinds of history – the history of art, for example, or the history of science – were not altogether excluded by the traditional paradigm, they were marginalized in the sense of being considered peripheral to the interests of 'real' historians.

The new history, on the other hand, has come to be concerned with virtually every human activity. 'Everything has a history,' as the scientist J. B. S. Haldane once wrote; that is, everything has a past which can in principle be reconstructed and related to the rest of the past.[7] Hence the slogan 'total history', so dear to the *Annales* historians. The first half of the century witnessed the rise of the history of ideas. In the last thirty years we have seen a number of remarkable histories of topics which had not previously been thought to possess a history, for example, childhood, death, madness, the climate, smells, dirt and cleanliness, gestures, the body (as Roy Porter shows in chapter 10 below), femininity (discussed by Joan Scott in chapter 3) reading (discussed by Robert Darnton in chapter 7), speaking, and even silence.[8] What had previously been considered as unchanging is now viewed as a 'cultural construction', subject to variation over time as well as in space.

The cultural relativism implicit here deserves to be emphasized. The philosophical foundation of the new history is the idea that reality is socially or culturally constituted. The sharing of this idea, or assumption, by many social historians and social anthropologists helps explain the recent convergence between these two disciplines, referred to more than once in the chapters which follow (pp. 98, 134). This relativism also undermines the traditional distinction between what is central in history and what is peripheral.

2. In the second place, traditional historians think of history as essentially a narrative of events, while the new history is more concerned with the analysis of structures. One of the most famous works of history of our time, Fernand Braudel's *Mediterranean*, dismisses the history of events *histoire événementielle*) as no more than the foam on the waves of the sea of history.[9] According to Braudel, economic and social changes over the long term *la longue durée*) and geo-historical changes over the very long term are what really matter. Although there has recently been something of a reaction against this view (discussed on p. 235 below) and events are no longer dismissed as easily as they used to be, the history of structures of various kinds continues to be taken very seriously.

3. In the third place, traditional history offers a view from above, in the sense that it has always concentrated on the great deeds of great men, statesmen, generals, or occasionally churchmen. The rest of humanity was allocated a minor role in the drama of history. The existence of this rule is revealed by reactions to its transgression. When the great Russian writer Alexander Pushkin was working on an account of a peasant revolt and its leader Pugachev, Tsar Nicholas's comment was that 'such a man has no history.' In the 1950s, when a British historian wrote a thesis about a popular movement in the French Revolution, one of his examiners asked him, 'Why do you bother with these bandits?'[10]

On the other hand (as Jim Sharpe shows in chapter 2), a number of the new historians are concerned with 'history from below', in other words with the views of ordinary people and with their experience of social change. The history of popular culture has received a great deal of attention. Historians of the Church are beginning to examine its history from below as well as from above.[11] Intellectual historians too have shifted their attention away from great books, or great ideas – their equivalent of great men – to the history of collective mentalities or to the history of discourses or 'languages', the language of scholasticism, for example, or the language of the common law (cf. Richard Tuck's essay, chapter 9 below).[12]

4. In the fourth place, according to the traditional paradigm, history should be based on the documents. One of Ranke's greatest achievements was his exposure of the limitations of narrative sources – let us call them chronicles – and his stress on the need to base written history on official records, emanating from governments and preserved in archives. The price of this achievement was the neglect of other kinds of evidence. The period before the invention of writing was dismissed as 'prehistory'.

However, the 'history from below' movement in its turn exposed the limitations of this kind of document. Official records generally express the official point of view. To reconstruct the attitudes of heretics and rebels, such records need to be supplemented by other kinds of source.

In any case, if historians are concerned with a greater variety of human activities than their predecessors, they must examine a greater variety of evidence. Some of this evidence is visual, some of it oral (see Ivan Gaskell and Gwyn Prins in chapters 8 and 6). There is also statistical evidence: trade figures, population figures, voting figures, and so on. The heyday of quantitative history was probably the 1950s and 1960s, when some enthusiasts claimed that only quantitative methods were reliable. There has been a reaction against such claims, and to some extent against the methods as well, but interest in a more modest quantitative history continues to grow. In Britain, for example, an Association for History and Computing was founded in 1987.

5. According to the traditional paradigm, memorably articulated by the philosopher-historian R. G. Collingwood, 'When an historian asks "Why did Brutus stab Caesar?" he means "What did Brutus think, which made him decide to stab Caesar?"'[13] This model of historical explanation has been criticized by more recent historians on a number of grounds, principally because it fails to take account of the variety of historians' questions, often concerned with collective movements as well as individual actions, with trends as well as events.

Why, for example, did prices rise in sixteenth-century Spain? Economic historians do not agree in their answer to this question, but their various responses (in terms of silver imports, population growth and so on) are very far from Collingwood's model. In Fernand Braudel's famous study of the sixteenth-century Mediterranean, first published in 1949, only the third and last part, devoted to the history of events, asks questions remotely like Collingwood's, and even here the author offers a very different kind of answer, emphasising the constraints on his protagonist, King Philip II, and the king's lack of influence on the history of his time.[14]

6. According to the traditional paradigm, History is objective. The historian's task is to give readers the facts, or as Ranke put it in a much-quoted phrase, to tell 'how it actually happened'. His modest disclaimer of philosophical intentions was interpreted by posterity as a proud manifesto for history without bias. In a famous letter to his international team of contributors to the *Cambridge Modern History*, published from 1902 onwards, its editor, Lord Acton, urged them that 'our Waterloo must be one that satisfies French and English, Germans and Dutch

alike' and that readers should be unable to tell where one contributor laid down his pen and another took it up.[15]

Today, this ideal is generally considered to be unrealistic. However hard we struggle to avoid the prejudices associated with colour, creed, class or gender, we cannot avoid looking at the past from a particular point of view. Cultural relativism obviously applies as much to historical writing itself as to its so-called objects. Our minds do not reflect reality directly. We perceive the world only through a network of conventions, schemata and stereotypes, a network which varies from one culture to another. In this situation, our understanding of conflicts is surely enhanced by a presentation of opposite viewpoints, rather than by an attempt, like Acton's, to articulate a consensus. We have moved from the ideal of the Voice of History to that of heteroglossia, defined as 'varied and opposing voices' (below, p. 239).[16] It is therefore quite appropriate that this volume should itself take the form of a collective work and that its contributors should speak different mother tongues.

Rankean history was the territory of the professionals. The nineteenth century was the time when history became professionalized, with its departments in universities and its trade journals like the *Historische Zeitschrift* and the *English Historical Review*. Most of the leading new historians are also professionals, with the distinguished exception of the late Philippe Ariès, who liked to describe himself as 'a Sunday historian'. One way to describe the achievements of the *Annales* group is to say that they have shown that economic, social and cultural history can meet the exacting professional standards set by Ranke for political history.

All the same, their concern with the whole range of human activity encourages them to be inter-disciplinary in the sense of learning from and collaborating with social anthropologists, economists, literary critics, psychologists, sociologists, and so on. Historians of art, literature and science, who used to pursue their interests more or less in isolation from the main body of historians, are now making more regular contact with them. The history-from-below movement also reflects a new determination to take ordinary people's views of their own past more seriously than professional historians used to do.[17] The same is true for some forms of oral history (below, p. 114). In this sense too heteroglossia is essential to the new history.

How New is the New History?

Who invented – or discovered – the new history? The phrase is sometimes used of developments in the 1970s and 1980s, a period in which the reaction against the traditional paradigm has become world-wide, involving historians in Japan, India, Latin America and elsewhere. The essays in this volume focus on this period in particular. It is clear, however, that many of the changes which have taken place in historical writing in these two decades are part of a longer trend.

For many people, the new history is associated with Lucien Febvre and Marc Bloch, who founded the journal *Annales* in 1929 to promote their approach, and in the next generation, with Fernand Braudel. It would indeed be difficult to deny the importance of the movement for the renewal of history led by these men. However, they were not alone in their revolt against the Rankeans. In Britain in the 1930s, Lewis Namier and R. H. Tawney both rejected the narrative of events for some kind of structural history. In Germany around the year 1900, Karl Lamprecht made himself unpopular in the profession by his challenge to the traditional paradigm. The contemptuous phrase *histoire événementielle*, 'event-centred history', was coined at this time, a generation before the age of Braudel, Bloch and Febvre.[18] It expresses the ideas of a group of scholars centred on the great French sociologist Emile Durkheim and his journal the *Année Sociologique*, a journal which helped inspire the *Annales*.

Even the phrase 'the new history' has a history of its own. The earliest use of the term known to me dates from 1912, when the American scholar James Harvey Robinson published a book with this title. The contents matched the label. 'History,' wrote Robinson, 'includes every trace and vestige of everything that man has done or thought since first he appeared on the earth.' In other words, he believed in total history. As for method, 'The New History' – I am quoting Robinson again – 'will avail itself of all those discoveries that are being made about mankind by anthropologists, economists, psychologists and sociologists.'[19] This movement for a new history was not successful in the United States at the time, but the more recent American enthusiasm for *Annales* becomes more intelligible if we remember this local background.

There is no good reason to stop in 1912, or even in 1900. It has been argued recently that the replacement of an old history by a new one (more objective and less literary) is a recurrent theme in the history of historical writing.[20] Such claims were made by the school of Ranke in the nineteenth century, by the great Benedictine scholar Jean Mabillon, who formulated new methods of source criticism in the seventeenth century, and by the Greek historian Polybius, who denounced some of his colleagues as mere rhetoricians a hundred and fifty years before the birth of Christ. In the first case at least, the claim to novelty was self-conscious. In 1867, the great Dutch historian Robert Fruin published an essay called 'The New Historiography', a defence of scientific, Rankean history.[21]

Attempts to write a wider history than that of political events also go back a long way. It was in the later nineteenth century that economic history was established in Germany, Britain and elsewhere as an alternative to the history of the state. In 1860 the Swiss scholar Jacob Burckhardt published a study of *The Civilization of the Renaissance in Italy*, concentrating on cultural history and describing trends rather than narrating events. The sociologists of the nineteenth century, such as Auguste Comte, Herbert Spencer – not to mention Karl Marx – were extremely interested in history but rather contemptuous of professional historians. They were interested in structures, not events, and the new history' owes a debt to them which is not often acknowledged.

They in turn owe a debt to predecessors they did not often recognize, the historians of the Enlightenment, among them Voltaire, Gibbon (despite the remark I quoted earlier), Robertson, Vico, Möser, and others. In the eighteenth century there was an international movement for the writing of a kind of history which would not be confined to military and political events but was concerned with laws, with trade, with the *manière de penser* of a given society, with its manners and customs, with the 'spirit of the age'. In Germany in particular there was a lively interest in world history.[22] Studies of the history of women were published by the Scotsman William Alexander and by Christoph Meiners, a professor at the University of Göttingen (a centre of the new social history in the late eighteenth century).[23]

Thus the alternative history discussed in this volume has a reasonably long ancestry (even if the great-great-grandparents might not recognize their descendants). What is new is not its existence so much as the fact that its practitioners are now extremely numerous and that they refuse to be marginalized.

Problems of Definition

The purpose of this volume is not to celebrate the new history (despite the agreement of the contributors that at least some kinds of it are worthwhile, indeed necessary) but to assess its strengths and weaknesses.

The movement for change has arisen from a widespread sense of the inadequacy of the traditional paradigm. This sense of inadequacy cannot be understood unless we look beyond the historian's craft, at changes in the wider world. Decolonization and feminism, for example, are two movements which have obviously had a great impact on recent historical writing, as the chapters by Henk Wesseling and Joan Scott make abundantly clear. In the future, the ecological movement is likely to have more and more influence on the way in which history is written.

Indeed, it has already inspired a number of studies. Braudel's famous monograph on the Mediterranean attracted attention when it was first published in 1949 by the amount of space it devoted to the physical environment – land and sea, mountains and islands. Today, however, Braudel's picture looks curiously static because the author did not seriously consider the ways in which the environment was modified by the presence of man destroying forests, for example, in order to build the galleys which figure so prominently in the pages of *The Mediterranean*.

A more dynamic eco-history has been offered by a number of writers. William Cronon has written a fine study of colonial New England focused on the effects of the arrival of the Europeans on the plant and animal communities of the region, noting the disappearance of beavers and bears, cedars and white pines and the increasing importance of European grazing animals. On a very different scale, Alfred Crosby has discussed what he calls 'the biological expansion of Europe' between 900 and 1900 and the place of European diseases in clearing the way for the successful establishment of 'Neo-Europes' from New England to New Zealand.[24]

For internal and external reasons alike, it is not unreasonable to speak of the crisis of the traditional paradigm of historical writing. However, the new paradigm also has its problems: problems of definition, problems of sources, problems of method, problems of explanation. These problems will recur in specific chapters but it may be worth offering a brief discussion of all of them at this point.

Problems of definition occur because the new historians are pushing into unfamiliar territory. They begin, as explorers of other cultures usually do, with a sort of negative image of what they are looking for. The history of the Orient has been perceived by occidental historians as the opposite of their own, eliminating differences between the Middle and Far East, China and Japan, and so on.[25] As Henk Wesseling points out below (chapter 4), world history has often been viewed – by westerners – as the study of the relations between the west and the rest, ignoring interactions between Asia and Africa, Asia and America, and so on. Again, history from below was originally conceptualized as the inversion of history from above, with 'low' culture in place of high culture. In the course of their research, however, scholars have become increasingly aware of the problems inherent in this dichotomy.

If popular culture, for example, is the culture of 'the people', who are the people? Are they everyone, the poor, the 'subordinate classes', as the Marxist intellectual Antonio Gramsci used to call them? Are they the illiterate or the uneducated? We cannot assume that economic, political and cultural divisions in a given society necessarily coincide. And what is education? Is it only the training handed out in certain official institutions like schools or universities? Are ordinary people uneducated or do they simply have a different education, a different culture from elites?

It should not of course be assumed that all ordinary people have the same experiences, and the importance of distinguishing women's history from that of men is underlined by Joan Scott in chapter 3. In some parts of the world, from Italy to Brazil, people's history is often called 'the history of the vanquished', thus assimilating the experiences of the subordinate classes in the west to those of the colonized.[26] However, differences between these experiences also need to be discussed.

The phrase 'history from below' seems to offer an escape from these difficulties, but it generates problems of its own. It changes its meaning in different contexts. Should a political history from below discuss the views and actions of everyone who is excluded from power, or should it deal with politics at a local or grass-roots' level? Should a history of the Church from below look at religion from the point of view of the laity, whatever their social status? Should a history of medicine from below concern itself with folk-healers as opposed to professional physicians, or with the patients' experiences and diagnoses of illness?[27] Should a military history from below deal with the ordinary soldier's Agincourt or Waterloo, as John Keegan has done so memorably, or should it concentrate on the civilian experience of war?[28] Should a history of education from below turn from the ministers and theorists of education to the ordinary teachers, as Jacques Ozouf has done, for example, or should it present schools from the point of view of the pupils?[29] Should an economic history from below focus on the small trader or the small consumer?

One reason for the difficulty of defining the history of popular culture is that the notion of 'culture' is if anything even more difficult to pin down than the notion of 'popular'. The so-called 'opera-house' definition of culture (as high art, literature, music and so on) was narrow but at least it was precise. A wide notion of culture is central to the new history.[30] The state, social groups, and even gender or society itself are considered to be culturally constructed. If we use the term in a wide sense, however, we have at least to ask ourselves, what does *not* count as culture?

Another example of a new approach which has run into problems of definition is the history of everyday life, *Alltagsgeschichte* as the Germans call it. The phrase itself is not new: *la vie quotidienne* was the title of a series launched by the French publishers Hachette in the 1930s. What is new is the importance given to everyday life in contemporary historical writing, especially since the publication of Braudel's famous study of 'material civilization' in 1967.[31] Once dismissed as trivial, the history of everyday life is now viewed by some historians as the only real history, the centre to which everything else must be related. The everyday is also at the crossroads of recent approaches in sociology (from Michel de Certeau to Erving Goffman), and philosophy (whether Marxist or phenomenological).[32]

What these approaches have in common is their concern with the world of ordinary experience (rather than society in the abstract) as their point of departure, together with an attempt to view daily life as problematic, in the sense of showing that behaviour or values which are taken for granted in one society are dismissed as self-evidently absurd in another. Historians, like social anthropologists, now try to uncover the latent rules of daily life (the 'poetics' of the everyday, as the Russian semiotician Juri Lotman puts it) and to show their readers how to be a father or a daughter, a ruler or a saint, in a given culture.[33] At this point social and cultural history seem to be dissolving into one another. Some practitioners describe themselves as 'new' cultural historians, others as 'socio-cultural' historians.[34] In any case, the impact of cultural relativism on historical writing seems inescapable.

However, as the sociologist Norbert Elias has pointed out in an important essay, the notion of the everyday is less precise and more complicated than it looks. Elias distinguishes eight current meanings of the term, from private life to the world of ordinary people.[35] The everyday includes actions – Braudel defines it as the realm of routine – and also attitudes, which we might call mental habits. It may even include ritual. Ritual, a marker of special occasions in the life of individuals and communities, is often defined in opposition to the everyday. On the other hand, foreign visitors frequently notice everyday rituals in the life of every society – ways of eating, forms of greeting, and so on – which the locals fail to perceive as rituals at all.

Equally difficult to describe or analyse is the relation between everyday structures and change. From within the everyday seems timeless. The challenge for the social historian is to show how it is in fact part of history, to relate everyday life to great events like the Reformation or the French Revolution, or to long-term trends like westernization or the rise of capitalism. The famous sociologist Max Weber coined a famous term which may be useful here: 'routinization' (*Veralltäglichung*, literally 'quotidianization'). One focus of attention for social historians might be the process of interaction between major events and trends on one side and the structures of everyday life on the other. To what extent, by what means, and over what period did the French or the Russian Revolution (say) penetrate the daily life of different social groups, to what extent and how successfully was it resisted?

Problems of Sources

The greatest problems for the new historians, however, are surely those of sources and methods. It has already been suggested that when historians began to ask new kinds of questions about the past, to choose new objects of research, they had to look for new kinds of sources to supplement official documents. Some turned to oral history, discussed in chapter 6; others to the evidence of images (chapter 8); others to statistics. It has also proved possible to re-read certain kinds of official records in new ways. Historians of popular culture, for example, have made great use of judicial records, especially the interrogations of suspects. Two famous studies of history from below are based on inquisition records, Le Roy Ladurie's *Montaillou* (1975), discussed in chapter 2, and Ginzburg's *The Cheese and the Worms* (1986).

However, all these sources raise awkward problems. Historians of popular culture try to reconstruct ordinary, everyday assumptions on the basis of the records of what were extraordinary events in the lives of the accused: interrogations and trials. They try to reconstruct what ordinary people thought on the basis of what the accused, who may not have been a typical group, were prepared to say in the unusual (not to say terrifying) situation in which they found themselves. It is therefore necessary to read the documents between the lines. There is nothing wrong with trying to read between the lines, particularly when the attempt is made by historians with the finesse of a Ginzburg or a Le Roy Ladurie.

All the same, the principles underlying such reading are not always clear. It is only fair to admit that to portray the socially invisible (working women, for example) or to listen to the inarticulate, the silent majority of the dead (however necessary as part of total history) is an enterprise more hazardous than is usually the case with traditional history. This is not always the case. The political history of the age of Charlemagne, for example, is based on sources at least as sparse and as unreliable as the history of popular culture in the sixteenth century.[36]

A good deal of attention has been given to oral evidence, some of it by historians of Africa, such as Jan Vansina, concerned with the reliability of oral traditions over centuries, and some of it by contemporary historians such as Paul Thompson, reconstructing the experience of life in the Edwardian era. The problem of the influence of the historian-interviewer and of the interview situation on the testimony of the witness has been discussed.[37] Yet it is only fair to admit that the criticism of oral testimonies has not yet reached the sophistication of the critique of documents, which historians have been practising for centuries. Some idea of the distance travelled in a quarter of a century – and of the long way still to go – may be gained by comparing the first edition of Vansina's study of oral tradition, first published in 1961, with the completely rewritten version of 1985.[38]

The situation is rather similar in the case of photographs, images and more generally the evidence of material culture. Recent work on photography (including film) has unmasked the assumption that the camera is an objective record of reality, emphasizing not only the selection made by photographers according to their interests, beliefs, values, prejudices and so on, but also their debt, conscious or unconscious, to pictorial conventions. If some Victorian photographs of rural life resemble seventeenth-century Dutch landscapes, this may well be because the photographers knew the paintings and posed their figures accordingly in order to produce, as Thomas Hardy put it in the subtitle to *Under the Greenwood Tree*, 'a painting of the Dutch school'. Like historians, photographers offer not reflections of reality but representations of it. Some important steps have been taken toward the source-criticism of photographic images, but here too there is still a long way to go.[39]

In the case of pictorial images, discussed below by Ivan Gaskell, the climate of enthusiasm for the decoding of their iconography or iconology in the middle of the twentieth century, the age of such virtuosos as Erwin Panofsky and Edgar Wind, has been succeeded by an ice age of relative scepticism. The criteria for the interpretation of latent meanings in particular are difficult indeed to formulate.[40] The problems of iconography become even more awkward when historians of other topics try to use pictures for their own purposes, as evidence of religious or political attitudes. It is all too easy to argue in a circle, reading an image by Albrecht Dürer (say) as a symptom of a spiritual crisis, and then presenting the image as an argument for the existence of the crisis.[41]

Material culture is of course the traditional province of the archaeologists, studying periods for which no written records exist. However, there is no good reason to restrict archaeological methods to prehistory, and archaeologists have in fact moved on to study the Middle Ages, the early Industrial Revolution, and more recently a wider range of periods, from colonial America to the consumer society of today.[42]

Historians are beginning to emulate them, if not by digging up the past (Versailles and other major buildings of the early modern period are happily in no need of excavation), then at least by paying more attention to physical objects. Arguments about the rise of individualism and privacy in the early modern period are now based not only on the evidence of diary-keeping, but also on such changes as the rise of individual cups (in place of communal bowls) and chairs (in place of communal benches) and the development of specialized bedrooms.[43]

In this instance, however, it is difficult not to wonder whether material culture is being utilized to do anything more than confirm a hypothesis founded in the first instance on literary evidence. Can the archaeology of the period since 1500 (in the West at least) aspire to anything more? The late Sir Moses Finley once suggested that 'certain kinds of documentation render archaeology more or less unnecessary,' sweeping industrial archaeology into the waste-basket in a single phrase.[44] His challenge deserves a serious response, but a thorough assessment of the value of the evidence of material culture for post-medieval history remains to be made.

Ironically enough, the history of material culture, an area which has attracted a great deal of interest in the last few years, is based less on the study of the artefacts themselves than on literary sources. Historians concerned with what has been called the social life of things' – or more exactly with the social life of groups as revealed by their use of things – rely heavily on such evidence as descriptions by travellers (which tell us much about the location and the functions of particular objects) or inventories of possessions, which are amenable to analysis by quantitative methods.[45]

The greatest – and the most controversial – innovation in method in the last generation has surely been the rise and spread of quantitative methods, sometimes described ironically as 'Cliometrics', in other words the vital statistics of the goddess of history. The approach is of course one of long standing among economic historians and historical demographers. What is or was new was its spread in the 1960s and 1970s to other kinds of history. In the United States, for example, there is a 'new political history' whose practitioners count votes, whether cast in elections or in parliaments.[46] In France, 'serial history' (*histoire sérielle*), so-called because the data are arranged in series over time, has gradually been extended from the study of prices (in the 1930s) to the study of population (in the 1950s) to the so-called 'third level' of the history of religious or secular mentalities.[47] One famous study of the so-called 'dechristianization' of modern France draws the bulk of its evidence from the declining figures for Easter communion. Another, focused on Provence in the eighteenth century, studies changing attitudes to death as they are revealed in trends in the formulae of some 30,000 wills, noting the decline in references to the 'court of heaven', or in bequests for elaborate funerals or for masses for the dead.[48]

In recent years statistics, aided by computers, have even invaded the citadel of Rankean history, the archives. The American National Archives, for example, now have a 'Machine-Readable Data Division', and archivists are beginning to worry about the conservation and storage of punched tapes as well as manuscripts. As a result, historians are more and more inclined to see earlier archives, such as the archives of the Inquisition, as 'data banks' which can be exploited by quantitative methods.[49]

The introduction into historical discourse of large numbers of statistics has tended to polarize the profession into supporters and opponents. Both sides have tended to exaggerate the novelty of the problems posed by the use of figures. Statistics can be faked, but so can texts. Statistics are easy to misinterpret, but so are texts. Machine-readable data are not user-friendly, but the same goes for many manuscripts, written in almost illegible hands or on the verge of disintegration. What is needed is an aid to discrimination, to discovering what sorts of statistics are most reliable, to what extent and for what purposes. The notion of the series, fundamental to serial history, needs to be treated as problematic, especially when changes are studied over the long term. The longer the period, the less likely it is that the units in the series – wills, records of Easter communions, or whatever – are homogeneous. But if they are subject to change themselves, how can they be used as measures of other changes?

In other words, what is required (as in the case of photographs and other new sources discussed already) is a new 'diplomatic' . This was the term used by the Benedictine scholar Jean Mabillon in his guide to the use of charters, at a time (the late seventeenth century) when the appeal to this sort of evidence was novel and aroused the suspicion of more traditional historians.[50] Who will be the Mabillon of statistics, photographs or oral history?

Problems of Explanation

It has already been suggested that the expansion of the historian's field entails rethinking historical explanation, since cultural and social trends cannot be analysed in the same way as political events. They require more structural explanation. Whether they like it or not, historians are having to concern themselves with questions which have long interested sociologists and other social scientists. Who are the true agents in history, individuals or groups? Can they successfully resist the pressures of social, political or cultural structures? Are these structures merely constraints on freedom of action, or do they enable agents to make more choices?[51]

In the 1950s and 1960s, economic and social historians were attracted by more or less determinist models of historical explanation, whether they gave primacy to economic factors, like the Marxists, to geography, like Braudel, or to population movements (as in the case of the so-called 'Malthusian model' of social change). Today, however, as Giovanni Levi suggests in his chapter on microhistory, the most attractive models are those which emphasize the freedom of choice of ordinary people, their strategies, their capacity to exploit the inconsistencies or incoherences of social and political systems, to find loopholes through which they can wriggle or interstices in which they can survive (cf. pp. 93 ff., below).

The expansion of the historical universe has had repercussions on political history as well, for political events too may be explained in various ways. Historians who study the French Revolution, say, from below, are likely to give it a rather different kind of explanation from those who concentrate on the actions and intentions of the leaders. Even the scholars who concentrate on leaders sometimes diverge from traditional models of historical explanation by invoking their unconscious as well as their conscious motives, on the grounds that these models overestimate the importance of consciousness and rationality.

For example, a group of so-called psychohistorians, most of them living in the United States (where psychoanalysis has penetrated the culture more deeply than elsewhere) have tried to incorporate the insights of Freud into historical practice. They range from the psychoanalyst Erik Erikson, who caused something of a sensation in the 1950s with his study of the identity problems of 'Young Man Luther', to the historian Peter Gay, who both preaches and practises psychohistory. It is scarcely surprising to find that their approach has stirred up controversy and that they have been accused of 'shrinking history', in other words of reducing the complexities of an individual adult (or a conflict between adults) to the relationship of an infant with his parents.[52]

To illustrate current controversies over historical explanation, it may be useful to take the example of Hitler. Earlier debates, such as the one between H. R. Trevor-Roper and A. J. P. Taylor about the relative importance of Hitler's long-term and short-term aims, assumed the validity of the traditional model of historical explanation in terms of conscious intentions. More recently, however, the debate has widened. In the first place, a few historians, such as Robert Waite, have offered interpretations of Hitler in terms of unconscious intentions and even of psychopathology, stressing his abnormal sexuality, the trauma of his mother's death (after treatment by a Jewish doctor), and so on.[53]

Another group of historians dismiss what they call 'intentionalism' altogether, in the sense that they treat the problem of Hitler's motives or drives as relatively marginal. According to these 'functionalists', as they have been called ('structural historians', as I would prefer to describe them), historical explanations of the policies of the Third Reich need to concentrate on the men around Hitler, on the machinery of government and the decision-making process, and on Nazism as a social movement.[54] There are also historians who combine structural with psychohistorical approaches, and concentrate on explaining what it was in the Nazis which attracted them to Hitler.[55]

What is at once exciting and confusing about the Hitler debate – like many other historical debates in recent years – is that it is no longer conducted according to the rules. The traditional agreement about what constitutes a good historical explanation has broken down. Is this a passing phase, to be replaced by a new consensus, or is it the way in which historical debates will in future be conducted?

If there is to be such a consensus, then the area of what may be called 'historical psychology' (collective psychology) is likely to be of particular importance, linking as it does the debates on conscious and unconscious motivation with those on individual and collective explanations. It is encouraging to see an increasing interest in this area. A recent cluster of monographs centre on the history of ambition, anger, anxiety, fear, guilt, hypocrisy, love, pride, security, and other emotions. All the same, the problems of method involved in the pursuit of these elusive objects of study are far from having been resolved.[56]

In attempting to avoid psychological anachronism, in other words the assumption that people in the past thought and felt just like ourselves, there is a danger of going to the other extreme and 'defamiliarizing' the past so thoroughly that it becomes unintelligible. Historians face a dilemma. If they explain differences in social behaviour in different periods by differences in conscious attitudes or social conventions, they risk superficiality. On the other hand, if they explain differences in behaviour by differences in the deep structure of the social character, they run the risk of denying the freedom and the flexibility of individual actors in the past.

A possible way out of the difficulty is to utilize the sociologist Pierre Bourdieu's notion of the 'habitus' of a particular social group. By the 'habitus' of a group, Bourdieu means the propensity of its members to select responses from a particular cultural repertoire according to the demands of a particular situation or field. Unlike the concept of 'rules', habitus has the great advantage of allowing its users to recognize the extent of individual freedom within certain limits set by the culture.[57]

All the same, problems remain. In my view, the new historians – from Edward Thompson to Roger Chartier – have been largely successful in revealing the inadequacies of traditional materialist and determinist explanations of individual and collective behaviour over the short term and in showing that in everyday life and in moments of crisis alike, it is culture that counts.[58] On the other hand, they have done little to challenge the importance of material factors, of the physical environment and its resources, over the long term. It still seems useful to regard these material factors as setting the agenda, the problems to which individuals, groups and, metaphorically speaking, cultures try to adapt or respond.

Problems of Synthesis

Although the expansion of the historian's universe and the increasing dialogue with other disciplines, from geography to literary theory, are surely to be welcomed, these developments have their price. The discipline of history is now more fragmented than ever before. Economic historians are able to speak the language of economists, intellectual historians the language of philosophers, and social historians the dialects of sociologists and social anthropologists, but, these groups of historians are finding it harder and harder to talk to one another. Do we have to endure this situation, or is there hope for a synthesis?

It is impossible to offer more than a partial, personal view of the problem. My own can be summed up into two opposite points, complementary rather than contradictory. In the first place, the proliferation of sub-disciplines is virtually inevitable. This movement is not confined to history. The historical profession simply offers one example among many of the increasing division of labour in our late industrial (or post-industrial) society. The proliferation has its advantages: it adds to human knowledge, and it encourages more rigorous methods, more professional standards.

There are costs as well as benefits, but we can do something to keep those intellectual costs as low as possible. Non-communication between disciplines or sub-disciplines is not inevitable. In the specific case of history, there are some encouraging signs of *rapprochement*, if not of synthesis.

It is true that, in the first flush of enthusiasm for structural history, the history of events was very nearly thrown overboard. In a similar way, the discovery of social history was sometimes associated with a contempt for political history, an inversion of the prejudice of traditional political historians. New fields such as women's history and the history of popular culture were sometimes treated as if they were independent from (or even opposed to) the history of learned culture and the history of men. Microhistory and the history of everyday life were reactions against the study of grand social trends, society without a human face.

In all the cases I have quoted, it is now possible to observe a reaction against this reaction, a search for the centre. Historians of popular culture are increasingly concerned to describe and analyse the changing relations between the high and the low, 'the intersection of popular culture and the culture of educated people'.[59] Historians of women have widened their interests to include gender relations in general and the historical construction of masculinity as well as femininity.[60] The traditional opposition between events and structures is being replaced by a concern for their interrelationship, and a few historians are experimenting with narrative forms of analysis or analytical forms of narrative (see below, pp. 233 ff.).

Most important of all, perhaps, the long-standing opposition between political and non-political historians is finally dissolving. G. M. Trevelyan's notorious definition of social history as 'history with the politics left out' is now rejected by almost everyone. Instead we find concern with the social element in politics and the political element in society. On one side, political historians no longer confine themselves to high politics, to leaders, to elites. They discuss the geography and sociology of elections and 'the republic in the village'.[61] They examine 'political cultures', the assumptions about politics which form part of everyday life but differ widely from one period or region to another. On the other side, society and culture are now viewed as arenas for decision-making, and historians discuss 'the politics of the family', 'the politics of language', or the ways in which ritual can express or even in some sense create power.[62] The American historian Michael Kammen may well be right in his suggestion that the concept of 'culture', in its wide, anthropological sense, may serve as 'a possible basis' for the 'reintegration' of different approaches to history.[63]

We are still a long way away from the 'total history' advocated by Braudel. Indeed, it would be unrealistic to believe that this goal could ever be attained – but a few more steps have been taken towards it.

NOTES

1 This essay owes a great deal to discussions with Raphael Samuel over many years; to Gwyn Prins and several generations of students at Emmanuel College Cambridge; and more recently to Nilo Odália and the lively audience at my lectures at the Universidade Estadual de São Paulo at Araraquara in 1989.

2 For a famous (and debatable) example, see R. W. Fogel and S. Engerman, *Time on the Cross* (Boston, 1974). There is a judicious assessment of the position of economic history today in D. C. Coleman, *History and the Economic Past* (Oxford, 1987).

3 J. Vincent, *The Formation of the British Liberal Party* (London, 1966).

4 Other varieties are surveyed in *What is History Today?* ed. J. Gardiner (London, 1988).

5 J. Le Goff, (ed.), *La nouvelle histoire* (Paris, 1978); J. Le Goff and P. Nora (eds), *Faire de l'histoire* (3 vols, Paris, 1974). Some of the essays in this collection are available in English: J. Le Goff and P. Nora, (eds), *Constructing the Past* (Cambridge, 1985).

6 T. S. Kuhn, *The Structure of Scientific Revolutions* (New York, 1961).

7 J. B. S. Haldane, *Everything has a History* (London, 1951).

8 P. Ariès, *Centuries of Childhood* tr. R. Baldick (London, 1962); P. Ariès, *The Hour of Our Death* tr. H. Weaver (London, 1981); M. Foucault, *Madness and Civilisation*, tr. R. Howard (London, 1967); E. Le Roy Ladurie, *Times of Feast, Times of Famine* tr. B. Bray (New York, 1971); A. Corbin, *The Foul and the Fragrant*, translation (Leamington, 1986); G. Vigarello, *Concepts of Cleanliness*, translation (Cambridge, 1988); J.-C. Schmitt, (ed.), *Gestures*, special issue, *History and Anthropology* 1 (1984); R. Bauman, *Let Your Words be Few* (Cambridge, 1984).

9 F. Braudel, *The Mediterranean and the Mediterranean World in the Age of Philip II*, tr. S. Reynolds, 2nd edn (2 vols, London 1972–3).

10 The examiner's name was Lewis Namier. R. Cobb, *The Police and the People*, (Oxford, 1970), p. 81.

11 E. Hoornaert et al., *Historia da Igreja no Brasil: ensaio de interpretação a partir do povo*, Petrópolis, 1977.

12 J. G. A. Pocock, 'The Concept of a Language', in *The Language of Political*

Theory, (ed.) A. Pagden (Cambridge, 1987). Cf. D. Kelley, 'Horizons of Intellectual History', *Journal of the History of Ideas* 48 (1987), pp. 143–69, and 'What is Happening to the History of Ideas?' *Journal of the History of Ideas?' Journal of the History of Ideas* 51 (1990), pp. 3–25.

13 R. G. Collingwood, *The Idea of History*, (Oxford, 1946), pp. 213ff.

14 Braudel (1949)

15 Quoted in *Varieties of History*, ed. F. Stern (New York, 1956), p. 249.

16 I take the term from the famous Russian critic Mikhail Bakhtin, in his *Dialogic Imagination*, tr. C. Emerson and M. Holquist (Austin, 1981), pp. xix, 49, 55, 263, 273. Cf. M. de Certeau, *Heterologies: Discourse on the Other*, tr. B. Massumi (Minneapolis, 1986).

17 See almost any issue of the *History Workshop Journal*.

18 Cf. P. Burke, *The French Historical Revolution*, (Cambridge, 1990), p. 113.

19 J. H. Robinson, *The New History* (New York, 1912); cf. J. R. Pole, 'The New History and the Sense of Social Purpose in American Historical Writing' (1973, reprinted in his *Paths to the American Past* (New York, 1979, pp. 271–98).

20 L. Orr, 'The Revenge of Literature', *New Literary History* 18 (1986), pp. 1–22.

21 R. Fruin, 'De nieuwe historiographie', reprinted in his *Verspreide Geschriften* 9 (The Hague, 1904), pp. 410–18.

22 M. Harbsmeier, 'World Histories before Domestication' *Culture and History* 5 (1989) pp. 93–131.

23 W. Alexander, *The History of Women* (London, 1779); C. Meiners, *Geschichte des weiblichen Geschlechts* (4 vols, Hanover, 1788–1800).

24 W. Cronon, *Changes in the Land* (New York, 1983); A. W. Crosby, *Ecological Imperialism* (Cambridge, 1986).

25 There are some sharp comments on this problem in E. Said, *Orientalism* (London 1978).

26 E. De Decca, *1930: o silêncio dos vencidos* (São Paulo, 1981).

27 Cf. R. Porter, 'The Patient's View: Doing Medical History from Below', *Theory and Society* 14 (1985), pp. 175–98.

28 On the ordinary soldiers, see J. Keegan, *The Face of Battle* (London, 1976).

29 J. Ozouf, (ed.), *Nous les maîtres d'école* (Paris, 1967) examines the experience of elementary school-teachers *c*.1914.

30 L. Hunt, (ed.), *The New Cultural History* (Berkeley, 1989).

31 F. Braudel, *Civilisation matérielle et capitalisme* (Paris, 1967); revised ed. *Les structures du quotidien* (Paris, 1979); *The Structures of Everyday Life*, tr. M. Kochan (London, 1981). Cf. J. Kuczynski, *Geschichte des Alltags des Deutschen Volkes* (4 vols, Berlin, 1980–2).

32 M. de Certeau, *L'invention du quotidien* (Paris, 1980); E. Goffman, *The Presentation of Self in Everyday Life* (New York, 1959); H. Lefebvre, *Critique de la vie quotidienne* (3 vols, Paris, 1946–81). Cf. F. Mackie, *The Status of Everyday Life* (London, 1985).

33 J. Lotman, 'The Poetics of Every day Behaviour in Russian Eighteenth-Century Culture', in *The Semiotics of Russian Culture*, ed. J. Lotman and

B. A. Uspenskii (Ann Arbor, 1984), pp. 231–56. A fuller discussion of the problem of writing the history of cultural rules is in P. Burke, *Historical Anthropology of Early Modern Italy* (Cambridge, 1987), pp. 5ff, 21ff.

34   L. Hunt, ed., *The New Cultural History* (Berkeley, 1989)

35   N. Elias, 'Zum Begriff des Alltags' in *Materiellen zur Soziologie des Alltags*, ed. K. Hammerich and M. Klein (Opladen, 1978), pp. 22–9.

36   Cf. P. Burke, *Popular Culture in Early Modern Europe* (London, 1978), chapter 3.

37   R. Samuel and P. Thompson, (eds), *The Myths We Live By* (London, 1990).

38   P. Thompson, *The Voice of the Past* 1978; revised ed., Oxford, 1988); J. Vansina, *Oral Tradition*, tr. H.M. Wright (London, 1965) and *Oral Tradition as History* (Madison, 1985).

39   P. Smith, (ed.), *The Historian and Film* (Cambridge, 1976); A. Trachtenberg, 'Albums of War', *Representations* 9 (1985) pp. 1–32; J. Tagg, *The Burden of Representation: Essays on Photographies and Histories* (Amherst, 1988).

40   E. Panofsky, *Essays in Iconology* (New York, 1939); E. Wind, *Pagan Mysteries in the Renaissance* (London, 1958). A more sceptical point of view is expressed by E. H. Gombrich, 'Aims and Limits of Iconology' in his *Symbolic Images* (London, 1972), pp. 1–22.

41   C. Ginzburg, 'Da Aby Warburg a E. H. Gombrich', *Studi medievali* 8 (1966) pp. 1015–65. His criticism was directed against Fritz Saxl in particular. On iconography for historians of mentalities see, M. Vovelle (ed.) *Iconographie et histoire des mentalités* (Aix, 1979).

42   K. Hudson, *The Archaeology of the Consumer Society* (London, 1983).

43   J. Deetz, *In Small Things Forgotten: the Archaeology of Early American Life* (New York, 1977).

44   M.I. Finley, *The Use and Abuse of History* (London, 1975), p. 101.

45   A. Appadurai, (ed.), *The Social Life of Things* (Cambridge, 1986).

46   W. Aydelotte, *Quantification in History* (Reading, Mass., 1971); A. Bogue, *Clio and the Bitch Goddess: Quantification in American Political History* (Beverly Hills, 1983).

47   P. Chaunu, 'Le quantitatif au 3e niveau' (1973: reprinted in his *Histoire quantitatif, histoire sérielle* (Paris 1978).

48   G. Le Bras, *Etudes de sociologie religieuse* (2 vols, Paris 1955–6): M. Vovelle, *Piété baroque et déchristianisation* (Paris, 1973).

49   G. Henningsen, 'El "Banco de datos" del Santo Oficio', *Boletin de la Real Academia de Historia* 174 (1977), pp. 547–70.

50   J. Mabillon, *De re diplomatica* (Paris, 1681).

51   C. Lloyd, *Explanation in Social History* (Oxford, 1986) offers a general survey. More accessible to non-philosophers is S. James, *The Content of Social Explanation* (Cambridge, 1984).

52   E. Erikson, *Young Man Luther* (New York, 1958); P. Gay, *Freud for Historians* (New York, 1985); D. Stannard, *Shrinking History* (New York, 1980).

53   R. G. L. Waite, *The Psychopathic God: Adolf Hitler* (New York, 1977).

54 I take the distinction between 'intentionalists' and 'functionalists' from T. Mason, 'Intention and Explanation' in *The Führer State, Myth and Reality*, ed. G. Hirschfeld and L. Kettenacker (Stuttgart, 1981), pp. 23–40. My thanks to Ian Kershaw for bringing this article to my attention.

55 P. Lowenberg, 'The Psychohistorical Origins of the Nazi Youth Cohort', *American Historical Review* 76 (1971), pp. 1457–502.

56 J. Delumeau, *La peur en occident* (Paris, 1978); and *Rassurer et protéger* (Paris, 1989); P. N. and C. Z. Stearns, 'Emotionology', *American Historical Review* 90 (1986), pp. 813–36; C. Z. and P. N. Stearns, *Anger* (Chicago, 1986); T. Zeldin, *France 1848–1945* (2 vols, Oxford 1973–7).

57 P. Bourdieu, *Outline of a Theory of Practice*, tr. R. Nice (Cambridge, 1977).

58 The argument is unusually explicit in G. Sider, *Culture and Class in Anthropology and History* (Cambridge and Paris, 1986).

59 A. Gurevich, *Medieval Popular Culture*, tr. J. M. Bak and P. A. Hollingsworth (Cambridge, 1988).

60 Editorial collective, 'Why Gender and History?' *Gender and History* 1 (1989) pp. 1–6.

61 M. Agulhon, *The Republic in the Village*, tr. J. Lloyd (Cambridge, 1982).

62 M. Segalen, *Love and Power in the Peasant Family*, tr. S. Matthews (Cambridge, 1983); O. Smith, *The Politics of Language 1791–1815* (Oxford, 1984); D. Cannadine and S. Price, (eds) *Rituals of Royalty* (Cambridge, 1987).

63 M. Kammen, 'Extending the Reach of American Cultural History' *American Studies* 29 (1984), pp. 19–42.

2

History from Below

Jim Sharpe

On 18 June 1815 a battle was fought near to the Belgian village of Waterloo. As everyone who has studied British history will know, the outcome of that battle was that an Allied army, commanded by the Duke of Wellington, with late but decisive assistance from Prussian forces led by Blücher, defeated a French army commanded by Napoleon Bonaparte, and the fortunes of Europe were thus decided. In the days following the battle, one of those who had helped determine the fate of a continent, Private William Wheeler of the British 51st Foot, wrote a number of letters home to his wife:

> The three days fight is over. I am safe, this is sufficient. I shall now and at every opportunity write the details of the great event, that is what came under my own observation . . . The morning of 18th June broke upon us and found us drenched with rain, benumbed and shaking with the cold . . . You often blamed me for smoking when I was at home last year, but I must tell you had I not had a good stock of tobacco this night I must have given up the Ghost.[1]

Wheeler went on to give his wife a description of the Battle of Waterloo from the sharp end: the experience of enduring French artillery fire, his regiment's destruction of a body of enemy cuirassiers with one volley, the spectacle of heaps of burnt corpses of British guardsmen in the ruins of the château of Hougoumont, the money plundered from a dead French hussar officer shot by a member of a detachment in Wheeler's charge. The history books tell us that Wellington won the battle of Waterloo. In a certain sense, William Wheeler and thousands like him also won it.

Over the past two decades a number of historians, working in a wide variety of periods, countries and types of history, have become aware of the potential for exploring new perspectives on the past offered by such sources as Private Wheeler's correspondence with his wife, and they have become attracted to the idea of exploring history from, as it were, the viewpoint of the private soldier and not the great commander. Traditionally, history has been regarded, from Classical times onwards, as an account of the doings of the great. Interest in broader social and economic history developed in the nineteenth century, but the main subject-matter of history remained the unfolding of elite politics. There were, of course, a number of individuals who felt unhappy with this situation, and as early as 1936 Bertolt Brecht, in his poem 'Questions from a Worker who Reads', offered what is still probably the most direct statement of the need for an alternative perspective to what might be termed 'top person's history'.[2] Yet it is probably fair to say that a serious statement of the possibility of translating this need into action did not come until 1966, when Edward Thompson published an article on 'History from Below' in *The Times Literary Supplement*.[3] Thereafter, the concept of history from below entered the common parlance of historians. By 1985 a volume of essays entitled *History from Below*[4] had been published, while in 1989 a new edition of a book dealing with the historiography of the English Civil Wars and their aftermath called a chapter about recent work on the radicals of the period 'History from Below'.[5] Thus, over the past twenty years or so, a label has been found for that perspective on the past offered by William Wheeler's letters.

This perspective has had an immediate appeal to those historians anxious to broaden the boundaries of their discipline, to open up new areas of research, and, above all, to explore the historical experiences of those men and women whose existence is so often ignored, taken for granted or mentioned in passing in mainstream history. Even today much of the history taught in Britain's sixth forms and universities (and, one suspects, in similar institutions elsewhere) still regards the experience of the mass of the people in the past as either inaccessible or unimportant, or fails to regard it as an historical problem, or, at best, regards the common people as 'one of the problems government has had to handle'.[6] The converse view was stated powerfully by Edward Thompson in 1965, in the preface to one of the major works of English history:

> I am seeking to rescue the poor stockinger, the luddite cropper, the 'obsolete' hand-loom weaver, the 'utopian' artisan, and even the deluded followers of Joanna Southcott, from the enormous condescension of posterity. Their crafts and traditions may have been dying. Their hostility to the new industrialism may have been backward-looking. Their communitarian

ideals may have been fantasies. Their insurrectionary conspiracies may
have been foolhardy. But they lived through these times of acute social
disturbance, and we did not.[7]

Thompson, therefore, identified not only the general problem of
reconstructing the experience of a body of 'ordinary' people. He also
grasped the necessity of trying to understand people in the past, as far as
the modern historian is able, in the light of their own experience and
their own reactions to that experience.

My object in this essay will be to explore, as far as possible with
reference to what might be regarded as a number of the key published
works, some of the potential and problems inherent in the writing of
history from below. In so doing I shall be aware of two rather different,
if in large measure inextricable, themes. The first of these is to introduce
the reader to the sheer diversity of subject-matter that work on what
might, in broad terms, be described as a history from below approach
has produced. It ranges from reconstructing the experiences of medieval
Pyrenean shepherds to those of the elderly former industrial workers
whose reminiscences form the staple of oral history. The second is to
isolate some of the issues, evidential, conceptual and ideological, which
are raised by the study of history from below. The notion of such an
approach to history is very appealing, but, as is so often the case, the
problems involved in studying the past rapidly become more complex
than might appear at first sight.

The prospect of writing history from below, of rescuing the past
experiences of the bulk of the population from either total neglect by
historians or from Thompson's 'enormous condescension of posterity'
is, therefore, an attractive one. But, as we have hinted, the attempt to
study history in this way involves a number of difficulties. The first
revolves around evidence. One has only to read Thompson's study of
the formative years of the English working class to realize that,
whatever criticisms may be made of his interpretation of the subject,
there is little doubt that it is based on a massively broad and rich body of
source material. Generally, however, the further back historians
seeking to reconstruct the experience of the lower orders go, the more
restricted the range of sources at their disposal becomes. As we shall
see, excellent work has been done on such materials as do remain for
early periods, yet the problem is a real one: diaries, memoirs and
political manifestos from which the lives and aspirations of the lower
orders might be reconstructed are sparse before the late eighteenth
century, a few periods (such as the 1640s and 1650s in England)

excepted. Secondly, there are a number of problems of conceptualization. Where, exactly, is 'below' to be located, and what should be done with history from below once it has been written?

The complications inherent in the question of precisely whose history comes from below are illustrated neatly in one of the growth areas of social history in recent years, the study of popular culture in early modern Europe. As far as I can see, apart from regarding it as some sort of residual category, no historian has yet come up with a fully comprehensive definition of what popular culture in that period actually was.[8] The fundamental reason for this is that 'the people', even as far back as the sixteenth century, were a rather varied group, divided by economic stratification, occupational cultures and gender. Such considerations render invalid any simplistic notion of what 'below' might mean in most historical contexts.[9]

The question of the wider significance or purposes of an approach to history from below is equally important. The problems are perhaps best illustrated by reference to the work of historians writing within the Marxist tradition or within the tradition of British labour history. Obviously, the contribution of Marxist historians, here as elsewhere, has been enormous: indeed, one Marxist philosopher has claimed that all of those writing history from below do so in the shadow of Marx's conceptualization of history.[10] Although such claims may seem a little hyperbolic, the social historian's debt to Marx's ideas and to Marxist historians must be acknowledged, and it is certainly not my intention to join the currently fashionable tendency to deprecate one of the world's richest intellectual traditions. Yet it would seem that Marxist historians, before others writing from different traditions suggested the breadth of subject-matter which the social historian might study, have tended to restrict study of history from below to those episodes and movements in which the masses engaged in overt political activity or in familiar areas of economic development. Although he was to transcend such limitations, this was to a large extent the starting-point of Thompson's 1966 essay. The historical background to such a line of thinking has been described more recently by Eric Hobsbawm. Hobsbawm argued that the possibility of what he terms 'grassroots history' was not really apparent before 1789 or thereabouts. 'The history of the common people as a special field of study,' he wrote, 'begins with the history of mass movements in the eighteenth century . . . For the Marxist, or more generally the socialist, interest in grassroots history developed with the growth of the labour movement.' As he went on to point out, this tendency 'imposed some quite effective blinkers on the socialist historians'.[11]

Something of the nature of these blinkers was suggested in a book published in 1957 which might well have been subtitled 'The Breaking of the English Working Class', Richard Hoggart's *The Uses of Literacy*. Discussing different approaches to the study of the working class, Hoggart urged caution on the readers of histories of working-class movements. Like many others, Hoggart came away from many such histories with the impression 'that their authors overrate the place of political activity in working-class life, that they do not always have an adequate sense of the grass-roots of that life.'[12] Thompson in 1966 noted a shift from the older concerns of labour historians with the institutions of labour and with approved leaders and ideology, although he also noted that this process was tending to rob labour history of some of its coherence.[13] Hobsbawm, writing in the light of the subsequent broadening of labour history, was able to make more focused comments on this point. The problem was (as Hoggart implied) that historians of the labour movement, Marxist or otherwise, had studied 'not just any common people, but the common people who could be regarded as ancestors of the movement: not workers as such, so much as Chartists, trade unionists, labour militants'. The history of the labour movement and other institutionalized developments, he averred, should not 'replace the history of the common people themselves'.[14]

Another limitation which mainstream labour history creates for history from below is that of a restriction in period. Readers of the early essay by Thompson and Hobsbawm's later contribution might easily be left (despite the intentions of the authors) with the impression that history from below can only be written for periods from the French Revolution onwards. Hobsbawm, as we have noted, felt that it was the development of mass movements in the late eighteenth century which first alerted scholars to the possibility of writing history from below, and he went on to declare that 'the French Revolution, especially since Jacobinism was revitalised by socialism and the Enlightenment by Marxism, has been the proving ground for this kind of history'. Asking at a slightly later point 'why so much modern grassroots history has emerged from the study of the French Revolution', Hobsbawm cited the mass action of the populace and the archives created by 'a vast and laborious bureaucracy', who documented the actions of the common people, and then turned to classifying and filing their records 'for the benefit of the historian'. This documentation provided a rich seam for later research, and was also, Hobsbawm noted, 'beautifully legible, unlike the crabbed hands of the sixteenth or seventeenth centuries'.[15]

History from below, however, has not merely been written about familiar modern political history by historians who are unable to cope with palaeographic challenges. Indeed, although the concept of history from below was essentially developed by English Marxist historians writing within the traditional chronological bounds of British labour history, perhaps the book using this perspective on the past which has had the widest impact was written by a French scholar and takes a medieval Pyrenean peasant community as its subject matter. Emmanuel Le Roy Ladurie's *Montaillou*, first published in France in 1975, enjoyed more attention, better sales and a wider readership than most works of medieval history.[16] It has, of course, attracted some criticism from within the scholarly community, and a number of questions have been raised about Le Roy Ladurie's methodology and his approach to his sources.[17] Historians working from below must, of course, be as rigorous in these matters as any others, yet *Montaillou* does stand as something of a landmark in writing history from that perspective. As its author pointed out, 'though there are extensive historical studies concerning peasant communities there is very little material available that can be considered the direct testimony of peasants themselves.'[18] Le Roy Ladurie circumvented this problem by basing his book on the inquisitorial records generated by Jacques Fournier, Bishop of Poitiers, during his investigation of heresy between 1318 and 1325. Whatever its drawbacks, *Montaillou* demonstrated not only that history from below could appeal to the general reading public, but also that certain types of official record could be used to explore the mental and material world of past generations.

Indeed, social and economic historians are becoming increasingly used to employing types of documentation whose very usefulness as historical evidence lies in the fact that its compilers were not deliberately and consciously recording for posterity. Many of these compilers, one imagines, would have been surprised, and perhaps disquieted, by the use which recent historians have made of the court cases, parish-register entries, wills and manorial land transactions which they recorded. Such evidence can be employed, as appropriate, to explore explicit actions and ideas or implicit assumptions and to provide a quantitative background to past experiences. As Edward Thompson has noted:

> People were taxed: the hearth-tax lists are appropriated, not by historians of taxation, but by historical demographers. People were tithed: the terriers are appropriated as evidence by historical demographers. People were customary tenants or copyholders: their tenures were enrolled and surrendered in the rolls of the manorial court: these essential sources are interrogated by historians again and again, not only in pursuit of new evidence but in a dialogue in which they propose new questions.[19]

As this quotation suggests, such materials are very varied. Occasionally, as with the materials upon which *Montaillou* was based, they allow the historian to get almost as close to people's words as do the tape-recordings of the oral historian. Oral history has been much used by historians trying to examine the experience of ordinary people, although, of course, there is no self-evident reason why the oral historian should not record the memories of duchesses, plutocrats and bishops as well as miners and factory workers.[20] Yet the oral historian has obvious problems in dealing with people who either died before they were recorded or whose memory has been lost to their successors, and the type of direct testimony they can obtain is denied to historians of earlier periods. Conversely, as we have suggested, sources exist which permit historians of such periods to get close to the experiences of the lower orders.

Le Roy Ladurie used one such source, Jacques Fournier's register. Another work showing how this type of legal record could be employed for a rather different type of history from below came in 1976, with the publication of the Italian edition of Carlo Ginzburg's *The Cheese and the Worms*.[21] Ginzburg's objective was not to reconstruct the mentality and way of life of a peasant community, but rather to explore the intellectual and spiritual world of one individual, a miller named Domenico Scandella (nicknamed Menocchio), born in 1532, who lived in Friuli in north-eastern Italy. Menocchio fell foul of the Inquisition (he was eventually executed, probably in 1600) and the voluminous documentation dealing with his case allowed Ginzburg to reconstruct much of his belief system. The book itself is a remarkable achievement, while Ginzburg's preface provides a useful discussion of the conceptual and methodological problems of reconstructing the culture of the subordinate classes in the pre-industrial world. In particular, he was insistent that 'the fact that a source is not "objective" (for that matter, neither is an inventory) does not mean that it is useless . . . In short, even meagre, scattered and obscure documentation can be put to good use,'[22] and that studying individuals in this sort of depth is as valuable as the more familiar aggregative approaches to social history. The problem remains, of course, of the typicality of such individuals, yet, properly handled, case-studies of this sort can be immensely illuminating.

But historians have used other types of official or semi-official documentation than a single rich source in their efforts to study history from below. One example is Barbara A. Hanawalt, who has made extensive use of one of the great neglected sources of English social history, the coroner's inquest, in reconstructing medieval peasant family life.[23] Hanawalt argues that these records are free of the bias found in the records of the royal, ecclesiastical or manorial courts, and also makes the important point (to return to an earlier theme) that the details of material life and family activities recorded in them are incidental to the main purpose of the records and hence unlikely to be distorted. As so often when dealing with official records, they are at their most useful when employed for purposes that their compilers would never have dreamt of. Combined with other forms of documentation, Hanawalt used the inquests to build up a picture of the material environment, household economy, stages in the life cycle, patterns of child-rearing, and other aspects of the everyday life of medieval peasants. In a sense, her work demonstrates an alternative strategy to that followed by Le Roy Ladurie and Ginzburg: the sifting of a broad body of documentation rather than the construction of a case study based on one exceptionally rich source. But the net result is a demonstration of how yet another form of official documentation can be used to construct history from below.

This broadening of the chronological range of history from below, and the movement towards a wider range of historical concerns than the political actions and political movements of the masses, has led to a search for models other than those provided by traditional Marxism or the older style of labour history. The need to maintain a dialogue with Marxist scholars is essential, but it remains clear that the application of even such a basic Marxist concept as class to the pre-industrial world is problematic, while it is difficult to imagine a distinctly Marxist line on a sixteenth-century Yorkshire defamation suit or a seventeenth-century Wiltshire skimmington. Unfortunately, the search for an alternative model (admittedly, as yet barely begun) has so far achieved very little success. Many historians, especially in continental Europe, have been inspired by the French *Annales* school.[24] Without doubt, many of the varied works produced by writers working within the *Annales* tradition have not only deepened our knowledge of the past, but also provided tremendous methodological insights into showing how innovative use can be made of familiar forms of documentation and how new questions about the past can be formulated. Moreover, the Annalistes' clarification of the concept of *mentalité* has proved invaluable to historians who have attempted to reconstruct the mental world of the lower orders. I would contend, however, that the greatest contribution of the *Annales* approach has been in demonstrating how to build up the context within which history from below might be written. The knowledge of, for example, a run of grain prices in a given society over a given period helps provide essential background to understanding the experience of the poor: such quantified evidence, however, cannot be the whole story.

Others have sought models in sociology and anthropology. Here too, in skilled and sensitive hands, the gains have been great, although even in these hands some problems have remained, while in other hands some disasters have occurred. Sociology, it might be argued, is of greater relevance to historians of industrial society, while some of its assumptions have not always been too readily applicable to the type of microstudy favoured by practitioners of history from below.[25] Anthropology has attracted a number of historians working on medieval and early modern topics, although here too the outcome has not been without problems.[26] Some of the issues are illuminated by Alan Macfarlane's work on witchcraft accusations in Tudor and Stuart Essex.[27] Macfarlane set out to write what could be described as a history of witchcraft from below. The top person's interpretation of the subject had been set out at an earlier point by Hugh Trevor-Roper, who in his own study of early modern European witchcraft declared his lack of interest in 'mere witch-beliefs: those elementary village credulities which anthropologists discover in all times and in all places'.[28] Macfarlane, conversely, immersed himself in 'mere witch-beliefs' and produced a book which constituted a major breakthrough in our understanding of the subject. One of the more striking elements in his project was the application of anthropological studies to historical material. The result was a deepening of our insights into the function of witchcraft inside village society and of how witchcraft accusations were generated most often by a fairly patterned set of interpersonal tensions. Yet the anthropological approach did little to help readers to understand those wider dimensions of the topic which lay outside the village community: why it was that a statute was passed in parliament allowing the prosecution of malefic witchcraft in 1563 and why other legislation making the legal prosecution of witchcraft impossible was passed in 1736. The microhistorical approach favoured by anthropological models can easily obscure the more general problem of where power is located in society as a whole and the nature of its operation.

Behind all of our discussion there has lurked a fundamental question: does history from below constitute an *approach* to history or a distinctive *type* of history? The point could be argued from either direction. As an approach, history from below arguably fulfils two important functions. The first is to serve as a corrective to top person's history, to show that the Battle of Waterloo involved Private Wheeler as well as the Duke of Wellington, or that the economic development of Britain, which was in full swing by 1815, involved what Thompson has described as 'the poor bloody infantry of the Industrial Revolution without whose labour and skill it would have remained an untested hypothesis'.[29] The second is that, by offering this alternative approach, history from below opens the possibility of a richer synthesis of historical understanding, of a fusion of the history of the everyday experience of the people with the subject-matter of more traditional types of history. Conversely, it could be argued that the subject-matter of history from below, the problems of its documentation, and, possibly, the political orientation of many of its practitioners makes it a distinctive type of history. In a sense, of course, it is difficult to maintain a clearcut division between a type of history and an approach to the discipline in general: economic history, intellectual history, political history, military history and so on are at their least effective when confined in hermetically sealed boxes. Any type of history benefits from breadth in the thinking of the historian writing it.

It would seem, then, that history from below is at its most effective when it is set in a context. Thus, in the first issue of a periodical devoted in large measure to this type of history, the editorial collective of *History Workshop Journal* declared that 'our socialism determines our concern with the common people in the past, their life and work and thought and individuality, as well as the context and shaping causes of their class experience,' and continued 'equally it determines the attention we shall pay to capitalism.'[30] As such sentiments remind us, the term 'history from below' does imply that there is something above to relate to. This assumption in turn assumes that the history of 'the common people', even when aspects of their past experience which are explicitly political are involved, cannot be divorced from the wider considerations of social structure and social power. This conclusion in its turn leads to the problem of how history from below is to be fitted into wider conceptions of history. To ignore this point, when dealing with history from below or any other sort of social history, is to risk the emergence of an intense fragmentation of historical writing, perhaps even of some sort of latter-day antiquarianism. The dangers were well stated in 1979 by Tony Judt. One need not share Judt's position in its entirety to sympathize with his concern that 'there is no place for political ideology in most modern social history, any more than there was in the sociology from which the latter derived . . . social history, as I suggested earlier, has been transformed into a sort of retrospective cultural anthropology.'[31]

The type of history from below introduces another issue, that of broadening the audience of the professional historian, of allowing a wider access to history of a professional standard than that normally afforded by the academic historian's peers and their students. In his 1966 article Thompson noted that Tawney and other historians of his generation had 'an unusually wide, participatory relationship with an audience outside the groves of academe', and obviously regretted that this was something which more recent practitioners of history lacked.[32] This issue has been raised more recently by somebody working from a rather different ideological position from Thomson, David Cannadine. Noting the massive expansion of history as a university discipline in postwar Britain, Cannadine commented that

> much of this new, professional version of British history was completely cut off from the large lay audience, the satisfaction of whose curiosity about the national past had once been history's prime function. One paradoxical result of this unprecedented period of expansion was that more and more academic historians were writing more and more academic history which fewer and fewer people were actually reading.[33]

One of the major objectives of those writing history from below, particularly those working from a socialist or labour history position, was to attempt to remedy this situation by broadening their audience and, possibly, providing a people's version of that new synthesis of our national history whose passing Cannadine lamented. So far their efforts have not been successful, and top person's history still seems to be very much the public taste. Hobsbawm himself professed bafflement at the wide readership for biographies of leading political figures.[34]

Even so, the notion of broadening access to an awareness of our past through history from below is still an attractive one. The danger remains, however, of falling into something like that fragmentation of historical knowledge and that de-politicization of history which so vexed Judt. Popular interest in history from below, as anybody who has had to field questions on such topics at Historical Association branch meetings will know, is often restricted to what might be termed an 'Upstairs, Downstairs' view of past society, this problem being exacerbated by some aspects of what these days we are becoming accustomed to describing as public history. Such a view is aware that people did different (and hence by implication slightly odd) things in the past, and that many of them suffered material deprivation and endured hardship, which allows us to compare past unpleasantness with our current easier conditions. But there is little attempt to push matters further or to approach historical problems on a level much higher than anecdote or isolated local experience. Even those with a more developed view of the people's past have not escaped from those charges of antiquarianism which academic historians are so fond of throwing at their less conceptually or ideologically well equipped brethren. Thus Roderick Floud, criticising the position of a group with very sharply defined ideas on the importance of people's history, could claim that 'at times, indeed, the style of History Workshop has verged on the antiquarianism of the left, the collection and publication of ephemera of working class life.'[35] Although one may not be in sympathy with the overall drift of Floud's argument, there can be little doubt that he has isolated a genuine problem.

A possible response to this criticism is, of course, that until some 'antiquarianism of the left' has permitted the building up of a solid body of relevant materials, even through the collection and publication of ephemera, there can be little hope of developing a mature synthesis or a meaningful broader view. A second, and perhaps more valid, response might be that isolated case studies or other similar studies, if contextualized, might lead to something more significant than antiquarianism. Under appropriate circumstances (Carlo Ginzburg's study of Domenico Scandella would seem to furnish a good example) the writer of history from below can benefit greatly from the use of what anthropologists might describe as thick description.[36] The intellectual problem which such a technique raises will be familiar to social historians: that of placing a social event within its full cultural context, so that it can be studied on an analytical rather than merely a descriptive level. But obviously, this process can be reversed, and once a grasp of the society in question has been established, the isolated social event or individual (as it were, a single but well documented Friulian miller) can be used to provide a pathway to a deeper understanding of that society. The historian need not adopt the semiotic concept of culture advocated by such anthropologists as Clifford Geertz to appreciate the potential usefulness of this technique. And the basic problem which Geertz addresses, that of how we are to understand people culturally different from ourselves, and of how we are to translate a social reality into the scholarly constructs of books, articles or lectures, is surely one which is familiar to the student of history from below.

It is hoped that the preceding pages will, if nothing else, have convinced the reader that the writing of history from below is a project which has proved unusually fruitful. It has attracted the attention of historians working on a number of past societies, both geographically varied and ranging chronologically from the thirteenth to the twentieth centuries. These historians have been drawn from a number of countries and from a number of intellectual traditions and ideological positions. In writing history from below, these historians have sought succour in forms as varied as quantification with the aid of the computer and anthropological theory, and their findings have appeared in formats as disparate as the technical scholarly article and the best-selling book. The point has now come to draw up some general conclusions about the labours which have taken place in this fruitful if confusing corner of Clio's vineyard.

It is at least clear that a number of historians have been successful in overcoming the not inconsiderable obstacles which impede the practice of history from below. More specifically, a number of scholars have recognized the need to make a conceptual leap to further their understanding of the lower orders in past societies, and have then gone on to perform that feat of intellectual gymnastics successfully. Edward Thompson, Carlo Ginzburg, Emmanuel Le Roy Ladurie and the rest, from differing starting-points and with different historical objectives in view, have all been able to demonstrate how imagination can interact with scholarship to broaden our view of the past. Moreover, the work of these and other historians has shown how the historical imagination can be applied not only to forming new conceptualizations of the subject-matter of history, but also to asking new questions of documents and doing different things with them. Two or three decades ago many historians would have denied the possibility, on evidential grounds, of writing serious history about a number of subjects which are now familiar ones: crime, popular culture, popular religion, the peasant family. From medievalists trying to reconstruct the life of peasant communities to oral historians recording and describing the life of earlier generations in the twentieth century, historians working from below have shown how the imaginative use of source materials can illuminate many areas of history that might otherwise have been thought of as doomed to remain in darkness.

Yet the significance of history from below is deeper than merely providing historians with an opportunity to show that they can be imaginative and innovatory. It also provides a means for restoring their history to social groups who may have thought that they had lost it, or who were unaware that their history existed. As we have noted, the initial setting of history from below in the history of the French Revolution or in the history of the British labour movement causes some problems here, although it remains true that work on the eighteenth-century crowd or the nineteenth-century working class has provided some of the most powerful examples of how the unexpected history of sections of the population can be uncovered. The purposes of history are varied, but one of them is to provide those writing or reading it with a sense of identity, with a sense of where they came from. On the broadest level, this can take the form of history's role, through being part of the national culture, in the formation of a national identity. History from below can play an important part in this process by reminding us that our identity has not been formed purely by monarchs, prime ministers and generals. This point has further implications. In a book written on the history of a group which was undeniably 'below', black slaves in the pre-Civil War United States, Eugene D. Genovese noted that his main objective was to explore 'the question of nationality – of "identity" [which] has stalked Afro-American history from its colonial beginnings'.[37] Once more, as, for example, with Thompson's work on the English working class, the use of history to help self-identification is fundamental. But it should be noted that Genovese's book is subtitled 'The World the Slaves Made'. To Genovese, the human beings who formed his subject-matter, although undoubtedly socially inferior, were capable of making a world for themselves: thus they were historical *actors*, they *created* history, rather than just being a 'problem' which helped involve white politicians and soldiers in a civil war, and which white politicians were eventually to 'solve'. Most of those who have written history from below would, in a broad sense, accept the view that one of the outcomes of their following this approach has been to demonstrate that members of the lower orders were agents whose actions affected the (sometimes limited) world in which they lived. We return to Edward Thompson's contention that the common people were not just 'one of the problems which government has had to handle'.

But we must admit, regretfully, that although the concept has been with us for over two decades, history from below has so far had comparatively little impact on mainstream history or on altering the perspectives of mainstream historians. To take the problem on one of its basic levels, the initial primers on history have little to say on the subject. Most students wanting to find out what history is about, or how it should be done, still turn or are directed to what is now a rather elderly work, E. H. Carr's *What is History?* There they will find a rather limited view of what the answer to this intriguing question might be. In particular, they will find that Carr did not have the breadth of imagination as to history's subject-matter which later historians have shown, and which Braudel and other writers of the early *Annales* tradition had already established before he wrote. Thus his statement that 'Caesar's crossing of that petty stream, the Rubicon, is a fact of history, whereas the crossing of the Rubicon by millions of people before or since interests nobody at all' suggests that the history of transport, migration and geographical mobility had not occurred to him. Similarly, his problems with accepting the kicking to death of a gingerbread vendor at Stalybridge Wakes in 1850 as an historical fact (one suspects the gingerbread vendor may have had a more focused view of the subject) demonstrates that he had not envisaged the history of crime as a subject.[38] If a work is ever written to replace Carr's as a basic history primer, it is obvious that its author, in the light of history from below and the broader recent development of social history, will have to take a broader view of the past.

Our final point, therefore, must be that however valuable history from below might be in helping to establish the identity of the lower orders, it should be brought out of the ghetto (or peasant village, working-class street, slum or tower block) and used to criticize, redefine and strengthen the historical mainstream. Those writing history from below have not only provided a body of work which permits us to know more about the past: they have also made it plain that there is a great deal more, much of its secrets still lurking in unexplored evidence, which could be known. Thus history from below retains its subversive aura. There is a distant danger that, as happened with the *Annales* school, it may become a new orthodoxy, but at the moment it still cocks a snook at the mainstream. There will certainly be historians, both academic and popular, who will contrive to write books which implicitly or explicitly deny the possibility of a meaningful historical re-creation of the lives of the masses, but their grounds for so doing will become increasingly shaky. History from below helps convince those of us born without silver spoons in our mouths that we have a past, that we come from somewhere. But it will also, as the years progress, play an important part in helping to correct and amplify that mainstream political history which is still the accepted canon in British historical studies.

NOTES

1 *The Letters of Private Wheeler 1809–1828* ed. B. H. Liddell Hart (London, 1951), pp. 168–72.

2 Bertolt Brecht, *Poems*, ed. John Willett and Ralph Manheim (London, 1976), pp. 252–3.

3 E. P. Thompson, 'History from Below', *The Times Literary Supplement*, 7 April 1966, pp. 279–80. For a discussion of the background to Thompson's thought see Harvey J. Kaye, *The British Marxist Historians: an Introductory Analysis* (Cambridge, 1984).

4 *History from Below: Studies in Popular Protest and Popular Ideology*, ed. Frederick Krantz (Oxford, 1988). This was the English edition of a collection first published in Montreal in 1985.

5 R. C. Richardson, *The Debate on the English Revolution Revisited* (London, 1988), chapter 10, 'The Twentieth Century: "History from Below"'.

6 Thompson, 'History from Below', p. 279.

7 E. P. Thompson, *The Making of the English Working Class* (London, 1965), pp. 12–13.

8 See, for example, the discussions in: Peter Burke, *Popular Culture in Early Modern Europe* (London, 1978), pp. 23–64; and Barry Reay, 'Introduction: Popular Culture in Early Modern England', in *Popular Culture in Seventeenth-Century England*, ed. B. Reay (London, 1985).

9 A way round this problem is to examine the experience of different sections of the lower orders, sometimes through the medium of the isolated case study. For two works using this approach, both of them constituting important contributions to history from below, see: Natalie Zemon Davis, *Society and Culture in Early Modern France* (London, 1975) and David Sabean, *Power in the Blood: Popular Culture and Village Discourse in Early Modern Germany* (Cambridge, 1984).

10 Alex Callinicos, *The Revolutionary Ideas of Karl Marx* (London, 1983), p. 89. Conversely, it should be noted that there is no reason why the Marxist approach should not produce very effective 'history from above': see the comments of Perry Anderson, *Lineages of the Absolutist State* (London, 1979), p. 11.

11 E. J. Hobsbawm, 'History from Below – Some Reflections', in *History from Below*, ed. Krantz, p. 15.

12 Richard Hoggart, *The Uses of Literacy: Aspects of Working-Class Life with Special Reference to Publications and Entertainments* (Harmondsworth, 1958), p. 15.

13 Thompson, 'History from Below', p. 280.

14 Hobsbawm, 'Some Reflections', p. 15.

15 Ibid., p. 16. Despite the scepticism which might be felt about the uniqueness of the contribution of historians of the French Revolution, it remains clear that works based on that period have made a substantial contribution to the canon of history from below, ranging from such pioneering studies as Georges Lefebvre, *Les Paysans du Nord* (Paris, 1924) and *The Great Fear of 1789* (Paris, 1932; English trans., New York, 1973), to the more recent work of Richard Cobb.

16 Published in English as *Montaillou: Cathars and Catholics in a French Village 1294–1324* (London, 1978).

17 See, for example: L. E. Boyle, 'Montaillou Revisited: *Mentalité* and Methodology', in *Pathways to Medieval Peasants*, ed. J. A. Raftis (Toronto, 1981) and R. Rosaldo, 'From the Door of his Tent: the Fieldworker and the Inquisitor', in *Writing Culture: the Poetics and Politics of Ethnography*, ed. J. Clifford and G. Marcus (Berkeley, 1986).

18 Le Roy Ladurie, *Montaillou*, p. vi.

19 E. P. Thompson, *The Poverty of Theory and Other Essays* (London, 1978), pp. 219–20. For a broader discussion of the types of record upon which historians of England might base history from below, see Alan Macfarlane, Sarah Harrison and Charles Jardine, *Reconstructing Historical Communities* (Cambridge, 1977).

20 Some impressions of the type of subject areas covered by oral historians can be gained from reading the regular reports of work in progress contained in *Oral History: the Journal of the Oral History Society*, which has appeared since 1972.

21 Published in English, translated by Anne and John Tedeschi, as *The Cheese and the Worms: the Cosmos of a Sixteenth-Century Miller* (London, 1980). Another work by Ginzburg, *The Night Battles: Witchcraft and Agrarian Cults in the Sixteenth and Seventeenth Centuries* (London, 1983: Italian edition, 1966), also demonstrates how inquisitorial records can be used to throw light on popular beliefs.

22 Ginzburg, *The Cheese and the Worms*, p. xvii.

23 Barbara A. Hanawalt, *The Ties that Bound: Peasant Families in Medieval England* (New York and Oxford, 1986). For a briefer statement of Hanawalt's objectives see her article 'Seeking the Flesh and Blood of Manorial Families', *Journal of Medieval History* 14 (1988), pp. 33–45.

24 The best introduction to the work of this school is Traian Stoianavitch, *French Historical Method: the Annales Paradigm* (Ithaca and London, 1976).

25 For general discussions of the relationship between the two disciplines see: Peter Burke, *Sociology and History* (London, 1980) and Philip Abrams, *Historical Sociology* (Shepton Mallet, 1982).

26 Two classic statements of the importance of the possible links between history and anthropology are E. E. Evans-Pritchard, *Anthropology and History* (Manchester, 1961) and Keith Thomas, 'History and Anthropology', *Past and Present* 24 (1963), pp. 3–24. For a more sceptical view see E. P. Thompson, 'Anthropology and the Discipline of Historical Context', *Midland History* 3 no. 1 (Spring 1972), pp. 41–56.

27 Alan Macfarlane, *Witchcraft in Tudor and Stuart England: a Regional and Comparative Study* (London, 1970). Macfarlane's work should be read in conjunction with Keith Thomas, *Religion and the Decline of Magic: Studies in Popular Beliefs in Sixteenth and Seventeenth-Century England* (London, 1971), a wider-ranging work which also derives considerable insights from anthropology.

28 H. R. Trevor-Roper, *The European Witch-Craze of the Sixteenth and Seventeenth Centuries* (Harmondsworth, 1967), p. 9.

29 Thompson, 'History from Below', p. 280.

30 'Editorial', *History Workshop* 1 (1971), p. 3.

31 Tony Judt, 'A Clown in Regal Purple: Social History and the Historian', *History Workshop* 7 (1979), p. 87.

32 Thompson, 'History from Below', p. 279.

33 David Cannadine, 'British History: Past, Present – and Future', *Past and Present* 116 (1987), p. 177. Cannadine's piece prompted 'Comments' by P. R. Coss, William Lamont, and Neil Evans, *Past and Present* 119 (1988), pp. 171–203. Lamont's views, notably those expressed on pages 186–93, imply a history from below approach to a new national history, while Evans, p. 197,

states explicitly that 'British history . . . needs to be fashioned from below and to work up to an understanding of the state.'

34 Hobsbawm, 'Some Reflections', p. 13.
35 Roderick Floud, 'Quantitative History and People's History', *History Workshop* 17 (1984), p. 116.
36 See Clifford Geertz, *The Interpretation of Cultures* (New York, 1973), chapter 1, 'Thick Description: Toward an Interpretative Theory of Culture'.
37 Eugene D. Genovese, *Roll, Jordan, Roll: the World the Slaves Made* (London, 1975), p. xv.
38 E. H. Carr, *What is History?* (Harmondsworth, 1961), pp. 11, 12.

3

Women's History

Joan Scott

The history that you could write of women's studies belongs also to the
movement; it is not a metalanguage, and will act either as a conservative
moment or a subversive moment . . . there is no theoretically neuter
interpretation of the history of women's studies. The history will have a
performative part in it.[1]

Jacques Derrida, 1984

Women's history has emerged as a definable field mainly in the last two
decades. Despite vast differences in resources allocated to it, in its
institutional representation and its place in the curriculum, in the status
accorded it by universities and disciplinary associations, there seems no
longer any question that women's history is an established practice in
many parts of the world. While the United States may be unique for the
extent to which women's history has achieved a visible and influential
presence in the academy, there is clear evidence – in articles and books,
in the self-identification of historians whom one meets at international
conferences, and in the informal networks that transmit scholarly news –
of international participation in the women's history movement.

I use the term "movement" deliberately to distinguish the current
phenomenon from earlier scattered efforts by individuals to write about
women in the past, to suggest something of the dynamic quality involved
in cross-national and cross-disciplinary exchanges by historians of
women, and to evoke associations with politics.

The connection between women's history and politics is at once
obvious and complex. In one of the conventional narratives of the
origins of this field, feminist politics are the starting-point. These
accounts locate the origin of the field in the 1960s, when feminist
activists called for a history that would provide heroines, proof of
women's agency, and explanations of oppression and inspiration for
action. Academic feminists are said to have responded to the call for
"herstory" by directing their scholarship to a larger political agenda;

there was a direct connection between politics and scholarship in the early days. Later – sometime in the mid to late seventies the account continues, women's history moved away from politics. It enlarged its field of questions by documenting all aspects of the lives of women in the past and so acquired a momentum of its own. The accumulation of monographs and articles, the appearance of internal controversies and ongoing interpretive dialogues, and the emergence of recognized scholarly authorities were the familiar markers of a new field of study, legitimized in part it seemed, by its very distance from political struggle. Finally, (so the story goes), the turn to gender in the 1980s was a definitive break with politics and so enabled this field to come into its own, for gender is a seemingly neutral term devoid of immediate ideological purpose. The emergence of women's history as a field of scholarship involves, in this rendition, an evolution from feminism to women to gender; that is from politics to specialized history to analysis.

To be sure, this story has significant variations depending on who tells it. In some versions the evolution is viewed positively as a rescue of history from either narrowly interested politics, too exclusive a focus on women, or philosophically naive assumptions. In others, the interpretation is negative, the "retreat" to the academy (to say nothing of the turn to gender and to theory) viewed as a sign of depoliticization. "What happens to feminism when the women's movement is dead?" Elaine Showalter asked recently. "It becomes women's studies – just another academic discipline."[2] Despite the different valences put on the account, however, the story itself is shared by many feminists and their critics, as if it were, incontestably, the way things had happened.

I would like to argue that the story needs some critical reflection because it is not only too simple, but also because it misrepresents the history of women's history and its relationship both to politics and to the discipline of history. The history of this field requires not a simple linear narrative, but a more complex one that takes into account the changing position not only of women's history, but of the feminist movement and the discipline of history as well. Although women's history is surely associated with the emergence of feminism, feminism has not disappeared either as a presence in the academy or in the society at large, though the terms of its organization and existence have changed. Many of those who use the term gender, in fact, call themselves feminist historians. This is not only a political allegiance, but a theoretical perspective that leads them to see gender as a better way of conceptualizing politics. Many of those writing women's history consider themselves involved in a highly political effort to challenge prevailing authority in the profession and the university and to change the way history is written.

And much current women's history, even as it works with concepts of gender, addresses itself to the contemporary concerns of feminist politics (among them in the US these days, welfare, childcare and abortion rights). Indeed, there is as much reason to argue that developments in women's history are strongly related to "the growing strength and legitimacy of feminism as a political movement"[3] as there is to insist that there has been increasing distance between academic work and politics. But to take women's history simply as a reflection of the growth of feminist politics outside the academy also misses the point. Rather than posit a simple correlation, we need to think about this field as a dynamic study in the politics of knowledge production.

The word politics is used these days in several senses. First, in its most typical definition it can mean activity directed by or at governments or other powerful authorities, activity that involves an appeal to collective identity, mobilization of resources, strategic calculation, and tactical maneuver. Second, the term politics is also used to refer to relations of power more generally and the strategies aimed at maintaining or contesting them.[4] Third, the word politics is applied even more broadly to practices that reproduce or challenge what is sometimes labelled "ideology", those systems of belief and practice which establish individual and collective identities, which form the relations between individuals and collectivities and their world, and which are taken to be natural or normative or self-evident.[5] These definitions correspond to different kinds of action and different spheres of activity, but my use of the word "politics" to characterize them all suggests that definitional and spatial boundaries are blurred, and that inevitably any usage has multiple resonances. The story of women's history that I want to tell depends on these multiple resonances; it is always a story about politics.

"Professionalism" versus "Politics"

Feminism has been an international movement in the last decades, but it has particular regional and national characteristics. It seems to me useful to focus on the details of the case I know best – the United States – in order to make some general observations.

In the United States feminism re-emerged in the 1960s, stimulated in part by the Civil Rights movement and by government policies aimed at providing womanpower for anticipated economic expansion across the society and including the professions and the academy. It fashioned its appeal and its self-justification within the terms of the prevailing rhetoric of equality. In the process, feminism assumed and created a collective identity of women, female subjects with a shared interest in ending subordination, invisibility, and powerlessness, by creating equality and winning control over their bodies and their lives.

In 1961, at the behest of Esther Peterson, head of the Women's Bureau in the Department of Labor, President Kennedy established a Commission on the Status of Women. Its report in 1963 documented the fact that American women were denied equal rights and opportunities and recommended the creation of fifty state commissions. In 1964, when the Equal Employment Opportunity Commission (EEOC) was established under the Civil Rights Act, sex discrimination was included in its jurisdiction (added by a hostile legislator to discredit Title VII of the Act). In 1966, delegates to the third meeting of the National Conference of State Commissions on the Status of Women voted down a resolution which urged the EEOC to enforce the prohibition against sex discrimination as seriously as it did that against race discrimination. The women who had offered the defeated amendment then met to decide on their next action and formed the National Organization of Women.[6] At about the same time, young women in Students for a Democratic Society and the Civil Rights movement began articulating their grievances, demanding recognition of the role of women as active (and equal) participants in political movements for social change.[7] In the realm of traditional politics, women had become an identifiable group (for the first time since the suffrage movement at the turn of the century).

During the 1960s, too, colleges, graduate schools and foundations began to encourage women to get PhDs by offering fellowships and a great deal of verbal support. "It is apparent," commented one author, "that women constitute a major untapped source for colleges and universities in need of good teachers and researchers."[8] While writers as diverse as college presidents and feminist academics acknowledged that there had been "prejudices against women in the learned professions," they tended to agree that obstacles would fall away if women pursued higher education.[9] It is interesting (in the light of subsequent theoretical discussions) that women's agency was here assumed; as freely choosing, rational actors, women were called upon to enter professions that had previously excluded or underutilized them.

In the space opened by the recruitment of women, feminism soon appeared to claim more resources for women and to denounce the persistence of inequality. Feminists in academia argued that prejudices against women did not disappear, even when they had academic or professional credentials, and they organized to demand a full share of the rights to which their degrees presumably entitled them. In the associations of academic disciplines women formed caucuses to press their demands. (These included greater representation in the associations and at scholarly meetings, attention to salary differentials between women and men, and an end to discrimination in hiring, tenure, and promotion.) The new collective identity of women in the academy posited a shared experience of discrimination based on sexual differentiation and it also assumed that women historians as a group had particular needs and interests that could not be subsumed in the general category of historians. By suggesting that female historians were different from (male) historians, and that their gender influenced their professional chances, feminists disputed the universal and unitary terms which usually designated professionals and drew the charge that they had "politicized" previously non-political organizations.

In 1969, the newly formed Coordinating Committee on Women in the Historical Profession offered resolutions aimed at improving the status of women at the business meeting of the American Historical Assocation (AHA) in a tense, highly charged atmosphere. Ordinarily devoted to discussions of by-laws and organizational policy – the business (not the politics) of the association – these meetings were usually a model of good fellowship and decorum. Disagreements, when they occurred, could be attributed to differences of individual opinion, taste, or even political persuasion, to institutional or regional priority, but none of them were fundamental, none the platform of an identifiable "interest" at odds with the whole. By their tone, their sense of embattlement and their claim to represent a collective entity systematically denied its rights, women disrupted the procedures and challenged the implications of "business as usual." Indeed, they charged that business as usual was itself a form of politics because it ignored and thus perpetuated the systematic exclusion (on grounds of gender and race) of qualified professionals. The attack on entrenched power had at least two results: it won concessions from the AHA in the form of an *ad hoc* committee to look into the questions raised (a committee that issued a report in 1970 acknowledging women's inferior status and recommending a number of corrective measures, including the creation of a standing committee on women), and it led to criticism of the women's conduct as unprofessional.

The opposition between "professionalism" and "politics" is not a natural one, but part of the self-definition of a profession as a skilled practice resting on shared possession of extensive knowledge acquired through education. There are two distinct, but usually inseparable, aspects of the definition of a profession. One involves the nature of the knowledge produced, in this case what counts as history. The other involves the gate-keeping functions that set and enforce the standards kept to by members of the profession, in this case historians. For professional historians in the twentieth century, history is that knowledge of the past arrived at through disinterested, impartial investigation (interestedness and partiality are the antithesis of professionalism) and universally available to anyone who has mastered the requisite scientific procedures.[10] Access then rests on this mastery, the possession of which is supposed to be evident to those who are already professionals and which they alone can judge. Mastery cannot be a matter of strategy or power, but only of education and training. Membership in the historical profession confers responsibility on individuals, who become the guardians of that knowledge which is their special province. Guardianship and mastery are then the basis for autonomy and for the power to determine what counts as knowledge and who possesses it.

And yet, of course, professions and professional organizations are structured hierarchically; dominant styles and standards work to include some and exclude others from membership. "Mastery" and "excellence" can be both explicit judgments of ability *and* implicit excuses for bias; in fact judgments of ability are often intertwined with assessments of an individual's social identity that are irrelevant to professional competence.[11] How to separate these judgments, indeed whether they can be separated at all, are matters not only of strategy but of epistemology. The opposition between "politics" and "professionalism" worked to obscure the epistemological issue.

In the AHA women, blacks, Jews, Catholics and "persons not gentlemen" were systematically under-represented for years.[12] This situation was periodically noted and protested, and some historians made concerted efforts to redress discrimination, but the terms and style of protest were different from those used after 1969. In the earlier periods, whether refusing to attend a convention held in a segregated hotel or insisting that women be included at professional meetings, protesting historians argued that discrimination based on race, religion, ethnicity or sex prevented the recognition of otherwise qualified individual historians. Accepting the notion of what a profession should be, they argued that politics had no place in it; their action, they claimed, was aimed at realizing truly professional ideals. In contrast, the implication of the protests in 1969 and after was that professions *were* political organizations (in the multiple meanings of the term "political"), however decorous their members' behavior, and that only collective action could change prevailing power relationships. During the 1970s, women in the AHA (and other professional associations) linked their local struggles for recognition and representation with national women's campaigns, especially the one for the Equal Rights Amendment to the

Constitution and they insisted that professional associations as a whole take a stand on these national issues. They rejected the suggestion that the ERA was irrelevant to the business of the AHA on the grounds that silence was not neutrality, but complicity with discrimination. Within the organizations, sacred notions like "scholarly excellence" and "quality of mind" were assaulted as so many covers for discriminatory treatment that ought to be replaced by quantitative measures of affirmative action. Professional standards of impartiality and disinterestedness were being overthrown by particularistic interests, or so it seemed to those holding the normative view.

Another way of looking at the matter, however, is to treat the women's challenge as a matter of professional redefinition, for the presence of organized women contested the notion that the profession of history was a unitary body. By insisting that there was a collective identity of women historians at odds with that of men (and suggesting as well that race divided white male historians from black), feminists questioned whether there could ever be impartial assessments of mastery, implying that they were nothing more than the hegemonic gesture of an interested viewpoint. They did not discard professional standards; indeed they continued to champion the need for education and judgments of quality (setting up, among other things, prize competitions for outstanding work in women's history). Although one can surely cite evidence of tendentiousness among historians of women, that did not characterize the field as a whole, nor was it (or is it) peculiar to feminists. And even the tendentious did not advocate deliberate distortion of facts or suppression of information for the sake of the "cause."[13] Most historians of women did not reject the quest for mastery and knowledge that is the ultimate rationale for a profession. Indeed, they accepted the laws of academia and sought recognition as scholars. They employed the rules of language, accuracy, evidence and inquiry which make communication among historians possible.[14] And in the process, they sought and acquired standing as professionals in the field of history. At the same time, however, they challenged and subverted those rules by questioning the constitution of the discipline and the conditions of its production of knowledge.[15] Their presence contested the nature and effects of a uniform and inviolable body of professional standards and of a single (white male) figure to represent the historian.

In effect, feminist historians insisted that there was no opposition between "professionalism" and "politics" by introducing a set of profoundly troubling questions about the hierarchies, foundations, and assumptions governing the historical enterprise: Whose standards, whose definitions of "professionalism" are in operation? Whose consensus do they represent? How was consensus arrived at? What other viewpoints were excluded or suppressed? Whose perspective determines what counts as good history or, for that matter, as history?

"History" versus "Ideology"

The emergence of women's history as a field of study accompanied the feminist campaigns for improved professional status and it involved the expansion of the boundaries of history. But this was not a direct or straightforward operation, not simply a matter of adding something that had been previously missing. Instead there is a troubling ambiguity inherent in the project of women's history for it is at once an innocuous supplement to and a radical replacement for established history.

This double edge is apparent in many of the declarations made by proponents of the new field in the early 1970s, but it was best expressed by Virginia Woolf in 1929. In *A Room of One's Own* Woolf turned to the issue of women's history, as many of her contemporaries were doing in the period following the enfranchisement of women in England and the United States.[16] She muses about the inadequacies of existing history, a history that needs rewriting, she says because it "often seems a little queer as it is, unreal, lop-sided," that is lacking, insufficient, incomplete. Apparently drawing back from rewriting history, she tentatively offers what appears to be another solution: "Why . . . not add a supplement to history? calling it, of course, by some inconspicuous name so that women might figure there without impropriety?" Woolf's invocation of a supplement appears to offer a compromise, but it does not. The delicate sarcasm of her comments about an "inconspicuous name" and the need for propriety suggest a complicated project (she calls it "ambitious beyond my daring"), that, even as she tries to circumscribe the difficulties, evokes contradictory implications.[17] Women are both added to history and they occasion its rewriting; they provide something extra and they are necessary for completion, they are superfluous and indispensable.

Woolf's use of the term supplement calls to mind Jacques Derrida's analysis, which helps me to analyze the relationship of women's history to history. In the project of deconstructing Western metaphysics, Derrida has pointed to certain "markers" that resist and disorganize binary oppositions "without ever constituting a third term" or dialectical resolution. They are disruptive because of their undecidability: they simultaneously imply contradictory meanings which are impossible ever to classify separately. The supplement is one of these "undecidables." In

French, as in English, it means both an addition and a substitute. It is
something added, extra, superfluous, above and beyond what is already
fully present; it is also a replacement for what is absent, missing,
lacking, thus required for completion or wholeness. "The supplement is
 neither a plus nor a minus, neither an outside nor the complement of an
inside, neither accident nor essence."[18] It is (in Barbara Johnson's
words) "superfluous and necessary, dangerous and redemptive." "On
the level of both signifier and signified it is not possible to pin down the
distinction between excess and lack, compensation and corruption."[19]

I would like to argue that by thinking in terms of the contradictory
logic of the supplement we can analyze the ambiguity of women's
history and its potentially critical political force, a force that challenges
and destabilizes established disciplinary premises but without offering
synthesis or easy resolution. The discomfort attendant on such
destabilization has led not only to resistance from "traditional"
historians, but also to a desire for resolution on the part of historians of
women. There is no simple resolution, however, only the possibility of
constant attention to the contexts and meanings within which subversive
political strategies are formulated. It is within this kind of analytic frame
that we can better understand the contests about power and knowledge
that characterize the emergence of this field.

Most women's history has sought somehow to include women as
objects of study, subjects of the story. It has taken as axiomatic the
notion that the universal human subject could include women and
provided evidence and interpretations about women's varied actions
and experiences in the past. Since, however, in modern Western
historiography, the subject has most often been embodied as a white
male, women's history inevitably confronts (what the American legal
theorist Martha Minow calls) "the dilemma of difference."[20] This
dilemma arises because difference is constructed "through the very
structure of our language, which embeds . . . unstated points of
comparison inside categories that bury their perspective and wrongly
imply a natural fit with the world."[21] "Universal" implies a comparison
with the specific or the particular, white men with others who are not
white or not male, men with women. But these comparisons are most
often stated and understood as natural categories, separate entities,
rather than as relational terms. Hence to make a claim about the
importance of women in history is necessarily to come up against
definitions of history and its agents already established as "true" or at
least as accurate reflections of what happened (or what mattered) in the
past. And it is to contend with standards secured by comparisons that
are never stated, by points of view that are never expressed as such.[22]

Women's history, implying as it does a modification of "history," scrutinizes the way the meaning of that general term has been established. It questions the relative priority given to "his-story" as opposed to "her-story," exposing the hierarchy implicit in many historical accounts. And, more fundamentally, it challenges both the sufficiency of any history's claim to tell a whole story and the completeness and self-presence of history's subject – universal Man. Although all historians of women do not ask these questions directly, their work implies them: By what processes have men's actions come to be considered a norm, representative of human history generally, and women's actions either overlooked, subsumed, or consigned to a less important, particularized arena? What unstated comparisons are implicit in terms like "history" and "the historian"?. Whose perspective establishes men as primary historical actors? What is the effect on established practices of history of looking at events and actions from other subject positions, that of women, for example? What is the relationship of the historian to the subjects s/he writes about?

Michel de Certeau puts the problem this way:

> That the particularity of the place where discourse is produced is relevant will be naturally more apparent where historiographical discourse treats matters that put the subject-producer of history into question: the history of women, of blacks, of Jews, of cultural minorities, etc. In these fields one can, of course, either maintain that the personal status of the author is a matter of indifference (in relation to the objectivity of his or her work) or that he or she alone authorizes or invalidates the discourse (according to whether he or she is "of it" or not). But this debate requires what has been concealed by an epistemology, namely the impact of subject-to-subject relationships (women and men, blacks and whites, etc.) on the use of apparently "neutral" techniques and in the organization of discourses that are, perhaps, equally scientific. For example, from the fact of the differentiation of the sexes, must one conclude that a woman produces a different historiography from that of a man? of course, I do not answer this question, but I do assert that this interrogation puts the place of the subject in question and requires a treatment of it unlike the epistemology that constructed the "truth" of the work on the foundation of the speaker's irrelevance.[23]

De Certeau's point here is *not* that only women can write women's history, but that women's history throws open all the questions of mastery and objectivity on which disciplinary norms are built. The seemingly modest request that history be supplemented with information about women suggests not only that history as it is is incomplete, but also that historians' mastery of the past is necessarily partial. And, more disturbingly, it opens to critical scrutiny the very nature of history as a subject-centered epistemology.[24]

The discussion of these disturbing philosophical issues has, for the most part, been displaced onto another kind of terrain. So-called "traditional" historians have defended their power as guardians of the discipline (and by implication their mastery of history) by invoking an opposition between "history" (that knowledge gained through neutral inquiry) and "ideology" (knowledge distorted by considerations of interest). "Ideology" is described as, by its very nature, infecting and so disqualifies intellectual work. The label "ideological" attaches to dissenting views a notion of unacceptability and gives prevailing views the status of unassailable law or "truth."[25]

Norman Hampson would never admit that his dismissive characterization of a book on nineteenth-century French women as "uterine history" implied for him a contrast with phallic history; for him the contrast was with "real" history. And Richard Cobb's gratuitous attack on Simone de Beauvoir in a review of the same book implied that feminists could not be good historians. Lawrence Stone's ten commandments for women's history were far more accepting of the field as a whole, but they stressed the dangers of "distorting evidence" to "support modern feminist ideology," as if the meaning of evidence were unequivocal and otherwise presented no problems about the position, point of view, and interpretations of historians. With a similar refusal of these issues Robert Finlay has charged Natalie Davis with disregarding the "sovereignty of sources" and transgressing "the tribunal of documents" for the purpose of promoting a feminist reading of the story of Martin Guerre.[26] It need hardly be said that feminists' attempts to expose the "male biases" or "masculinist ideology" embedded in historical writing have often met with ridicule or rebuttal as expressions of "ideology."[27]

Unequal power relations within the discipline made charges of "ideology" dangerous for those who sought professional status and disciplinary legitimacy. This (and the rules of disciplinary formation) initially discouraged many historians of women from confronting the most radical epistemological implications of their work; instead they emphasized women as additional historical subject matter and not their challenge to the methodological presuppositions of the discipline. (At that moment, we sought to appear as law-abiding citizens, not as agents of subversion.) Women's history was a fresh area of inquiry like area studies or international relations, I argued for example, when defending new courses on women before a university curriculum committee in 1975.[28] In part this was a tactical ploy (a political move) that attempted in a specific context to detach women's studies from too close an association to the feminist movement. In part, it stemmed from the belief that the accumulation of enough information about women in the past would inevitably achieve their integration into standard history. This latter motive was encouraged by the emergence of social history with its focus on the collective identities of a wide range of social groups.

The existence of the relatively new field of social history provided an important vehicle for women's history; the association of a new topic with a new set of approaches strengthened the claim for the importance, or at least the legitimacy, of the study of women. Appealing to some disciplinary preconceptions about disinterested scientific analysis, it nonetheless pluralized the objects of historical inquiry, granting social groups like peasants, workers, teachers and slaves status as historical subjects. In this context, historians of women could point to the reality of women's lived experience, and assume its inherent interest and importance. They located women in political organizations and at workplaces, and introduced new arenas and institutions – families and households – as worthy of study. Some women's history sought to demonstrate the similarity of women's and men's agency, some of it stressed women's difference; both approaches took "women" as a fixed social category, a separate entity, a known phenomenon – these were biologically female persons who moved in and out of different contexts and roles, whose experience changed, but whose essential being – as women – did not.[29] Thus social historians (myself among them) documented the effects of industrialization on women, a group whose common identity we assumed. (We asked less often in those days about the historical variability of the term "women" itself, how it changed, how in the course of industrialization, for example, the designation of "women workers" as a separate category from "workers" created new social understandings of what it meant to be a woman.)[30] Others turned to women's culture as the tangible product of women's social and historical experience and they, too, tended to assume that "women" was a homogeneous category.[31] As a result, the category "women" took on existence as a social entity apart from its historically situated conceptual relationship to the category "men."[32] Women's history spent less time documenting women's victimization and more time affirming the distinctiveness of "women's culture," thereby creating a historical tradition to which feminists could appeal for examples of women's agency, for proof of their ability to make history.[33]

The documentation of the historical reality of women echoed and contributed to the discourse of collective identity that made the women's movement possible in the 1970s. This discourse produced a shared female experience that, while it took social differences into account, stressed the common denominator of sexuality and the needs and interests that attached to it. Consciousness-raising involved the discovery of the "true" identity of women, the shedding of blinders, the achievement of autonomy, individuality, and, therefore, emancipation. The women's movement assumed the existence of women as a separate, definable social category, whose members needed only to be mobilized (rather than seeing a disparate collection of biologically similar people whose identity was in the process of being created by the movement). Women's history thus confirmed the reality of the category "women", its existence prior to the contemporary movement, its inherent needs, interests and characteristics, by giving it a history.

The emergence of women's history, then, was intertwined with the emergence of the category of "women" as a political identity and this was accompanied by an analysis that attributed women's oppression and their lack of historical visibility to male bias. Like "women," "men" were deemed a homogeneous interest group whose resistance to demands for equality were attributed to an intentional desire to protect the power and resources their dominance gave them. Attention to diversity, to class, race, and culture, yielded variations on the theme of patriarchy but nonetheless fixed the man/woman opposition. There was less attention to the conceptual underpinnings of "patriarchy," to the ways in which sexual difference was built into cultural knowledge, than there was to the effects of systems of male dominance on women, and women's resistance to them. The antagonism men versus women was a central focus of politics and history and this had several effects: it made an influential and widespread political mobilization possible at the same time that it implicitly affirmed the essential nature of the binary opposition male versus female. The ambiguity of women's history seemed to be resolved by this straightforward opposition between two separately constituted, conflicting interest groups.

Paradoxically, although this kind of conflict was anathema to those who conceived of professions as unified communities, it was acceptable as a characterization of history. (This was so at least in part because the field itself was changing, its foci shifting, its reigning orthodoxies challenged and displaced.) Indeed, it might be said that women's history achieved a certain legitimacy as an historical enterprise as it affirmed the separate nature, the separate experience of women, as, that is, it consolidated the collective identity of women. This had the double effect of securing a place for women's history in the discipline and affirming its difference from "history." Women's history was tolerated (at least in part because pressure from feminist historians and students made it worth tolerating) by liberal pluralists who were willing to grant credence to the historical interest of many topics; but it remained outside the dominant concerns of the discipline, its subversive challenge seemingly contained in a separate sphere.

"Politics" versus "Theory"

The apparent containment and segregation of women's history was never complete, but it began to be obviously undermined in the late 1970s by a number of strains, some of them from within the discipline, others from the political movement. These combined to challenge the viability of the category of "women" and introduced "difference" as a problem to be analyzed. The focus on difference made explicit some of the ambiguity that was always implicit in women's history by pointing to the inherently relational meanings of gender categories. It brought to the fore questions about the links between power and knowledge and it demonstrated the interconnections between theory and politics.

The goal of historians of women, even as they established the separate identity of women, was to integrate women into history. And the push for integration proceeded with funding from government and private foundations in the 1970s and early eighties. (These agencies were interested not only in history but also in the light historical studies could throw on contemporary policy about women.) Integration assumed not only that women could be fit into established histories, but that their presence was required to correct the story. Here the contradictory implications of the supplementary status of women's history were at work. Women's history – with its compilations of data about women in the past, with its insistence that accepted periodizations didn't work when women were taken into account, with its evidence that women influenced events and took part in public life, with its insistence that private life had a public, political dimension – implied a fundamental insufficiency: the subject of history was not a universal figure, and historians who wrote as if he were could no longer claim to tell the whole story. The project of integration made these implications explicit.

Undertaken with great enthusiasm and optimism, integration proved difficult to achieve. There seemed more to the resistance of historians than simple bias or prejudice, although that surely figured in the problem.[34] Rather, historians of women themselves found it difficult to write women into history and the task of rewriting history called for reconceptualizations that they were not initially prepared or trained to undertake. What was needed was a way of thinking about difference and how its construction defined relations between individuals and social groups.

"Gender" was the term used to theorize the issue of sexual difference. In the United States, the term is borrowed both from grammar, with its implications about (man-made) conventions or rules of linguistic usage, and from sociology's studies of social roles assigned to women and men. Although sociological uses of "gender" can carry with them functionalist or essentialist overtones, feminists chose to emphasize the social connotations of gender in contrast to the physical connotations of sex.[35] They also stressed the relational aspect of gender: one could not conceive of women except as they were defined in relation to men, nor of men except as they were differentiated from women. In addition, since gender was defined as relative to social and cultural contexts, it was possible to think in terms of different gender systems and the relations of those to other categories such as race or class or ethnicity, as well as to take account of change.

The category of gender, used first to analyze differences between the sexes, was extended to the issue of differences within difference. The identity politics of the 1980s brought multiple allegiances into being that challenged the unitary meaning of the category of "women." Indeed, the term "women" could hardly be used without modification: women of color, Jewish women, lesbian women, poor working women, single mothers were only some of the categories introduced. They all challenged the white middle class heterosexual hegemony of the term "women," arguing that fundamental differences of experience made it impossible to claim a single identity.[36] The fragmentation of a universal notion of "women" by race, ethnicity, class, and sexuality was compounded by serious political differences within the women's movement on issues ranging from Palestine to pornography.[37] The increasingly visible and vehement differences among women called into question the possibility for a unified politics and suggested that women's interests were not self-evident, but a matter of contest and debate. In effect, all the demands for recognition of the experiences and histories of diverse kinds of women, played out the logic of supplementarity, this time in relation to the universal category of women, to the sufficiency of any general women's history, and to the ability of any historian of women to cover all the ground.

The issue of differences within difference brought to the fore a debate about how and whether to articulate gender as a category of analysis. One of these articulations draws on work in the social sciences about gender systems or structures; it assumes a fixed opposition between men and women and separate identities (or roles) for the sexes, that operate consistently in all spheres of social life. It also assumes a direct correlation between the social categories male and female and the subject identities of men and women, and attributes their variation to other established social characteristics such as class or race. It extends the focus of women's history by attending to male/female relationships and to questions about how gender is perceived, what the processes are that establish gendered institutions, and to the differences that race, class, ethnicity and sexuality have made in the historical experiences of women. The social science approach to gender has pluralized the category of "women" and produced a flourishing set of histories and collective identities; but it has also run into a seemingly intractable set of problems that follow from acknowledging differences among women. If there are so many differences of class, race, ethnicity and sexuality, what constitutes the common ground on which feminists can organize coherent collective action? What is the conceptual link for women's history or women's studies courses among what seems to be an infinite proliferation of different (women's) stories. (The two problems are linked: is there a common identity for women and is there a common history of them that we can write?)

Some feminists have tried to address these questions by analyzing gender with the literary and philosophical approaches that, as diverse as they are, are jointly grouped under the rubric of poststructuralism. Here the emphasis changes from documenting the binary opposition male versus female to asking how it is established, from assuming a pre-existing identity of "women" to inquiring into the processes of its construction, from granting an inherent meaning for categories like "men" and "women" to analyzing how their meaning is secured. This analysis takes signification as its object, examining the practices and contexts within which the meanings of sexual difference are produced. It often uses psychoanalytic theory (particularly Lacanian readings of Freud) to discuss the complexity and instability of any subject identifications. Masculinity and femininity are taken to be subject positions not necessarily restricted to biological males or females.[38]

Most important have been the ways feminists have appropriated poststructuralism to think about difference. Difference lies at the heart of linguisitic theories of signification. All meanings are said to be produced differentially, through contrasts and oppositions, and hierarchically, through the assignment of primacy to one term, subordination to another. The interconnectedness of the asymmetrical relationship is important to take into account because it suggests that change is more than a matter of the adjustment of social resources for a subordinated group, more than a question of distributive justice. If Man's definition rests on the subordination of Woman, then a change in the status of Woman requires (and brings about) change in our understanding of Man (a simple cumulative pluralism won't work). The radical threat posed by women's history lies exactly in this kind of challenge to established history; women can't just be added on without a fundamental recasting of the terms, standards and assumptions of what has passed for objective, neutral and universal history in the past because that view of history included in its very definition of itself the exclusion of women.

Those who draw on the teachings of poststructuralism argue that power must be understood in terms of the discursive processes which produce difference. How is knowledge of difference produced, legitimated and disseminated? How are identities constructed and in what terms? Feminist historians find answers to these questions in particular, contextual instances, but they do not simply produce separate stories. Rather the common ground, politically and academically, is one on which feminists produce analyses of difference and organize resistance to the exclusion, domination, or marginality that are the effects of systems of differentiation.

Unlike the social science approach which takes the identity and experience of women for granted, the poststructuralist approach relativizes identity and deprives it of its basis in an essentialized "experience," both crucial elements, in most standard definitions of politics, for the mobilization of political movements. By problematizing the concepts of identity and experience, feminists using poststructuralist analyses have offered dynamic interpretations of gender that stress contest, ideological contradiction, and the complexities of changing power relationships. In many ways their work insists on greater historical variability and contextual specificity for the terms of gender itself than does the work of those relying on social scientific conceptualizations. But work influenced by poststructuralism runs into some of the same problems encountered by those who prefer social scientific approaches. If, as Denise Riley has argued, the category of "women," and so women's identity and experience, are unstable because historically variable, what are the grounds for political mobilization? How to write coherent women's history without a fixed, shared notion of what women are? Riley answers, rightly I think, that it is possible to think about and organize politics with unstable categories, that indeed it has always been done, but exactly how is something that needs discussion. Ironically, however, rather than acknowledge the similarity of dilemmas confronted by feminist historians in the 1980s, dilemmas that stem from our need to think about politics in new terms, there has developed instead a polarized debate about the usefulness of poststructuralism for feminism that is cast as a contest between "theory" and "politics."

Feminists hostile to poststructuralism have generalized their critique as a denunciation of "theory" and they have labelled it as abstract, elitist, and masculinist. They have, in contrast, insisted that their position is concrete, practical, and feminist, and so politically correct. Whatever is theoretical about feminism is renamed as "politics" in this opposition because, (according to one recent account), its insights come "straight out of reflection on our own, that is, women's experience, out of the contradictions we felt between the different ways we were represented even to ourselves, out of the inequities we had long experienced in our situations."[39] By casting the problem in terms of an intractable binary opposition, this formulation rules out the possibility of considering the usefulness of various theoretical approaches for feminist history and feminist politics, as well as the possibility of conceiving of theory and politics as inextricably linked.

I think the opposition between "theory" and "politics" is a false one that seeks to silence debates we must have about *which* theory is most useful for feminism by making only one theory acceptable as "politics." (In the language of those who use this dichotomy "politics" really means good theory; "theory" means bad politics.)[40] The "good" theory takes "women" and their "experience" as the self-evident facts that are the origin of collective identity and action. In effect, (in a move that is the inverse of history's reaction to women's history) those who use this opposition establish "politics" as the normative position, for some the ethical test of the validity of feminism and of women's history. And historians of women who reject "theory" in the name of "politics" are curiously allied with those traditional historians who find poststructuralism (and found women's history) antithetical to the tenets of their discipline.[41] In both cases these historians are defending the concept of "experience" by refusing to problematize it; by opposing "theory" and "politics" they remove "experience" from critical scrutiny and protect it as the foundational and unproblematic ground of politics and historical explanation.[42]

Yet the concept of experience has been rendered problematic for historians and needs to be critically discussed. Not only has poststructuralism questioned whether experience has a status outside linguistic convention (or cultural construction), but the work of women's historians, too, has pluralized and complicated the ways historians have conventionally appealed to experience. In addition, and most important for my argument here, the diverse world of the feminist political movement in the 1980s has made a single definition of women's experience impossible. As has always been the case, the questions posed for theory are questions about politics: Is there an experience of women that transcends the boundaries of class and race? How do differences of race or ethnicity affect the "experience of women" and the definitions of female needs and interests around which we can organize or about which we write? How can we determine what that "experience" is or was in the past? Without some way to think theoretically about experience, historians cannot answer these questions; without some way to think theoretically about the relationship of women's history to history, the potentially critical and destabilizing effects of feminism will be too easily lost and we will forsake the opportunity to radically transform the knowledge that constitutes the history and politics we practice.

Poststructuralism is not without its dilemmas for feminist historians. I think those who insist that poststructuralism can't deal with reality or that its focus on texts excludes social structures miss the point of the theory. But I do think that it does not give ready answers for historians to some of the problems it raises: how to invoke "experience" without implicitly endorsing essentialized concepts; how to describe political mobilization without appealing to essentialized, ahistorical identities; how to depict human agency while acknowledging its linguistic and cultural determinations; how to incorporate fantasy and the unconscious into studies of social behavior; how to recognize differences and make processes of differentiation the focus of political analysis without either ending up with unconnected, multiple accounts or with overarching categories like class or "the oppressed;" how to acknowledge the partiality of one's story (indeed of all stories) and still tell it with authority and conviction. These are problems not solved by dismissing "theory" or declaring it antithetical to "politics;" rather they require sustained and simultaneous discussion (discussion that is at once theoretical and political) for in the end they are the problems of all those who write women's history, whatever their approach.

They are common problems because they follow from the logic of supplementarity that characterizes women's history and that has given it its critical force. As feminist historians have undertaken to produce new knowledge, they have necessarily called into question the adequacy not only of the substance of existing history, but also of its conceptual foundations and epistemological premises. In this they have found allies among historians and other scholars in the humanities and the social sciences who are debating among themselves issues of causality and explanation, agency and determination. Yet feminists have, for the most part, not been considered full partners in these debates.[43] Even in these critical discourses, their position remains supplementary: at once a particular example of a general phenomenon *and* a radical commentary upon the (in)sufficiency of its terms and practices. The supplementary position is one of recurring indeterminacy and potential destabilization. It requires constant attention to relationships of power, a certain vigilance in the face of attempts to implement one or another of its contradictory positions. Women's historians constantly find themselves protesting attempts to relegate them to positions that are merely extraneous; they also resist arguments that dismiss what they do as so different that it does not qualify as history. Their professional lives and their work are, for this reason, necessarily political. In the end there is no way to detach politics – relations of power, systems of belief and practice – from knowledge and the processes that produce it; women's history is for this reason an inevitably political field.

In this paper I have turned to the operations of the logic of the supplement to help me understand and analyze the inherently political nature of the field of women's history; ultimately, I would argue, it is such "theory" that can illuminate for us the politics of our practice.

NOTES

I would like to thank Clifford Geertz for first posing some of the questions that led to the formulation of this paper and for his clarifying comments on an early version of it. Donald Scott helped me articulate many crucial points and Elizabeth Weed provided invaluable critical suggestions. I also appreciate the comments and advice of Judith Butler, Laura Engelstein, Susan Harding, Ruth Leys, and Mary Louise Roberts. The criticisms of Hilda Romer, Tania Urum, and Karin Widerberg posed difficult challenges that have improved and strengthened the argument. I am grateful for them.

1   "Women in the Beehive: A seminar with Jacques Derrida," transcript of the Pembroke Center for Teaching and Research Seminar with Derrida, in *Subjects/Objects* (Spring 1984), p. 17.
2   Cited in Karen Winkler, "Women's Studies After Two Decades: Debates over Politics, New Directions for Research," *The Chronicle of Higher Education*, September 28, 1988, p. A6.
3   Nancy Fraser and Linda Nicholson, "Social Criticism Without Philosophy," unpublished ms. 1987, p. 29.
4   "Politics in the profound sense, as the ensemble of human relations in their real, social structure, in their ability to construct the world." Roland Barthes, *Mythologies* (Paris 1957), p. 230. See also Michel Foucault, *The History of Sexuality* Vol. I *An Introduction* (New York, 1980), pp. 92–102.
5   Gayatri Chakravorty Spivak, "The Politics of Interpretation," in W. J. T. Mitchell, *The Politics of Interpretation*, Chicago, 1983, pp. 347–66; Mary

Poovey, *Uneven Developments: The Ideological Work of Gender in mid-Victorian England*, (Chicago, 1988). See also "ideology" in the glossary of Louis Althusser and Etienne Balibar, *Reading Capital*, tr. Ben Brewster, (London, 1979), p. 314.

6   Jo Freeman, "Women on the Move: Roots of Revolt," in Alice S. Rossi and Ann Calderwood (eds.), *Academic Women on the Move* (New York, 1973), pp. 1–37. See also the essays by Alice Rossi and Kay Klotzburger in this same volume.

7   Sara Evans, *Personal Politics* (New York, 1979).

8   Quotation from Barnaby Keeney, President of Brown University, *Pembroke Alumnae* 27:4 (October 1962), p. 1.

9   Keeney, ibid. pp. 8–9; Jessie Bernard, *Academic Women* (Cleveland, 1966); Lucille Addison Pollard, *Women on College and University Faculties: A Historical Survey and a Study of their present Academic Status*, (New York, 1977). See especially, p. 296.

10 Peter Novick, *That Noble Dream: The "Objectivity Question" and the American Historical Profession* (New York, 1988).

11 On the issue of access see Mary G. Dietz, "Context is All: Feminism and Theories of Citizenship;" Jill K. Conway, "Politics, Pedagogy, and Gender;" and Joan W. Scott, "History and Difference;" all in *Daedalus* (Fall 1987), pp. 1–24, 137–52, 93–118, respectively.

12 Howard K. Beale, "The Professional Historian: His Theory and His Practice," *Pacific Historical Review* 22 (August 1953), p. 235.

13 This issue has come up in many different ways, most recently in connection with the Sears case. In the course of a sex discrimination suit brought against the Sears Roebuck and Company retail chain, two historians of women, Rosalind Rosenberg and Alice Kessler-Harris, testified on opposite sides. The case created tremendous controversy among historians about the political implications of women's history and about the political commitments of feminist historians. There have been accusations of bad faith on both sides, but the most recent (and by far the most vindictive) charges, by Sanford Levinson and Thomas Haskell in defense of Rosenberg, insist that Kessler-Harris deliberately distorted history in the interests of politics while Rosenberg bravely defended "truth." The opposition between "politics" and "truth," "ideology" and "history" structures their essay (and gives it its seemingly objective, dispassionate tone) while allowing them to gloss over all the difficult epistemological issues the case raised (and that they gesture to in footnote 136). See "Academic Freedom and Expert Witnessing: Historians and the Sears Case," *Texas Law Review*, 66:7 (October 1988), pp. 301–31. On the Sears case see also, Ruth Milkman, "Women's History and the Sears Case," *Feminist Studies* 12 (Summer 1986), pp. 375–400; and Joan W. Scott, "The Sears Case," in Scott, *Gender and the Politics of History* (New York, 1988), pp. 167–77.

14 Ellen Somekawa and Elizabeth A. Smith, "Theorizing the Writing of History or, 'I can't think why it should be so dull, for a great deal of it must

be invention,'" *Journal of Social History* 22:1 (Fall 1988), pp. 149–61.

15 On the potential of women's history to transform history see Ann Gordon, Mari Jo Buhle, and Nancy Schrom Dye, "The Problem of Women's History," in Berenice Carroll, (ed.), *Liberating Women's History* (Urbana, 1976); Natalie Zemon Davis, "Women's History in Transition: The European Case," *Feminist Studies* 3 (1976), pp. 83–103; Joan Kelly, *Women, History, and Theory* (Chicago, University of Chicago Press, 1984); Carl Degler, "What the Women's Movement has done to American History," *Soundings* 64 (Winter 1981), p. 419.

16 Among these were Ivy Pinchbeck, *Women Workers and the Industrial Revolution 1750–1850* (London, 1930) and Mary Beard, *On Understanding Women* (New York, 1931) and *America Through Women's Eyes* (New York, 1934).

17 Virginia Woolf, *A Room of One's Own* (New York, 1929), p. 47.

18 Jacques Derrida, *Positions*, tr. Alan Bass (Chicago, 1981), p. 43. See also Derrida, *Of Grammatology*, tr. Gayatri Chakravorty Spivak (Baltimore, 1974), pp.141–64.

19 Barbara Johnson, introduction to her translation of Derrida's *Disseminations*, (Chicago, 1981), p. xiii.

20 Martha Minow, "The Supreme Court 1986 Term: Foreword: Justice Engendered," *Harvard Law Review* 101, no. 1 (November 1987), pp. 9–95.

21 Ibid., p. 13.

22 On the question of history's representations see, Gayatri Chakravorty Spivak, "Can the Subaltern Speak?" in Cary Nelson and Lawrence Grossberg, *Marxism and the Interpretation of Culture* (Urbana, 1988), pp. 271–313.

23 Michel de Certeau, "History: Science and Fiction," in *Heterologies: Discourse on the Other* (Minneapolis, 1986), p. 217–18.

24 Mary Hawkesworth, "Knower, Knowing, Known . . . " *Signs* (Spring 1989), pp. 533–557.

25 "Ideological success is achieved when only dissenting views are regarded as ideologies; the prevailing view is the truth." Martha Minow, "Justice Engendered," *Harvard Law Review* 101 (November 1987), p. 67.

26 Norman Hampson, "The Big Store," *London Review of Books* (21 January–3 February 1982), p. 18; Richard Cobb, "The Discreet Charm of the Bourgeoisie," *New York Review of Books* (December 17, 1981) p. 59; Lawrence Stone, "Only Women," *New York Review of Books* (April 11, 1985), pp. 21–7; Robert Finlay, "The Refashioning of Martin Guerre," and Natalie Zemon Davis, "'On the Lame'", both in the *American Historical Review* 93:3 (June 1988), pp. 553–71, and 572–603, respectively.

27 "Western liberalism's intractability to right struggles based on gender and race . . . displays something that feminists have come to know well: the liberal individual's – Man's – resistance to intimations of deficiency, especially when those intimations are themselves expressed through gender." Elizabeth Weed, Introduction to *Coming to Terms: Feminism, Theory, Politics* (New York, 1988), p. 6 (of typed transcript).

28   Testimony of Joan Scott to University of North Carolina – Chapel Hill
     Curriculum Committee, May, 1975, cited in Pamela Dean, *Women on the
     Hill: A History of Women at the University of North Carolina* (Chapel Hill,
     1987), p. 23.
29   I do not mean to underestimate the variety of approaches to women's
     history and the different interpretive and theoretical positions taken.
     Within women's history there was/is a great deal of divergence among
     Marxist-feminists, liberal feminists, those who use the insights of varying
     psychoanalytic schools, etc. My point here is not to review the variety, but
     to indicate some of the common ground among them all – the preoccupation
     with woman as subject, with women's identity – as well as the relation of the
     field as a whole to the discipline of history. I have reviewed the diversity
     elsewhere. See Joan W. Scott, "Women's History: The Modern Period,"
     Past and Present 101 (1983), pp. 141–57; and "Gender: A Useful Category
     of Historical Analysis," *American Historical Review* 91:5 (December 1986),
     pp. 1053–75.
30   For histories of women's work, see Louise A. Tilly and Joan W. Scott,
     Women, Work and Family (New York, 1978; 1987); Alice Kessler-Harris
     Out to Work: A History of Wage-Earning Women in the United States (New
     York, 1982; Thomas Dublin, *Women at Work: The Transformation of
     Work and Community in Lowell, Massachusetts*, 1826–60 (New York, 1979;
     Sally Alexander, "Women's Work in Nineteenth-Century London: A Study
     of the Years 1829–50," in Juliet Mitchell and Ann Oakley, (eds), *The
     Rights and Wrongs of Women* (London, 1976); Patricia A. Cooper, *Once a
     Cigar Maker: Men, Women, and Work Culture in American Cigar Factories*,
     1900–1919 (Urbana, 1987).
31   Linda Kerber, "Separate Spheres, Female Worlds, Woman's Place: The
     Rhetoric of Women's History," *Journal of American History* 75:1 (June
     1988), pp. 9–39.
32   This is not to say that historians of women didn't write about women in
     relationship to men – as wives, lovers, mothers, daughters, employees,
     patients, etc. It is to say that they tended to disregard the conceptual issue –
     that "women" has no intrinsic definition but only a contextual one (one that
     is always contested in its idealization and actualization) and one that cannot
     be elaborated except through contrast, usually to "men." On this see
     Denise Riley, *"Am I that name?" Feminism and the Category of "women" in
     History* (London and Minneapolis, 1988).
33   See, for example, the symposium on "Women's Culture" and politics in
     Feminist Studies 6 (1980), pp.26–64.
34   Susan Hardy Aiken, et al., "Trying Transformations: Curriculum Integration
     and the Problem of Resistance," *Signs* 12:2 (Winter 1987), pp. 255–75. See
     also in the same issue Margaret L. Anderson, "Changing the Curriculum in
     Higher Education," pp. 222–254.
35   See, Gail Rubin, "The Traffic in Women: Notes on the Political Economy
     of Sex," in Rayna R. Reiter, (ed.), *Towards an Anthropology of Women*
     (New York, 1975). See also, Joan W. Scott, "Gender: A Useful Category

of Historical Analysis," *American Historical Review* 91:5 (December 1986); and Donna Haraway, "Geschlecty, Gender, Genre: Sexualpolitik eines Wortes," in *Viele Orte uberall? Feminismus in Bewegung* (Festschrift fur Frigga Haug), ed. Kornelia Hauser (Berlin, 1987), pp. 22–41.

36 Teresa de Lauretis, "Feminist Studies/ Critical Studies: Issues, Terms, and Contexts,"; Cherrie Moraga, "From a Long Line of Vendidas: Chicanas and Feminism;" Biddy Martin and Chandra Talpade Mohanty, "Feminist Politics: What's Home Got to Do with It?," all in Teresa de Lauretis (ed.), *Feminist Studies/Critical Studies* (Bloomington, 1986), pp. 1–19, 173–190, 191–212, respectively. See also, The Combahee River Collective, "A Black Feminist Statement," in Gloria T. Hull, Patricia Bell Scott and Barbara Smith, (eds), *But Some of Us are Brave: Black Women's Studies* (New York, 1982); Barbara Smith, (ed.), *Home Girls; A Black Women's Anthology* (New York, 1983). See also, Barbara Smith, "Toward a Black Feminist Criticism;" Deborah E. McDowell, "New Directions for Black Feminist Criticism;" Bonnie Zimmerman, "What has Never Been; An Overview of Lesbian Feminist Criticism;" all in Elaine Showalter (ed.) *The New Feminist Literary Criticism: Essays on Women, Literature, Theory* (New York, 1985), pp. 168–224; Nancy Hoffman, "White Women, Black Women: Inventing an Adequate Pedagogy," *Women's Studies Newsletter* 5 (Spring 1977) pp. 21–4; Michele Wallace, "A Black Feminist's Search for Sisterhood," *Village Voice*, July 28, 1975, p. 7; Teresa de Lauretis, "Displacing Hegemonic Discourses: Reflections on Feminist Theory in the 1980s," *Inscriptions* nos. 3/4 (1988), pp.127–41.

37 Some of the fracturing came in the wake of the defeat of the Equal Rights Amendment to the US Constitution, a campaign that provided a united front among different groups of feminists. Of course the ERA campaign itself showed how profound were differences between feminists and anti-feminists and called into question any notion of an inherent female solidarity. Some of the differences were attributed to "false consciousness", but not entirely. On the ERA campaign, see Mary Frances Berry, *Why ERA Failed* (Bloomington, 1986); Jane Mansbridge, *Why We Lost the ERA* (Chicago, 1986); Donald G. Mathews and Jane Sherron de Hart, *ERA and the Politics of Cultural Conflict: North Carolina* (New York, 1989).

38 See Judith Butler, *Gender Trouble: Feminism and the Subversion of Identity* (New York, 1989).

39 Judith Newton, "History as Usual?: Femninism and the 'New Historicism'," *Cultural Critique*, 9 (1988), p. 93.

40 The opposition between "theory" and "politics" also suggests an opposition between idealism and materialism which misrepresents the philosophical issues currently at stake. On the invalidity of the idealism/materialism opposition see Joan Scott, "A Reply to Criticism," *International Labor and Working Class History* 32 (Fall 1987), pp. 39–45. The "theory" versus "politics" opposition also refers obliquely to the question of human agency, much insisted upon these days by historians. Poststructuralist theory doesn't deny that people act or that they have some control over their

actions; rather it criticizes the liberal individual theory that assumes that individuals are fully autonomous, rational, self-creating actors. The issue is not agency *per se*, but the limits of the liberal theory of agency.

41 The irony is striking. Historians of women who have accepted the discipline's notions of universality (adding the universal category "women" to the existing one of "men") and of mastery (assuming that historians can achieve disinterested or complete knowledge of the past) nonetheless characterize their position as "political" – a term that indicates their subversive relationship to the discipline. I think this is yet another example of the logic of the supplement, women's historians (whatever their epistemological position) are neither fully of nor fully out of the profession of history.

42 See John Toews , "Intellectual History After the Linguistic Turn: The Autonomy of Meaning and the Irreducibility of Experience," *American Historical Review*, 92, (October 1987), pp. 879–907.

43 One example of this neglect of feminist contributions to historiographical debates can be found in the special forum on history and critical theory in *American Historical Review* 94 (June 1989). None of the articles acknowledges the impact that feminist history (or African American history or gay and lesbian history) has had on the epistemological questions confronting the discipline. See David Harlan, "Intellectual History and the Return of Literature," David Hollinger, "The Return of the Prodigal: The Persistence of Historical Knowing," and Alan Megill, "Recounting the Past: 'Description,' Explanation, and Narrative in Historiography," pp. 581–609, 610–21, and 627–53, respectively.

4

Overseas History

Henk Wesseling

This contribution is on overseas history, an interesting but by no means an easy subject. For what *is* overseas history? Strictly speaking there is no proper definition of it or rather what it is depends on where one stands. From the British perspective, for example, practically all history is overseas history, including part of the history of the UK itself. To paraphrase a well-known French expression: everybody's history is overseas history for somebody else. This is obviously not what we have in mind when we use the term, so what is it? A practical solution of this problem can be found by examining the contents of publications which carry this term in their title. The French *Revue française d'histoire d'outre-mer*, published by the society of the same name, is essentially a journal devoted to the history of European, and particularly French, expansion overseas and of former French possessions. This is not surprising, as its original name was *Revue d'histoire des colonies*. In the same vein the French as well as the Belgian *Académies des sciences d'outre-mer* used to be known as *Académies des sciences coloniales*. The German language series of *Beiträge zur Kolonial- und Überseegeschichte* combines the two terms. The British are lucky enough to have their Commonwealth, which is why there is a *Journal of Imperial and Commonwealth History*, a much more elegant combination than 'Imperial and Overseas History'. In the Netherlands the Royal Colonial Institute changed its name to the Royal Tropical Institute but somehow 'tropical history' was not accepted.

It is not difficult to understand what was going on here. After 1945 the term 'colonial' became increasingly unattractive and institutes that wanted to continue their existence had to find different (preferably more neutral) names. However, it was not simply a matter of changing names. There was also a change of approach and interest. Overseas history developed into a much broader field of study than colonial history used to be. It deals not only with colonial systems and the encounter between Europeans and non-Europeans in general, but also with the economic, social, political and cultural history of the non-European peoples. It is precisely here that problems arise, because not only theoretically but also in actual practice overseas history has developed into such a vast subject as to become unidentifiable. Of course there are some elements that give a certain cohesion to the field. In the first place the overseas historian normally deals with two types of sources, on the one hand European, mostly archival, sources and on the other non-European, written or, as is often the case in African history, non-written sources. Because of the lack of traditional sources the assistance of other disciplines is necessary, hence the role of disciplines like archaeology, linguistics and anthropology in overseas history. Overseas history therefore tends to be interdisciplinary.

Apart from this the overseas historian must also familiarize himself with civilizations other than his own. This generally supposes a broader – and somewhat different – education than is normally the case, as well as a greater demand for linguistic skills. This is the reason why overseas historians are often found in orientalist or Africanist departments, at least in Europe (the situation in the US is different). And even when they are appointed in history departments overseas historians feel the need to collaborate with other specialists on the same area, such as linguists, anthropologists, or art historians. This is not the case with historians of Europe. A specialist in French history will not normally work in a department of French studies nor will he feel the urge to go to conferences on French studies. As it is typical for overseas historians to learn about civilizations other than their own, they have to collaborate with other disciplines to reach a better understanding of that particular civilization or society. But they also have to keep in touch with other historians in order to understand what is going on in their own discipline. The tension between the area approach and the disciplinary approach is a well-known phenomenon.

There is another reason why, historically speaking, there is a certain unity in the field of overseas history. Most of the overseas world formerly belonged to the colonial world and is now supposed to form part of the Third World. This is why in some circles the expression 'Third World history' is in use.[1] But the very idea of a 'Third World' is now disintegrating, as it no longer reflects reality. In retrospect it even seems strange that countries like India and Indonesia were supposed to form one world with Sudan and Mali for the sole reason that they were all former colonies and are still relatively poor. To equate overseas history with Third World history therefore does not seem to be a good idea, all the more so as the history of the US clearly belongs to overseas and indeed to colonial history but not to Third World history.

The question can be raised whether overseas history, if it is supposed to include the history of the whole world apart from Europe (or 'the West'), is a subject of study at all. This problem is the result of the success of overseas history after World War Two, when the rise of overseas history was to some extent due to a reaction to former colonial history. A great backlog had to be made up, and a great leap forward was made. The new nations vindicated their own national past. The 'people without history' finally found one and the results of this movement were impressive. Overseas history has become so vast and so varied that it cannot be considered any longer as one specific field of history. In order to survive, overseas history will need some form of reconceptualization. Before discussing this we should sketch a brief outline of the history of the subject.

The History of Overseas History: a Survey

In one form or another history has been practised in most civilizations. In Indonesia the chronicles or *babads* go back very far. The Hindus in India took little interest in history, but the Muslims had a greater interest and a stronger sense of chronology, though they too only drew up chronicles of events. In Japan and China a historiography was developed comparable to traditional European history, which, in its modern scientific form, was only developed in the West in the nineteenth century. It is characterized by what is called 'the historical method' (chronology, philology, textual criticism, hermeneutics) as well as a particular type of historical thinking. Awareness of the uniqueness of events, the notion of development and succession over time but also the notion that each period has a specific character with its own values and standards, are characteristic of this. The German historical school played a major role in this development which is why some of the most famous historical notions are still best known in their German form: *Historismus*, *Verstehen*, *Zeitgeist*.

The historical interpretation which resulted from this was extremely Eurocentric. *Weltgeschichte* in fact came down to European history, for in the framework of general history non-European peoples played no role. They were considered as people without history (Hegel) or people of eternal standstill (Ranke). Apart from the traditional ancient civilizations, they came into the picture only at the moment they submitted to and were conquered by the Europeans. This does not mean that there was no interest at all in civilizations other than western ones for this existed in the form of what was known as oriental studies. The impetus for these studies was on one hand the Bible and linguistics, on the other colonialism. After the Renaissance many European universities not only created chairs of Greek and Latin but also Hebrew and Arabic. Later on departments of Middle Eastern and/or Arabic studies emanated from these subjects. Comparative and historical linguistics, a popular subject in the nineteenth century, stimulated the study of Sanskrit, which in turn gave rise to chairs and institutes for the study of Indian civilization.

An even more important stimulus came from colonialism. The training of colonial civil servants became a part of university education in the nineteenth century. Courses on languages and colonial administration could be found alongside courses on imperial or colonial history. While they focused primarily on the European point of view, these courses also paid some attention to overseas peoples. It is interesting to see that already in 1897 a search committee for a chair in the history of the Netherlands Indies gave preference to a candidate because he could also pay attention 'to the indigenous point of view'.[2] Apart from the colonial subjects themselves other overseas peoples became objects of study. In the Netherlands, for example, the Chinese were studied because of the important Chinese community in the East Indies, the Japanese because of the 'yellow peril' and Islam because of the danger of 'Muslim fanaticism'. The result of this was that two groups of historians came into being: a small group in departments of oriental studies who studied other civilizations in their own right, and a much larger one who taught history proper, that is, the history of Europe and its colonies. Even though they were based in the same university the two groups would rarely collaborate.

The situation changed drastically after 1945, partly for external and partly for internal reasons. The external reasons are obvious: decolonization, the decline of Europe, the emergence of the new superpowers. All this led to a rethinking of the role of Europe in world history and a questioning of the Euro-centric approach. The decline of Europe became as important a subject of study as its rise. The Dutch historian Jan Romein proclaimed the end of the *European Era* and the beginning of the *Asian Century*.[3]

But apart from political and ideological reasons there were also internal developments, changes in the way history was studied. The post-war period witnessed the rise of social and economic history. Historians became less interested in political and military history and more interested in subjects such as material civilization, *mentalités*, everyday life, the common man etc. In this respect, at least until the eighteenth century, European history was not so different from non European history. Under the impact of the *Annales* school history became less teleological, less 'whiggish'. Structure replaced evolution as the central preoccupation. Continuity became as important as change and therefore the opposition between Europe (change) and Asia (continuity) became less relevant. In this approach the nation state was not the central unit of historical analysis any more, therefore the opposition of motherland and colony was less important. The new approach was more in terms of villages, towns, regions, social groups. This made the antagonism between the colonialist and the nationalist approach less sharp, and there were also practical changes. A growing influence came from American historians, for their departments of history had always been less parochial than European ones, and they played an increasing role in Asian and African history. Moreover, the former colonies themselves developed their own history departments. To be sure, for a long time western historians still dominated the field, as they were better educated and had easy access to important holdings in European archives. The indigenous elites were more interested in fields other than history. The task of developing the economy and building the nation was more urgent – and more rewarding – than that of writing history.

A curious situation resulted from this. On one hand the impact of Europe on the concept of history itself became even stronger than before. Historians from Asia and Africa often came to Europe to study history or at least to finish their education. They worked in western archives and they turned to western models to learn how history was to be studied and written. Thus, like the Japanese after the Meiji revolution, they learned history from the West.[4] In their own civilization they found no references. On the other hand, their interpretation was of course very different and sometimes strongly anti-western. The young nations needed 'a usable past' and 'usable' meant nationalistic and anti-colonial.[5] Thus the question was not only one of colonialist versus nationalist historiography. It concerned the place of the West in world history in general. European historians themselves also questioned the Eurocentric approach to overseas history. A new impulse for this debate came from the discussion about the origins of under-development stemming from the disappointment of post-colonial change. The original optimism about a bright new future now that colonialism was over faded away when it became clear that the economic and social problems of the former colonies were permanent (or structural) rather

than temporary. Liberal optimism was replaced by radical pessimism, to
paraphrase A. G. Hopkins's happy formulation.[6] This time the
opposition was not that of colonialism versus nationalism but of Left
versus Right. The neo-Marxist critique of colonialism became very
influential in the western world itself.

Thus the development of overseas history after 1945 was a dialectical
process. First there was an emancipation movement in non-western
historiography, which resulted in an impressive explosion of historical
research and production in Asia and Africa. The non-European
countries discovered their own past and offered their own interpretation
of it, but it was precisely then that the problem of overseas history
manifested itself in a new form. Today everybody accepts that Africans
and Asians have their own history, as rich and interesting as that of
Europe. The question, however, is whether we can stop here and simply
consider world history as the sum of a great number of autonomous
regional histories. Most historians would agree that we should try to do
more and study how, in one way or another, these various civilizations
have become interconnected, how today's world situation has come into
being. The real challenge of overseas history is to offer a modern form
of world history. This is an ambitious goal but, as Fernand Braudel has
said, we need ambitious historians.[7] The first outline of this can perhaps
be found in the new history of European expansion that has developed
in the last three decades or so. Before examining this we shall look first
at the spectacular development of Asian and African history in the same
period.[8]

Asian and African History

Both in India and Indonesia history in its modern scientific form was
introduced by the colonial power. In India the foundation of the Asiatic
Society of Bengal in 1784 can be considered as the starting-point. The
official British historiography of India was highly Anglocentric. As
Nehru once remarked about the British: 'Real history for them begins
with the advent of the Englishman to India; all that went before it is in
some mystic kind of way a preparation for this divine consummation.'[9]
However, an interest in historical studies soon began to develop in the
milieu of the new Indian intelligentsia. In the middle of the nineteenth
century, as a reaction to the rather condescending approach of the
colonial historians, Indian historians developed their own historiography,
and in the late nineteenth century the rise of the nationalist movement
gave a strong impetus to this so that by the 1920s and 1930s there existed

a considerable group of professional historians. The names of well known scholars such as R. K. Mookerji and R. C. Majumdar bear witness to this. Therefore, when independence came in 1947 Indian professional historiography was already in a strong position. The transfer of power itself also stimulated the writing of history, and there was a demand for popular texts and schoolbooks. The government stimulated the study of the recent past and particularly of the nationalist movement. In 1952 the Ministry of Education ordered the compilation of a history of the Indian freedom movement, and R. C. Majumdar was appointed director of the project. Majumdar's conclusions were very different from what the government had expected, but he published his interpretation all the same. This debunking of the nationalist myth was a clear indication of the high standard of professionalism that had been reached by the Indian historians.[10] Although British historians are still playing a leading, if not *the* leading, role in Indian history, Indian historians themselves have become increasingly important. The *Cambridge Economic History of India* as well as the *New Cambridge History of India* are convincing demonstrations of this.

In Indonesia the development was somewhat different. Compared to India, there were fewer university-trained persons in general and practically no professional historians at all during the colonial period. The nationalist movement was also weaker than it was in India, and nationalist intellectuals expressed their feelings in literary rather than scholarly works. Thus there were practically no professional Indonesian historians before independence. The government of the Republic stimulated the study of the past but from a clear political perspective (ideological pressures were strong). In 1957 the first national congress of historians was held. There it became clear how little research had yet been done, but from then on history as a scholarly discipline was being developed. The main figure in this was Sartono Kartodirdjo who introduced a new social-science-inspired form of history which pays special attention to rural history.[11]

In the meantime it was Indonesian history that led to an interesting debate about a new Asiacentric approach to Asian history. John Bastin, in his inaugural lecture at Kuala Lumpur in 1959 about *The Study of Modern Southeast Asian History* greatly stimulated this discussion,[12] but the question itself had already been raised much earlier. It was introduced by J. C. van Leur in the dissertation about early Asian trade which was published in 1934.[13] Van Leur, who died very young, at the age of thirty-four, in the Battle of the Java Sea, was to have a lasting influence on Indonesian history and indeed on Asian history in general. The originality of his work lies in two things: the abandonment of the

Eurocentric viewpoint and the application of sociological categories. He reacted against the exclusively colonial approach, which constituted a distorted perspective and ignored vast areas of historical reality. 'Most historians,' he wrote, 'see the Asiatic world through the eyes of the Dutch ruler: from the deck of the ship, the rampart of the fortress, the high gallery of the trading house.'[14]

However, Van Leur's criticism is at the same time more general and more fundamental. He questions the periodization of history and the place in it allotted to Asia. For instance, in a well-known article he examines why period labels such as 'the eighteenth century' were applied to Indonesian history. He concludes that there was no point in this since none of the great changes which typify European history of this period can be traced in the Indonesian past. Up to 1800 it simply remains part of Asia.[15]

This leads us to the second main characteristic of Van Leur's historical approach, namely the application of concepts from sociology, in particular those of Max Weber. Using Weber's concept of the ideal type – for example, those of 'peasant culture', 'patrimonial bureaucratic states', 'peddling trade' – he attempts to describe Asian history as part of universal history, but with its own character. In this way it is possible to do justice to the peculiarities of various cultures without either wrapping them up entirely in too abstract and too general a set of categories or discussing them as merely exotic and incomprehensible.

The question of the role of Europe in Asian history was of course of vital importance for the post-independence historiography. In this respect one can distinguish two schools, the minimalist and the sentimentalist. The minimalist school minimalizes the role of the western factor in Asian history claiming that this was virtually non-existent while the sentimentalist school maximizes the crimes and misdeeds of the West. Although, logically speaking, the two views seem to be contradictory they can sometimes both be found in the work of one scholar (for example the Dutch sociologist W. F. Wertheim or the Indian historian K. M. Panikkar).[16] Thus the debate was not altogether clear and the concepts themselves are ambiguous. But the two questions: 'Was western influence good or bad? Was its impact great or small?' are still intensively debated today and understandably so. They are vital for our interpretation of the past as well as our understanding of the present, as we shall see later.

In the nineteenth century the European approach to Asian history became increasingly dominated by feelings of European superiority and a conviction of Asian backwardness. This, however, was only a fairly recent phenomenon since European historians had traditionally shown a great respect for the ancient civilizations of Asia. This was very different from the European attitude towards Africa, which had always been regarded as an ahistorical continent and African people as people without civilization and thus without history. The most famous formulation of this opinion is to be found in the Jena lectures given by Hegel in 1830–1 and published as the *Philosophy of History*. Here he wrote: 'At this point we leave Africa, not to mention it again. For it is no historical part of the World; it has no movement or development to exhibit . . . What we properly understand by Africa is the Unhistorical, Undeveloped Spirit, still involved in the conditions of mere nature, which had to be presented here only as on the threshold of the World's history.'[17]

Hegel had of course a great influence on Karl Marx and classical Marxist writings reflect the same line of thought. A late echo of this can be found in the work of the Hungarian Marxist historian of Africa, Endre Sik, who wrote in 1966:

> Prior to their encounter with Europeans the majority of African peoples still lived a primitive, barbaric life, many of them even on the lowest level of barbarism. Some of them lived in complete, or almost complete, isolation: the contacts, if any, of others were but scattered skirmishes with neighbouring peoples. The *State*, taken in the real sense of the word, was a notion unknown to most African peoples, as classes did not exist either. Or rather – both existed already, but only in embryo. Therefore it is unrealistic to speak of their 'history' – in the scientific sense of the word – before the appearance of the European invaders.[18]

There is no doubt that such opinions were by no means a monopoly of Marxist historians. Just one year before Sik's book appeared, the Regius Professor of Modern History at Oxford, H. R. Trevor-Roper, compared the histories of Britain and Africa, decribing the latter as being little more than 'the unrewarding gyrations of barbarous tribes in picturesque but irrelevant quarters of the globe'.[19]

How things have changed in twenty years! Nobody in his right mind would argue any more that African history does nto exist, not even in Oxford. The development of African history has been spectacular. Perhaps it has been the most vivid, dynamic and innovative field of history since the emergence of the new social and economic history in the 1920s and 1930s. One could argue that the *Journal of African History* has been the most innovative journal since the founding of the *Annales*. Indeed the two developments are to a certain extent comparable. Social historians, such as those of the *Annales* and others, began to ask questions that had not been asked before and of which no mention was made in traditional sources. New sources had to be discovered and new techniques developed to re-examine old sources in a new light. The same situation exists with African history. Sources are scarce, at least traditional ones. For cultural reasons the Africans have produced less written material on African history than the Europeans and for climatic reasons, little of this has been handed down to us. This means that most of the sources are exogenous. They come from foreigners, be they Greek, Roman or Arabic travellers, geographers, European merchants or administrators. Technically speaking, much of African history is pre- or protohistory (or ethno-history as it has sometimes been called).[20]

The very scarcity of sources has given an enormous stimulus to the development of new techniques and methods. The past had to be interrogated with other means. Again, the comparison with the *Annales* and its *nouvelle histoire* is relevant. In both cases archaeology, cartography, linguistics, onomastics have been applied. Anthropology has also played a major role in African history. Indeed the distinction between the anthropologist and the historian is by no means very sharp.

The most famous of the techniques developed in order to provide new sources for African history was of course the study of oral tradition. Here the publication of Jan Vansina's *De la tradition orale. Essai de méthode historique* in 1961 was epoch-making. Quickly translated into English (*Oral tradition*, 1965) the book had a tremendous impact on African history.[21] Halfway between the naive and the sceptic, Vansina developed a method for using oral tradition in a critical way and thus for employing it in serious history writing. Vansina divided the oral tradition into five categories (formulae, poetry, lists, tales, commentaries) each with its various subdivisions. He argued that oral tradition should not be accepted at face value and that it should only be used after critical examination, paying attention to the impact of social significance, cultural values and the personality of the writers. It should also, as far as possible, be checked with other sources, for example, archaeological findings or written documents. Some historians (and anthropologists) were more sceptical about oral tradition and believed, with due respect for Vansina, that he overestimated its possibilities, but it is undeniable that his work and ideas have greatly influenced African history.[22]

Whatever possibilities oral tradition and other unorthodox sources offer, the fact remains that as far as written documents are concerned Africa is rather deprived. It is of course true that this also goes for certain periods of European history for which documents are also very scarce, as well as for pre-Columbian America, pre-Cookian Australia etc. and that therefore African history is exceptional but not unique. All the same a historiography of Africa comparable to that of Europe seems impossible. Long-term developments can be studied but a strictly factual or *événementiel* history is often impossible. At the moment the structural or long-term approach is in vogue in European history as well, but this is a matter of choice. In Africa structural history is not a choice but the only possibility. One is not seduced by it, but condemned to it.[23]

In the last decades a number of African historians have appeared in the international forum, and their role is becoming increasingly prominent. All the same one should acknowledge that the great leap forward in African history was mostly due to European and American historians, especially British ones. The *Journal of African History* – the first issue of which appeared in 1960 – was, as Terence Ranger has said, 'the combined manifesto, charter, programme and shop-window for the field'.[24] Roland Oliver's seminar at the London School of Oriental and African Studies has been called 'the premier setting in the world for the presentation of new work on Africa's past'.[25] Oliver's and Fage's *Short History of Africa* sold over a million copies and was probably the single most influential book on African history.

French historians also played an important role, albeit a more modest one. In 1961 Henri Brunschwig, a former student of Marc Bloch and Lucien Febvre at Strasbourg, was invited by Fernand Braudel to introduce African history at the École des Hautes Études. His seminar became a meeting place for French and African scholars. Yves Person, the author of a monumental and innovative history of Samori, and Catherine Coquery-Vidrovitch not only wrote important books themselves but also brought the subject to the University of Paris.[26] Other universities (Aix, Bordeaux) also offered courses and seminars in African history, and a great number of African students presented doctoral dissertations at French universities.

The contribution of American universities was significant, particularly that of the three main schools of Yale, UCLA and, above all, Madison (Wisconsin). Those American historians who played a leading role in the second and third generations of African historians were mostly former students of Curtin and Vansina at Madison. At the moment important historical schools also exist at various universities in Africa itself (Nigeria, Kenya, Zaïre). The period of European dominance is clearly over.

In retrospect much of the debate about the possibilities and impossibilities of African and Asian history looks rather futile, not only because of the decrease in the feeling of European superiority but also due to the changes in the study of history itself. The antagonism of colonialist versus nationalist makes sense within the framework of political history, but in other fields of history we find a different approach. Social history is studied at the level of the village, the region, the ethnic group. Cultural history is analysed on a much bigger scale than that of the nation state. Concepts like Hindu or Javanese civilization or 'the world of Islam' are relevant here. Economic history works with large unities like the Indian Ocean, or South-east Asia or even the world economy. In this type of approach the opposition-colonial versus anti-colonial does not make much sense.

Does this mean that the impact of colonialism on overseas history is over and that western and non-western attitudes have found a complete equilibrium? Not necessarily, for in two respects there still exists a western dominance. In the first place, as a result of colonial expansion a great quantity of books, documents and other material about the overseas world has been brought over to Europe and is now available in European archives and libraries. This means that in order to study their own past non-European historians will have to continue to come to Europe. In the second place, and also to a large extent as a consequence of colonialism, in the western world a great tradition has been founded in the field of non-western studies, in which it still plays a major role. On the other hand there are practically no African or Asian historians who study European history and society. As long as the West has its Orientalists but the East has no 'Occidentalists' there can be no real equilibrium.

On balance one can say that the development of African and Asian history was a natural and a necessary phenomenon. But it also leaves us with a problem. While it is true that African and Asian history is to a large extent autonomous, it is also true that since about 1500 the history of Africa and Asia has become connected to that of Europe. Asian history is much more than an extension of the history of Europe, but it cannot be completely isolated from European history either. The central development of modern history is the increasing interconnec-tion and interweaving of various formerly isolated civilizations and economies. This has resulted in the 'modern world system' (Wallerstein) and the 'civilization of modernity' (Eisenstadt) that we have today. One cannot understand this process by considering only isolated parts of history, for that would be missing the central theme of modern world history. World history cannot be considered as identical to European or western history; neither can it be conceived of as a series of isolated developments. To tackle this problem is the central concern of the history of European expansion as it has developed in the post-decolonization period.

Expansion and Reaction

The study of European expansion was also influenced by external as well as internal factors. The rapid fall of the colonial empires, for example, led to a questioning of their previous apparent stability. The rise of the American empire, an empire without colonies, stimulated a rethinking of both informal and formal techniques of imperialism. The emergence of China led to a reappraisal of the country's scientific and naval possibilities and thus to new questions about the differences between Chinese and early European expansion.

On the other hand internal factors changed the nature of expansion studies as well, and the general trend in favour of social and economic history also manifested itself in this field. Questions about monetarization, shipping, gold and silver, the profits of empire etc. were asked in a new way and these could often be answered with the aid of a computer.[27] Social history became a fashionable subject and this stimulated the study of migration, the slave trade, race relations, urbanization and *mentalités*. Political science influenced political history by suggesting the study of such topics as decision-making, public opinion, the role of special interest groups etc.

Although at the theoretical level the traditional distinction between a first and a second phase of expansion was questioned, in actual practice the division of labour between modernists and students of contemporary history is still very visible. Traditionally in early modern expansion the emphasis is on the great discoveries, ships and navigation, companies and trade, migration, plantation systems and slave societies. Charles Boxer and J. H. Parry wrote successful books aiming at an overview of the seaborne empires.[28] The Minnesota series on the history of *Europe and the World in the Age of Expansion* also offered a series of textbooks on these topics. In many of these fields new approaches were offered, new questions were asked and new techniques applied. Glamann, Steensgaard and Chaudhuri published path-finding studies of the Indian Companies, Curtin did pioneer work on the slave trade, Chaunu on the Atlantic world, Bailyn on migration and many more could and should be mentioned.[29] Many of the questions discussed here are closely related to major topics of debate in European history such as theories about the origins of capitalism, 'Phase I and II', the general depression of the seventeenth century, the price revolution etc. It should however be acknowledged that no general theory of European expansion was offered. While in the history of nineteenth- and twentieth-century expansion the debate was dominated by the concept of imperialism, there was no such thing in early expansion studies, at least not until Immanuel Wallerstein launched his theory about the modern world system.

Wallerstein's World System

Immanuel Wallerstein, a social scientist from Columbia University, first studied African decolonization and development problems. His way of thinking about these topics was influenced by *dependencia* and by underdevelopment theories. However, Wallerstein turned to history because he believes that these problems of development can only be fully understood in their global context and in a historical perspective. The historical work he feels most familiar with is that of the *Annales* group and particularly that of Fernand Braudel. There is indeed a strong similarity between Wallerstein's ideas and the conceptual framework of the third volume of Braudel's work on *Material Civilization, Economy and Capitalism.*[30] Wallerstein's main publication so far is a (planned) four-volume study of what he calls *The Modern World System*. The first volume, which came out in 1974, offered the analytic framework of the project.[31] It was a source of inspiration for many other scholars and led to an interesting debate on the origins of European expansion and capitalism.

Wallerstein argues that the world economy of today goes back to the end of the fifteenth century. Here we find the beginnings of a world system that developed fully in the sixteenth and seventeenth centuries and was already mature before the Industrial Revolution. The 'systemic turning point' can be located in the resolution of the crisis of feudalism which occurred approximately between 1450 and 1550. By the period 1550–1650 all the basic mechanisms of the capitalist world system were in place. In view of this the Industrial Revolution of about 1760 to 1830 can no longer be considered as a major turning-point in the history of the capitalist world economy.

The world system according to Wallerstein is characterized by an international economic order and an international division of labour. It consists of a core, a semi-periphery and a periphery, the location of which changes over time (regions can ascend to the core or descend to the periphery). Modern history is in fact the history of the continuing integration into this world system of ever more parts of the world. The world system works in such a way as to make the centre receive the profits, thus exploiting the periphery. This is brought about by international trade, which is considered as a zero-sum game: the profits of one party equal the losses of the other. The profits of international trade made the Industrial Revolution possible, which in turn only confirmed existing unequal relations and reinforced the development of underdevelopment.

Wallerstein's work was well received by social scientists but rather more critically by historians who in particular criticized the great weight given to international trade in the model. Some argued that pre-industrial economies were not able to produce such a significant surplus as to make an important international trade possible. Before the steamships transport facilities were very limited. Around 1600 the combined merchant fleets of the European states only had the tonnage of one or two (around 1800 of seven or eight) of today's supertankers.[32] Even in trading nations *par excellence* such as Britain and the Dutch Republic trading for export represented a very small percentage of the GNP (and export to the periphery only a small percentage of the total overseas trade).[33] The capital accumulated in Britain as a consequence of overseas trade cannot have represented more than 15 per cent of the gross expenditure undertaken during the Industrial Revolution.[34] Generally speaking, the effects of European expansion on overseas regions were not very important. In Asia the impact of overseas trade was only regional. Both in India (textile) and Indonesia (cash crops) only limited regions were affected by European demand. As far as Africa is concerned the trade in products was very limited. Much more important was the Atlantic slave trade. Recent research however tends to minimize the long-term demographic consequences of this. In the Americas and the Caribbean the impact of European expansion was the most dramatic, not so much because of trade but because of the demographic decline of the original population.

An interesting point of Wallerstein's theory is his questioning of the very concept of an Industrial Revolution and thus of the distinction between pre-industrial and industrial colonialism. This distinction was a central argument in the classical theory of imperialism, a theory that has dominated the historiography of late nineteenth- and twentieth-century European expansion.

Imperialism

Although the word imperialism had been in existence since the 1860s, imperialism as a historical concept only began with the publication of J. A. Hobson's *Imperialism: a Study* in 1902.[35] In order to explain imperialism Hobson argued that as a consequence of the capitalist system the British economy suffered from underconsumption. This meant that surplus capital could not be profitably invested in England herself. Therefore, in his famous words, the capitalists were 'seeking foreign markets and foreign investments to take the goods and capital they cannot sell or use at home'.[36] Thus the theory of capitalist imperialism was born.

Hobson's theory was soon taken over, adapted and made more sophisticated by Marxist thinkers, especial Germans such as Karl Hilferding and Rosa Luxemburg. In doing so, these authors also changed Hobson's argument. Whereas to Hobson the flight of capital was a typical but not a necessary consequence of capitalism, for the Marxists imperialism became an inevitability. The most famous formula is to be found with Lenin, who in 1916 called imperialism 'the highest stage of capitalism'. Although the differences between Hobson and Lenin are evident, it soon became commonplace to refer to the 'Hobson-Lenin thesis'. In fact, this became a standard explanation of European imperialism during the 1920s and 1930s.

Only in the 1960s was the general discussion on imperialism reopened. Clearly, decolonization as well as the rise of the American economic empire had much to do with this. In 1961 the British historians J. Gallagher and R. Robinson published the book that was to be the single most influential re-examination of British imperialism: *Africa and the Victorians*.[37] The year before, Henri Brunschwig had published *Mythes et réalités de l'impérialisme colonial français, 1871–1914*, an essay which set the tone for all later studies on French imperialism.[38] New interpretations of Belgian, German, Italian, Portuguese and, eventually, Dutch imperialism followed. We might speak of a historiographical revolution, the conclusions of which can be summarized here only very briefly for the two major powers involved.

Gallagher and Robinson, continuing along the lines they had developed in their article 'The Imperialism of Free Trade',[39] argued that the so-called imperialist period (1880–1914) was only different from the preceding, allegedly anti-imperialist, mid-Victorian period of free trade in its means and not in its ends: the mid-Victorians could do without political measures; the late Victorians had to formalize their empire. This formalization was prompted by local crises and frontier situations creating political vacuums which had to be filled by the British. Their actions had a strategic and not an economic background, and their policy was essentially defensive and reluctant. Gallagher and Robinson, in short, demolished the concept of an imperialist period as well as the economic explanation which had traditionally been connected with it.

Although his conclusions were in some respects similar, Brunschwig's revision of French imperialism was rather different. Brunschwig did accept that, in the case of France, there was a definite imperialist period, viz. roughly 1880 to 1914. This indeed could hardly be denied, But while he was traditional in this respect, he was revolutionary in the interpretation of the phenomenon. After a careful examination of the economic interests of French colonialists, as well as the economic balance sheet of French imperialism, he reached the conclusion that to explain it in economic terms would be a myth. The empire did not pay, there was no link between protectionism and imperialism, and the French imperialists had no economic motives or interests. Consequently, there must be a different explanation. According to Brunschwig, this is to be found in the rising tide of nationalism in the Third Republic, deeply wounded by the defeat of 1870. Thus, like that of Gallagher and Robinson, his book is basically a refutation of the economic theory of imperialism.

The books mentioned above did away with the traditional simple explanation of imperialism in terms of economic needs,though they did not give an analysis of the economic aspects of imperialism. In order to tackle this immense question it is not only necessary to solve a great number of theoretical and methodological problems, but also to collect and analyse an enormous amount of data. Again the computer made this possible. Two American historians, L. Davis and R. Huttenback, very appropriately connected with the California Institute of Technology, did precisely this for the subject of British imperialism. They collected a huge amount of data and analysed this with very sophisticated methods. Their book *Mammon and the Pursuit of Empire*[40] seems to offer the definite answer to the old and famous question: Did the Empire pay? The answer somewhat disappointingly is: No! After 1880 the initially high rates of profits on colonial investments fell below comparable returns from other overseas destinations or even Britain itself. Thus Hobson and Lenin were wrong about the relation between surplus capital and the urge of overseas expansion. The dependent colonies were not major recipients of City capital. There can be no doubt that this is not the whole answer, because Davis and Huttenback also argue that for some capitalists these investments were far from marginal.[41]

In France, under the influence of Brunschwig's arguments, even Marxist authors have accepted his vision that the economic aspects of French imperialism were negligible. In an attempt to rescue the Marxist interpretation they have argued that French imperialism was to be found elsewhere, in Russia, the Ottoman empire etc. This dialectical exercise resulted in the conclusion that French colonialism was not imperialist and French imperialism not colonial.[42] In order to find a

more empirical answer to the question of economy and empire
Professor Catherine Coquery-Vidrovitch took the initiative of setting up
a data bank of French colonial trade (1880–1960). Her Parisian
colleague, Jacques Marseille, was the first to make extensive use of this
rich documentation for his dissertation *Empire colonial et capitalisme
français: histoire d'un divorce.*[43] Marseille's conclusion is that there was
a break in the relation between capitalism and colonialism. In the initial
period, 1880–1930, French industry needed the outlet of the protected
colonial market, and the marriage of colonialism and capitalism was a
happy one. In the second period, 1930–60, protectionism became an
obstacle to sorely needed industrial modernization. Divorce became
inevitable. But decolonization was already under way. The end of
empire in 1960 was a blessing for capitalism.

So much for Europe, but what was the impact of imperialism on the
overseas world? This is a complicated subject on which a passionate
debate has been going on ever since the question was raised. There are
few things on which the debaters agree but one fact is undeniable: the
real impact of the West on the overseas territories took place after the
Industrial Revolution. What were the effects of this? Of course
colonialism was organized in such a manner as to promote the interests
of the colonial power. Of course this implied burdens of various kinds
for the colonized peoples. However, beyond the domain of basic truths
such as these there is a vast zone of problems that cannot be answered
simply. There is the well established phenomenon of de-industrialization
(notably in the case of the Indian textile industry). There is also the
problem of specialization in cash crops. On the other hand there are
long-term developments resulting from investment in infrastructure
(mining, roads, ports), the improvement of administration, education,
health. To draw an economic balance sheet of colonialism is extraordinarily difficult. Not only because of the lack of data but also because
of theoretical problems.

If, as modern research has convincingly demonstrated, the simple
explanation that imperialism was the result of capitalism is unacceptable,
the question remains: What *was* the reason? Why was there 'an age of
imperialism' at all? As far as Britain is concerned the answer to this
question was also given by Gallagher and Robinson. They argued that
there was none. The very concept of an age of imperialism (1880–1914)
is a fallacy. To consider this period as the zenith of British imperialism is
to misunderstand its real nature. The increasing number of red areas on
the world map during the 1880s and 1890s might seem to suggest that
Britain's power was increasing. In reality, however, this was not an
indication of strength but of weakness. Britain was more powerful in the

early nineteenth century when it ruled by informal means than in the later years of formal political rule.[44]

The concept of informal empire is very attractive and very inspiring because it explains a great number of important phenomena. It also gives a much broader meaning to the term imperialism. In this type of analysis imperialism exists in different periods and in different forms. The task of the historian is to explain the transition from one form to another. In Gallagher and Robinson's argument the reasons for this are not to be found with the politicians in Europe – who preferred informal empire anyway – but in changing situations overseas. Imperialism is considered as a system of collaboration between European and non-European forces. The changing forms of imperialism result from changes in terms of collaboration.[45] It is obvious that in such an analysis decolonization also loses much of its importance as a turning-point. If there exists an informal imperialism before Empire, logically there can also be an informal imperialism after Empire.[46] Here the debate on imperialism is connected to those on decolonization and underdevelopment.

Decolonization and After

Decolonization has only recently become a subject of historical analysis and debate. Of course a great deal had already been written about it, but all this was very much of an *événementiel* character and written from a clearly ideological perspective. The same song was sung everywhere. The colonized peoples wanted to become independent. After World War II they fought their oppressors and threw off the yoke of colonial rule. For a long time it seemed that there was nothing more to it. Recently a number of collective and comparative studies have been published that offer new interpretations and ask new questions. Decolonization is finally emerging as a subject for historical analysis rather than an act of God or the result of the laws of nature.[47]

The questions discussed are basically very simple ones. Why did decolonization occur when it occurred and why did it take on the various forms it did? Decolonization is no longer exclusively described as the history of the acts of political leaders in a short time-span (1947–62). Its long-term, structural and conjunctural aspects are also given attention. The analysis of the various forms of decolonization centres around the three forces that were at work, the colonial power, the situation in the colony and the international factor. The interaction of these forces decided the forms but not the outcome of the process because, whatever the differences, the outcome was always the same: independence. But here again a question arises. What did independence really mean? Was the end of Empire also the end of imperialism or was it the continuation of it by different means? Here the subject of decolonization is connected to another topic, the theory of dependency.

The *dependencia* theory was first put forward by the Argentinian economist Raúl Prebish in 1947 and then further developed in the 1960s by Latin-American scholars and by North Americans interested in Latin America. The theory was born from the observation of the permanency of Latin America's problems: poverty, inequality, slums, external debts, the dominance of foreign capital: in a word, dependency. The theory of dependency argues that this situation is not the result of a lack of development but of underdevelopment. Originating in Latin-American studies, the theory was further worked out and refined to become a universal one applicable not only to Latin America but to the entire Third World. The Third World is seen as the periphery of a world economic system in which the centre, that is to say, the West, is accumulating the profits and keeping the periphery in a situation of permanent dependency. Thus, underdevelopment is not a situation but a process. The Third World is not undeveloped, but it is being underdeveloped by the West. André Gunder Frank formulated its most catching formulation: 'the development of underdevelopment'.[48]

The theory of dependency was soon applied to various parts of the Third World, particularly to Africa. Samir Amin wrote extensively on the subject and Walter Rodney published his successful book about it with the arresting title *How Europe Underdeveloped Africa*.[49] The problem with the theory is that in order to explain the particular (under)development of Africa it has to make the continent dependent upon foreign influences during most of its history. This line of thought was somewhat contradictory of the main trend which developed in African history in the same period, which underlined the autonomy of African history. Africans were seen no longer as mere victims of European expansion but to a large extent as masters of their own destiny. While neo-Marxists embraced the theory of dependency, classical Marxist historians and anthropologists underlined the autonomy of African history and even tried to discover an 'African mode of production'.[50]

Both the theory of dependency and the concept of informal empire were of great heuristic value because they questioned some of the fundamental assumptions of overseas history and thus changed our interpretation. The very concept of an age of imperialism with a clearcut beginning and end can be disputed, at least as far as Britain is concerned. The zenith of the British Empire is now sometimes placed in the eighteenth century, its decline already beginning in the nineteenth. Not surprisingly the question has been asked: 'Why did the British Empire last so long?'[51] The danger with concepts and theories like these is that their meaning is overestimated and they become the new orthodoxy. It is a useful corrective to existing interpretations to relativize the importance of turning-points such as the beginning of imperialism or the transfer of power, but we should not also underestimate their historical significance. The loss and eventually recovery of political independence are important enough historical caesurae, and it is no use letting their concrete historical significance fade away in some rather abstract concept of dependency. Here we face another problem with concepts like this: they are formulated in such an abstract way that they cover all types of dominance. Ronald Robinson's most recent contribution to the theory of imperialism, the 'excentric' theory, with or without empire, suffers from this. In this, his latest model, imperialism is conceived in 'terms of the play of international economic and political markets in which degrees of monopoly and competition in relations at world, metropolitan and local levels decide its necessity and profitability'.[52] This is probably a correct but also a rather abstract description of imperialism. Asymmetry of power and changes in forms of collaboration are to be found throughout history. Perhaps it is more useful to stay somewhat closer to the concrete historical process and to give full attention to the specific and unique aspects of European expansion. This brings us back to the question we started with: 'What is overseas history?' or rather 'What will it be in the future?'

Conclusion

In 1979 when P. C. Emmer and I published a volume of essays entitled *Reappraisals in Overseas History* we also had to ask ourselves the question: 'What is overseas history?' We then argued that it is a much broader concept than the history of European expansion, for it 'deals not only with the encounters between Europeans and non-Europeans, but also with the economic, social, political and cultural systems of the non-Europeans themselves'.[53] This is true. As we have seen in this contribution, there are in fact two different and clearly distinct forms of overseas history, the autonomous history of Asia and Africa and the history of European expansion. But as we have also seen, this situation is not satisfactory. If there are autonomous histories of Africa, Asia, America, Australia etc. there is no point in throwing all these histories into one basket, for the sole reason that they are not European, and calling this 'overseas history'. The reason why this was done was that after 1945 overseas history had to find a new focus, and colonial historians and their students turned to Asian and African history itself. It was some time before these fields proved their right of existence. In the meantime the term 'overseas history' served as a neutral and therefore convenient cover for their activities. This form of overseas history can thus be considered as an emancipation movement. It can be compared with the emergence of women's history or black history or, in an earlier period, the history of the working classes, the peasants etc. As soon as the emancipation is completed the subject changes its character. From the professional historian's point of view it will continue to exist as a specialization, a special field of interest, but for the public it becomes part of 'general' history.

This is clearly also the case with African and Asian history. They have proved their right of existence, just like European or American history. So this particular branch of overseas history is bound to disintegrate into African or Asian history etc. But there is another side to it as well. Just as some but not all of European history can be understood as autonomous history, the same goes for the overseas world. Over the last five centuries or so the histories of various parts of the world have become interconnected and various civilizations have influenced one another. This is the other topic of overseas history and the importance of this aspect of modern history is increasingly understood. In this form overseas history has gained a distinct place in the field of modern history, not as a special discipline or subdiscipline but as a particular form of world history.

At the moment it seems that there are two approaches, two ways of dealing with the problem of world history. One of them can perhaps be labelled historical macrosociology. This type of history is characterized by a social-science approach. It singles out a specific social phenomenon or topic, like state formation or revolution or dictatorship, and analyses this in various historical contexts. Thus one can distinguish similarities and dissimilarities between, for example, events in sixteenth-century Europe and twentieth-century China. The aim of the game is to learn more about social processes in general.[54] The other approach is more traditional in so far as it tries to distinguish a certain pattern in the development of modern history and considers the writing of history as the description of concrete historical processes and events. History is also studied in a comparative way but within the framework of chronological developments. There is more interest in the differences between various developments and the uniqueness of certain events than in their similarities. The conceptual framework is that of the unification of the world as a consequence of the expansion of Europe and the rise of the West.[55] Both approaches are characterized by a strong desire to transcend traditional boundaries, parochial views and nationalist bias. In the end they have the same goal, to make the specific western discipline of history applicable to world history. This is necessary because 'our civilization is the first to have for its past the past of the world, our history is the first to be world history.' These words were written by Huizinga more than half a century ago.[56] The challenge of drawing the consequences from them is one we are still facing today.

NOTES

1   See, for example, M. Mörner and T. Svensson (eds), *The History of the Third World in Nordic Research* (Göteborg, 1986).

2   See C. Fasseur, 'Leiden and Empire: University and Colonial Office, 1825–1925' in W. Otterspeer (ed.), *Leiden Oriental Connections, 1850–1940* (Leiden, 1989), pp. 187–203.

3   J. Romein, *Aera van Europa* (Leiden, 1954) and *De eeuw van Azië* (Leiden, 1956).

4   L. Blussé, 'Japanese Historiography and European Sources' in P. C. Emmer and H. L. Wesseling (eds), *Reappraisals in Overseas History* (Leiden, 1979), pp. 193–222.

5   See T. O. Ranger, 'Towards a Usable African Past' in C. Fyfe (ed.), *African Studies Since 1945: a Tribute to Basil Davidson* (London, 1976), pp. 17–29.

6   See A. G. Hopkins, 'European Expansion into West Africa: a Historiographical Survey of English Language Publications since 1945' in Emmer and Wesseling, *Reappraisals*, p. 56.

7   F. Braudel, *La Méditerranée et le monde méditerranéen à l'époque de Philippe II* (2 vols, Paris, 1976) 3rd edn, vol. I, p. 17.

8   For both practical and theoretical reasons we will leave aside the history of the Americas and the Caribbean. As far as Asia is concerned we will restrict ourselves to the two former European colonies where the emancipation of a national historiography has been the most impressive, that is, India and Indonesia.

9   J. Nehru, *The Discovery of India* (London, 1956), p. 28.

10 See S. Ray, 'India: After Independence', *Journal of Contemporary History* 2 (1967) pp. 125–42.

11 H. A. J. Klooster, *Indonesiërs schrijven hun geschiedenis. De ontwikkeling van de Indonesische geschiedbeoefening in theorie en praktijk, 1900–1980* (Leiden, 1985).

12 J. Bastin, *The Study of Modern Southeast Asian History* (Kuala Lumpur, 1959). See also his *The Western Element in Modern Southeast Asian History* (Kuala Lumpur, 1963).

13 J. C. Van Leur, *Eenige beschouwingen betreffende den ouden Aziatischen handel* (Middelburg, 1934). A translation of this as well as of his other writings can be found in J. C. Van Leur, *Indonesian Trade and Society: Essays in Asian Social and Economic History* (The Hague/Bandung, 1955).

14 Van Leur, *Trade and Society*, p. 162.

15 Ibid., pp. 268–89.

16 K. M. Panikkar, *A Survey of Indian History* (London, 1947); W. F. Wertheim, 'Asian History and the Western Historian. Rejoinder to Professor Bastin', *Bijdragen tot de Taal-, Land- en Volkenkunde* 119 (1963), pp. 149–60.

17 G. W. F. Hegel, *The Philosophy of History* (New York, 1944), p. 99.

18 E. Sik, *The History of Black Africa* (2 vols, Budapest, 1966), vol. I, p. 17.

19 H. Trevor-Roper, *The Rise of Christian Europe* (London, 1965), p. 9.

20 H. Brunschwig, 'Un faux problème: l'ethnohistoire', *Annales E. S. C.* 20 (1965), pp. 291–300.

21 J. Vansina, *De la tradition òrale. Essai de méthode historique* (Tervueren, 1961). English translation: *Oral Tradition. A Study in Historical Methodology* (London, 1965).

22 In some of his later work Vansina himself seems to be more sceptical than before. See P. Salmon, *Introduction à l'histoire de l'Afrique* (Brussels, 1986), 126ff.

23 See H. Brunschwig 'Une histoire de l'Afrique noire est-elle possible?' in *Mélanges en l'honneur de Fernand Braudel* (2 vols, Toulouse, 1973), vol. I, pp. 75–87.

24 See T. Ranger, 'Usable Past', p. 17.

25 *The Blackwell Dictionary of Historians* (Oxford, 1988), p. 308 s.v. Oliver, R.

26 C. Coquery-Vidrovitch, *Le Congo au temps des grandes compagnies concessionnaires* (Paris, 1972); Y. Person, *Samori: une Révolution dyula* (3 vols, Dakar, 1968, 1970, 1976). See on this also: H. Brunschwig, 'French Historiography Since 1945 Concerning Black Africa' in Emmer and Wesseling, *Reappraisals*, pp. 84–97.

27 A useful report on this subject is T. Lindblad, 'Computer Applications in Expansion History: A Survey', *Second Bulletin of the ESF-Network on the History of European Expansion*. Supplement to *Itinerario* 12 (1988), pp. 2–61.

28 C. R. Boxer, *The Portuguese Seaborne Empire, 1418–1825* (New York, 1969); C. R. Boxer, *The Dutch Seaborne Empire, 1600–1800* (London, 1965); J. H. Parry, *The Spanish Seaborne Empire* (New York, 1966).

29 K. Glamann, *Dutch-Asiatic Trade 1620–1740* 2d edn (The Hague, 1980); N. Steensgaard, *The Asian Trade Revolution of the 17th Century. The East India Companies and the Decline of the Caravan Trade* (Chicago/London, 1974); K. N. Chaudhuri, *The Trading World of Asia and the English East India Company, 1660–1760* (Cambridge, 1978); P. Curtin, *The Atlantic Slave Trade: a Census* (Madison, Wis., 1969); P. and H. Chaunu, *Séville et l'Atlantique, 1504–1650* (12 vols, Paris, 1956–60); B. Bailyn, *Voyagers to the West; Emigration from Britain to America on the Eve of the Revolution*

(London, 1987). A recent synthesis is G. V. Scammell, *The First Imperial Age: European Overseas Expansion, c.*1400–1715 (London, 1989).

30 F. Braudel, *Civilisation matérielle, économie et capitalisme, XVe–XVIIIe siècle* (Paris, 1979).

31 I. Wallerstein, *The Modern World System: Capitalist Agriculture and the Origins of the European World-Economy in the Sixteenth Century* (New York, 1974).

32 See J. de Vries, *The Economy of Europe in an Age of Crisis, 1600–1750* (Cambridge, 1976), pp. 192–3.

33 See R. Floud and D. McCloskey (eds), *The Economic History of Britain since 1700* (2 vols, Cambridge, 1981), vol. I, pp. 87–92.

34 See P. O'Brien, 'European Economic Development: The Contribution of the Periphery', *Economic History Review*, 35 (1982), p. 9.

35 J. A. Hobson, *Imperialism: a Study* (London, 1902).

36 Ibid., p. 85.

37 R. Robinson, J. Gallagher (with A. Denny), *Africa and the Victorians: the Official Mind of Imperialism* (London, 1961).

38 H. Brunschwig, *Mythes et réalités de l'impérialisme colonial français, 1871–1914* (Paris, 1960).

39 R. Robinson and J. Gallagher, 'The Imperialism of Free Trade', *Economic History Review* 6 (1953), pp. 1–15.

40 L. A. Davis and R. A. Huttenback, *Mammon and the Pursuit of Empire: the Political Economy of British Imperialism, 1860–1912* (Cambridge, 1986).

41 See also the articles by P. J. Cain and A. G. Hopkins on this subject in *Economic History Review* 33 (1980), pp. 463–90; 39 (1986), pp. 501–525 and 40 (1987) pp. 1–26.

42 See J. Bouvier and R. Girault (eds), *L'Impérialisme français d'avant 1914* (Paris/The Hague, 1976).

43 J. Marseille, *Empire colonial et capitalisme français: histoire d'un divorce* (Paris, 1984).

44 Robinson and Gallagher, 'Imperialism of Free Trade' (see note 39).

45 R. Robinson, 'Non-European Foundations of European Imperialism: Sketch for a Theory of Collaboration' in R. Owen and B. Sutcliffe (eds), *Studies in the Theory of Imperialism* (London, 1972), pp. 117–40.

46 See W. J. Mommsen and J. Osterhammel (eds), *Imperialism and After: Continuities and Discontinuities* (London, 1986).

47 See H. L. Wesseling, 'Towards a History of Decolonization', *Itinerario* 11 (1987), pp. 94–106.

48 A. G. Frank, 'The Development of Underdevelopment' in R. I. Rhodes (ed.), *Imperialism and Underdevelopment: a Reader* (New York and London, 1960), pp. 5–16. See on this L. Blussé, H. L. Wesseling and G. D. Winius (eds), *History and Underdevelopment* (Leiden and Paris, 1980).

49 W. Rodney, *How Europe Underdeveloped Africa* (London, 1972).

50 There is a vast literature on this subject. For a brief introduction see A. G.

Hopkins, 'Clio-Antics: A Horoscope for African Economic History' in Fyfe, *African Studies*, pp. 31–48.

51 P. M. Kennedy, 'Why Did the British Empire Last So Long?' in P. M. Kennedy, *Strategy and Diplomacy, 1870–1945: Eight studies* (London, 1983), pp. 197–218.

52 R. Robinson, 'The Excentric Idea of Imperialism, With or Without Empire', in Mommsen and Osterhammel, *Imperialism and After*, pp. 267–89.

53 P. C. Emmer and H. L. Wesseling, 'What is Overseas History?' in Emmer and Wesseling, *Reappraisals*, p. 3.

54 See T. Skocpol and M. Somer, 'The Uses of Comparative History in Macrosocial Inquiry', *Comparative Studies in Society and History*, 22 (1980), pp. 174–97.

55 Next to Wallerstein Eric R. Wolf's *Europe and the People Without History* (Berkeley, 1982) and P. Curtin, *Cross Cultural Trade in World History* (Cambridge, 1985) as well as W. McNeill's *The Rise of the West: a History of the Human Community* (Chicago, 1963) are relevant for this.

56 J. Huizinga, 'A Definition of the Concept of History' in R. Klibansky and H. J. Paton (eds), *Philosophy and History* (Oxford, 1936), p. 8.

5

On Microhistory

Giovanni Levi

A doubt without an end is not even a doubt.
L. Wittgenstein, 1969

It is no accident that the debate over microhistory has not been based on theoretical texts or manifestos. Microhistory is essentially a historio-graphical practice whereas its theoretical references are varied and, in a sense, eclectic. The method is in fact concerned first and foremost with the actual detailed procedures which constitute the historian's work, so microhistory cannot be defined in relation to the micro-dimensions of its subject-matter. The reader may thus perhaps be surprised by the somewhat theoretical nature of this article. In fact, many historians who adhere to microhistory have been involved in continuous interchanges with the social sciences and established historiographical theories without, however, feeling any need to refer to any coherent system of concepts or principles of their own. Microhistory, in common with all experimental work, has no body of established orthodoxy to draw on. The wide diversity of material produced clearly demonstrates how limited the range of common elements is. However, in my opinion, such few common elements as there are in microhistory are crucial and it is these that I will here attempt to examine.

There are certain distinctive characteristics in microhistory which derive from that period in the 1970s when it arose out of a more general political and cultural debate. There is nothing particularly unusual in that since the 1970s and eighties were almost universally years of crisis for the prevailing optimistic belief that the world would be rapidly and radically transformed along revolutionary lines. At that time many of the hopes and mythologies which had previously guided a major part of the cultural debate, including the realm of historiography, were proving to be not so much invalid as inadequate in the face of the unpredictable consequences of political events and social realities – events and realities which were very far from conforming to the optimistic models proposed by the great Marxist or functionalist systems. We are still living through the initial dramatic phases of this process and historians have been forced to pose new questions about their own methodologies and interpretations. Above all, the assumption of the automatism of change has been undermined: more specifically, what has been called into question is the idea of a regular progression though a uniform and predictable series of stages in which social agents were considered to align themselves in conformity with solidarities and conflicts in some sense given, natural and inevitable.

The conceptual apparatus with which social scientists of all persuasions interpreted current or past change was weighed down by a burden of inherited positivism. Forecasts of social behaviour were proving to be demonstrably erroneous and this failure of existing systems and paradigms required not so much the construction of a new general social theory as a complete revision of existing tools of research. However banal and simplistic this statement may appear to be, this perception of crisis is so general that only the simplest reminder would seem to be necessary.

There were, however, a number of possible reactions to the crisis, and microhistory itself is nothing but one gamut of possible responses which laid emphasis on redefining concepts and profoundly analysing existing tools and methods. At the same time there have been other, altogether more drastic, solutions proposed which often veered towards a desperate relativism, neo-idealism or even the return to a philosophy riddled with irrationality.

Those historians who aligned themselves with microhistory[1] usually had their roots in Marxism, a political orientation to the left and a radical secularism with little inclination for metaphysics. Despite the fact that these characteristics were manifested in widely diverse ways, I believe that they served to anchor these historians firmly to the idea that historical research is not a purely rhetorical and aesthetic activity.

Their work has always centred on the search for a more realistic description of human behaviour, employing an action and conflict model of man's behaviour in the world which recognizes his – relative – freedom beyond, though not outside, the constraints of prescriptive and oppressive normative systems. Thus all social action is seen to be the result of an individual's constant negotiation, manipulation, choices and decisions in the face of a normative reality which, though pervasive, nevertheless offers many possibilities for personal interpretations and freedoms. The question is, therefore, how to define the margins – however narrow they may be – of the freedom granted an individual by the interstices and contradictions of the normative systems which govern him. In other words, an enquiry into the extent and nature of free will within the general structure of human society. In this type of enquiry the historian is not simply concerned with the interpretation of meanings but rather with defining the ambiguities of the symbolic world, the plurality of possible interpretations of it and the struggle which takes place over symbolic as much as over material resources.

Microhistory thus had a very specific location within the so-called new history. It was not simply a question of correcting those aspects of academic historiography which no longer appeared to function. It was more important to refute relativism, irrationalism and the reduction of the historian's work to a purely rhetorical activity which interprets texts and not events themselves.

'A doubt without an end is not even a doubt' according to Wittgenstein.[2] The problem lay in finding a way of both acknowledging the limits of knowledge and reason whilst at the same time constructing a historiography capable of organizing and explaining the world of the past. Therefore the main conflict is not one between new and traditional history, but rather one of the meaning of history seen as an interpretive practice.[3]

Microhistory as a practice is essentially based on the reduction of the scale of observation, on a microscopic analysis and an intensive study of the documentary material. This definition already gives rise to possible ambiguities: it is not simply a question of addressing the causes and effects of the fact that different dimensions coexist in every social system, in other words, the problem of describing vast complex social structures without losing sight of the scale of each individual's social space and hence, of people and their situation in life. It is not, therefore, a matter of conceptualizing the idea of scale as a factor inherent in all social systems and as an important characteristic of the contexts of social interaction including different quantitative and spatial dimensions. This problem has been amply discussed among anthropologists who have presented the concept of scale in just this perspective: scale as an object of analysis which serves to measure the dimensions in the field of relationships. For Fredrik Barth, for example, who organized a fundamental seminar on the theme, the problem is that of our 'ability to describe different combinations of scale in different empirical social organizations, to measure the part they play in the different sectors of the lives they shape'.[4] For microhistory the reduction of scale is an analytical procedure, which may be applied anywhere independently of the dimensions of the object analysed.

I want to look more closely at this problem for a moment because the idea that scale is an object of study is a source of misunderstanding for many people in discussions of microhistory. It is often assumed, for example, that local communities can be properly studied as objects of small-scale systems, but that the larger scales should be used to reveal connections between communities within a region, between regions within a country and so on. In actual fact, of course, it becomes immediately obvious that even the apparently minutest action of, say, somebody going to buy a loaf of bread, actually encompasses the far wider system of the whole world's grain markets. And only a paradoxical and significant distortion of perspective would suggest that the commercial life of one village is of no interest beyond its meaning on a local scale. An example of this kind of perspective can be glimpsed in an amusing diatribe of Franco Venturi against community studies and in particular against microhistory:[5]

> To study the chronicles of a village, as is done far too often nowadays, is completely meaningless. The historian's duty is to study the origins of those ideas which shape our lives, not to write novels. I need only to quote one example: there is a great deal of talk today about the need to return to the market. Who invented the market? The men of the eighteenth century. And in Italy who concerned themselves with it? The Enlightenment thinkers Genovesi and Verri. It is important to place firmly at the centre of our studies the roots of our modern life.

One could reply to this by paraphrasing Geertz: 'Historians do not study villages, they study in villages.'[6]

Naturally the description of differing albeit congruent combinations of scale in social phenomena is important, if only as a means of ascribing internal dimensions to the object of analysis. However it is self-evident, banal even, to state that the particular dimensions of the object of analysis do not necessarily reflect the distinctive scale of the problem posed. The idea that scale has its own existence in reality is accepted even by those who consider micro-analysis to work purely by example, that is to say as a simplified analytic process – the selection of a specific point of real life from which to exemplify general concepts – rather than the starting-point for a broader move towards generalization. What the dimensions of the social worlds of different categories of people and different structured fields of relationships demonstrate is the precise nature of the scale operating in reality. In this sense, therefore, the segmentation of complex societies is delineated without recourse to a priori assumptions and frameworks but this approach is only able to construct a generalization which is more metaphorical than argued, a generalization based merely on analogy. It seems to me, in other words, that we should discuss the problem of scale not only as one of the scale of observed reality, but also as a question of a variable scale of observation for experimental purposes. It is natural and right that the irreducibility of individual persons to the rules of large-scale systems should have placed the problem of scale at the core of the debate. Against an over-simple functionalism, it is important to emphasize the role of social contraditions in generating social change; in other words, emphasize the explanatory value of discrepancies between the constraints emanating from various normative systems (between, say, state and family norms) and of the fact that, in addition, any individual has a different set of relationships which determine his reactions to, and choices with regard to, the normative structure.

Although scale as an inherent characteristic of reality is certainly not an extraneous element in the microhistory debate it is, rather, tangential;[7] for the real problem lies in the decision to reduce the scale of observation for experimental purposes. The unifying principle of all microhistorical research is the belief that microscopic observation will reveal factors previously unobserved. Some examples of this intensive procedure are: a reinterpretation of the case against Galileo as a defence of Aristotelian notions of substance, and of the Eucharist, against an atomism which would have made impossible the transformation of wine and bread into blood and flesh;[8] focusing on a single painting and the identification of who its figures are as a means of investigating the cultural world of Piero della Francesca;[9] the study of consanguinary matrimonial strategies in a small village in the region of Como to reveal the mental universe of seventeenth-century peasants;[10] the introduction of the mechanical loom, as observed in a small textile village, to explain the general theme of innovation, its rhythms and effects;[11] one village's land transactions studied to discover the social rules of commercial exchange at work in a market which had yet to be de-personalized.[12]

Let us briefly examine the last example. There has been a great deal of discussion concerning the commercialization of land and it is a widely held belief that the precocity and frequency of land transactions which occurred in many Western European countries and in Colonial America indicate the early presence of capitalism and individualism. Two elements have prevented a more adequate assessment of this phenomenon. In the first place many interpretations have been based on aggregate data, an approach which has made it impossible to examine the concrete facts of the transactions themselves. Secondly, historians have been misled by their own modern mercantile mentality which led them to interpret the massive quantities of monetary land transactions they found in contemporary notarial deeds as evidence of the existence of a self-regulating market. Curiously, nobody had noticed or given weight to the fact that the prices involved were extremely variable, even allowing for the different qualities of land. Thus land prices and the general market were commonly referred to with the unquestioning assumption that the market forces were impersonal. It was only by reducing the scale of observation to an extremely localized area that it became possible to see that the price of land varied according to the kin relationship between the contractual parties. It also became possible to show that variable prices were charged for land of equal size and quality. It thus became possible to establish that one was looking at a complex market in which social and personal relationships played a determining role in establishing the price level, the timing, and the forms by which land changed hands. This example seems to me to be particularly revealing of the way microhistory proceeds in general. Phenomena previously considered to be sufficiently described and understood assume completely new meanings by altering the scale of observation. It is then possible to use these results to draw far wider generalizations although the initial observations were made within relatively narrow dimensions and as experiments rather than examples.

Despite having its roots within the circle of historical research, many of microhistory's characteristics demonstrate the close ties which link history with anthropology – particularly that 'thick description' which Clifford Geertz sees as the proper perspective of anthropological work.[13] Rather than starting with a series of observations and attempting to impose one law-like theory on them, this perspective starts from a set of signifying signs and tries to fit them into an intelligible structure. Thick description therefore serves to record in written form a series of signifying events or facts which would otherwise be evanescent, but which can be interpreted by being inserted in context, that is to say, in the flow of social discourse. This approach succeeds in using microscopic analysis of the most minute events as a means of arriving at the most far-reaching conclusions.

This, according to Geertz, is the procedure adopted by the ethnologist whose aims are both extremely ambitious and very modest. Ambitious in the sense that the ethnologist's authority to interpret material is practically limitless and most interpretation is the essence of ethnographical work. Anthropological writings are imaginative works in which the author's ability is measured by his capacity to bring us into contact with the lives of foreigners and to fix events or social discourse in such a way as to allow us to examine them clearly. The power of the interpreter thus becomes infinite, immeasurable, not susceptible of falsification.[14] Inevitably elements become introduced which are difficult to evaluate rationally, ranging from a sort of cold empathy to a literary communicative skill.

The danger of relativism is accentuated rather than minimized by the small place given to theory. For Geertz it is useless to search for laws and general concepts since culture is made up of a web of signifiers the analysis of which is not an experimental science groping towards universal laws but an interpretive science in search of meaning. What, then, is the role of theory? Geertz denies that the interpretive approach must renounce explicitly theoretical formulations. However, he immediately goes on to say 'that the terms in which such formulations can be cast are, if not wholly nonexistent, very nearly so . . . There are a number of characteristics of cultural interpretation which make the theoretical development of it more than usually difficult (p. 24). In the first place is 'the need for theory to stay rather closer to the ground than tends to be the case in sciences more able to give themselves over to imaginative abstraction' (p. 24). 'Theoretical formulations hover so low over the interpretations they govern that they don't make much sense or hold much interest apart from them' (p. 25). Thus theories are legitimate but of little use 'because the essential task of theory building here is not to codify abstract regularities but to make thick description possible, not to generalize across cases but to generalize within them' (p. 26). Something similar to clinical inference is going on: it is not a question of fitting observed cases to an existing law but rather of working from significant signs – which, in the case of ethnology, are symbolic acts – which have been organized 'within an intelligible frame', to allow the analysis of social discourse 'to ferret out the unapparent import of things'. It is therefore not a question of elaborating theoretical tools capable of generating predictions but of organizing a theoretical structure 'capable of continuing to yield defensible interpretations as new social phenomena swim into view . . . Theoretical ideas are not created wholly anew in each study . . . ; they are adopted from other, related studies, and, refined in the process, applied to new interpretive problems' (pp. 26–7).

'Our double task is to uncover the conceptual structures that inform our subjects' acts, the "said" of social discourse, and to construct a system of analysis in whose terms what is generic to those structures, what belongs to them because they are what they are, will stand out against the other determinants of human behaviour. In ethnography, the office of theory is to provide a vocabulary in which what symbolic action has to say about itself – that is, about the role of culture in human life – can be expressed.' Thus theory is 'a repertoire of very general, made-in-the-academy concepts and systems of concepts . . . woven into the body of thick-description ethnography in the hope of rendering mere occurrences scientifically eloquent' (p. 28). Concepts are therefore cold tools taken from the baggage of academic science: they are useful in interpretation but it is only in that function that they acquire concrete reality and specificity. Theories do not arise out of interpretation. Theory has only a small part to play as handmaiden to the much larger role of the interpreter. The systems of general concepts pertaining to academic language are inserted into the living body of thick description in the hope of giving scientific expression to simple events, not in order to create new concepts and theoretical abstract systems. The only importance, then, of general theory is as part of the construction of an ever-expanding repertoire of thickly described material, rendered intelligible by being contextualized, which will serve to broaden the universe of human discourse.

It seems to me that interpretive anthropology and microhistory have as much in common as have history and anthropology in general. Nevertheless I want here to underline two important differences, one deriving from anthropology's traditionally stronger use of intensive small scale research and the other deriving from an aspect I will try to explain below and which I may define as a kind of self-imposed limitation present in Geertz's thinking. These two differences concern the workings in practice of human rationality and the legitimacy of making generalizations in the social sciences.

Let us first examine the different way in which rationality is viewed. Since it denies the possibility of a specific analysis of cognitive processes interpretive anthropology assumes rationality as a datum, as something impossible to describe outside human action, outside human behaviour seen as meaningful, symbolic action or outside interpretation. Up to this point we may agree. However, Geertz draws from these considerations extreme conclusions. The only thing we can do is to first try to grasp and then make explicit, via thick description, the probable meanings of actions. Adherents of this approach do not believe it necessary to question the limitations, possibilities and measurability of rationality itself. Any such inherent limitations or confines are, rather, assumed to be set by the endless game of essentially unevaluable interpretations veering between idealism and relativism instead of being assessed by the standard of some definite conception of human rationality.

One can go further and state that Geertz's conception is revealed by certain characteristics which he has derived from Heidegger,[15] in particular the rejection of the possibility of total explicitation and the attempt to construct a hermeneutic of listening; listening, that is, to poetic language, in other words language caught in the effort of forging new meanings.[16] In fact, according to Geertz, man cannot formulate mental systems without recourse to the guidance of public, symbolic models of emotion so that these models are the essential elements with which he makes sense of the world. Furthermore, these symbolic models are not to be found in all human speech since speech has usually degenerated to a mere means of communication. Geertz, like Heidegger, finds these symbolic models in the quintessential language of poetry, which represents the foremost expression of the human experience of reality. Geertz specifically refers to the language of myth, ritual and art: 'In order to make up our minds we must know how we feel about things; and to know how we feel about things we need the public images of sentiment that only ritual, myth, and art can provide'.[17] Geertz's clear and lucid position is that the infinite repertoire of the symbolic possibilities of the human minds permits us to approach reality by a series of infinitely small steps, without, however, ever arriving. This view is consistent with Heidegger's anti-Hegelian theory that the knowing subject should not dissolve the existence of others into himself but rather that the proper function of thought as a 'hermeneutic classifier' is to allow other people to remain other. I believe this Heideggerian link is essential to an understanding both of the strength and subtlety of the interpretations and the relative weakness the explanations of the worlds in Geertz's interpretive anthropology. In this way Geertz manages to avoid the issue of rationality and its limits; limits which are defined by much more than simply differential access to information. The difference is that between 'authentic thought' and thought governed by the principle of 'sufficient reason'. In view of this it would seem that the ethnologist should perhaps be content to stop his research at the level of descriptions of meaning.

Clearly it must be accepted that, from a biological point of view, all men possess substantially equal intellects, but that intellect is completely dependent on cultural resources for its functioning. This emphasis on culture allows the avoidance of any theory of the superiority of civilized over primitive man. It also avoids considering the idea that culture is born at certain points ordered in evolutionary phases. Culture, defined as the capacity for symbolic thought, is part of man's very nature. Culture is not supplementary to, but an intrinsic ingredient of, human thought. Nevertheless, according to Geertz, the problem of avoiding 'absolute' cultural relativism – so making comparison between cultures possible – cannot be resolved and should not even be addressed. He confines himself to defining the function of the intellect as a 'search for information': an emotive elaboration using the materials common to members of a specific culture. 'In sum, human intellection, in the specific sense of directive reasoning, depends upon the manipulation of certain kinds of cultural resources in such a manner as to produce (discover, select) environmental stimuli needed – for whatever purpose – by the organism; it is a search for information' (p. 79), therefore a selective gathering of information. In fact human beings need constant affective and intellectual stimuli but, at the same time, these same stimuli require continuous cultural control which organizes than into a meaningful and intelligible order. Therefore it is not only a gathering of information but the emotive organization of which it is involved. The process, however, is not a private one since the meaning of symbols lies in the fact that they are shared and thus communicable among members of a small or large group: in the first instance thought is organized according to the public symbolic structures to hand and only after that does it become private. But Geertz cannot go beyond these considerations since a more specific enquiry into the functioning of reason would inevitably introduce threatening implications of a hierarchization of cultures.

Geertz defends the part played by cultural relativism in the destruction of ethnocentricity – and with this we can only agree. However, he goes so far as to identify cultural relativism with relativism *tout court* and he sees all anti-relativism as a dangerous tendency to see some cultures as hierarchically superior to others. In a revealing article of 1984,[18] 'Anti anti-relativism', he identifies all anti-relativism with that 'position in which cultural diversity, across space and over time, amounts to a series of expressions . . . of a settled, underlying reality, the essential nature of man'. Geertz sees in this vision of superficial diversity covering a deep underlying homogeneity a reliance on theories of human mind and human nature, which he rejects in that they lead inevitably to the re-establishment of mistaken concepts of 'primitive thought' and 'social deviance', in other words to the assumption of a hierarchy of beliefs and of forms of behaviour ranked according to different levels of rationality. So the neo-rationalist claim that it is possible to identify formal constancies (cognitive universals), developmental constancies (cognitive stages), and operational constancies (cognitive processes), in whatever form, only detracts from the power of concepts which rightly emphasize cultural diversity and otherness. 'It would be a large pity if now that the distance we have established and the elsewhere we have located are beginning to bite, to change our sense of sense and our perception of perception we should turn back to old songs' (p. 276). Geertz is declaring himself to be, not relativist, but rather anti anti-relativist in the sense that we are at a stage, perhaps transitory, in which only thick description and the elaborating of a repertoire of meanings are possible.

However, it does not seem to me that his reduction of every rationalist argument to a potential revival of hierarchical concepts of culture is tenable; and in fact it is difficult to consider Gellner, Lévi-Strauss, Needham, Winch, Horton and Sperber, to whom Geertz refers, as all exponents of a hierarchical ordering of cultures. Why should cognitive processes or cognitive universals lead only to an ethnocentric conclusion? Why should a description of rational processes in formal terms, or a concept of the limitations of rationality prove obstacles to a non-hierarchical description of culture? Why should formalization and generalization which allow for the possibility of comparison between cultures necessarily imply the destruction of otherness? Naturally the danger exists, but is the solution really to accept the paralysing irrationalist threat of relativism as the price for escaping ethnocentrism, a spectre in any case by now already largely exorcized? I believe, rather, that it is the very identification of uniform cognitive processes which enables one to accept cultural relativity whilst rejecting the absolute relativism of those who limit our possibilities of knowing reality, with the result of becoming entangled in an endless, gratuitous game of interpreting the interpretations.

It seems to me that one of the main differences of perspective between microhistory and interpretive anthropology is that the latter sees a homogeneous meaning in public signs and symbols whereas microhistory seeks to define and measure them with reference to the multiplicity of social representations they produce. The problem is thus not simply one of the functioning of the intellect. There is also a danger of losing sight of the socially differentiated nature of symbolic meanings and consequently of their partly ambiguous quality. This leads on also to the problem of defining the different forms of functioning of human rationality within the context of specific situations. Both the amount of information necessary to organize and define a culture, and the amount of information necessary for action, are historically mutable and socially variable. This then, is the problem which needs to be faced since the framework of public, symbolic structures is an abstraction. For, in the context of differing social conditions, these symbolic structures produce a fragmented and differentiated multiplicity of representations; and it is these which should be the object of our study.

Both the amount of information available and the opportunities for empirical observation are probably far wider and more complex in contemporary societies than in simple ones or in those of the past. Nevertheless the main problem is always the one stated in extraordinarily illuminating fashion by Foucault:[19] the problem of the selection from the range of alternative possible meanings which a dominant system of classification must impose; not to mention that selection of information which we may call self-protective, which allows us to give meaning to the world and to function effectively. The quantity and quality of such information is not, however, socially uniform and therefore it is necessary to examine the plurality of forms of the limited rationality at work in the particular reality under observation. This plurality exists as a result, among other things, of protective mechanisms deployed in the face of excess information, mechanisms enabling escape from the sheer quantity of information in order that decisions can be taken. One thinks, for example, of the processes of causal simplification, and of the use of simplified slogans in political choices, of the etiological systems used in popular medicine, or the techniques of persuasion employed by the advertising industry.

It seems to me, therefore, that it is not enough to conduct a general discussion of symbolic functioning on the basis of a Geertzian definition of culture as an endless search for information. I believe it is necessary to attempt to meausre and formalize the mechanisms of bounded rationality – a bounded rationality the location of whose boundaries varies with the various forms of access to information – in order to allow an understanding of the differences existing within the cultures of individuals, groups and societies in various times and places. The somewhat allusive quality of Geertz's important but incomplete system neglects this goal.

The proof of this inadequacy is exemplified in the abundance of autobiographical relativism which has appeared on the scientific scene in recent years under the guise of interpretive anthropology (Rabinow's *Reflections on Fieldwork in Morocco*[20] seems to me to be a prime example). There is further proof in the fact that the repertoire of thick descriptions has no comparative aim but remains simply a repertoire from which to pick out cases for clarification according to rules which are unspecified. Consequently, interpretation has often remained open, imponderable and limited. Certain examples of this imponderability appear more in Geertzians than in Geertz himself. A classic example seems to me to be the *Great Cat Massacre* by Robert Darnton.[21]

A second aspect which has already been mentioned is forgoing any attempt to construct models and state the formal rules of the interpretive and communicative games. Geertz concludes by proposing a tentative use of general, academic conceptualization only to revitalize the concepts in the concrete examples of thick descriptions. In this way a repertoire of concepts is woven into a repertoire of interpreted events in the hope that they will work together so that simple events may be made scientifically eloquent and conversely that far-reaching conclusions may be drawn from the density of simple facts. This method often results in a cultural history without social analysis, or in an extremely stereotyped social analysis drawn from an intensively investigated cultural history. The action is examined in depth but without a complex, formal reconceptualization of the social mechanisms involved and the analysis therefore stops short, as if frightened, at the very threshold of social history. For example, the charisma and symbolism of power in coronation ceremonial seems to speak the same language to everyone within a socially undifferentiated society.[22] Or, to take another example, cock-fighting is presented as having a single universal significance for the whole society even though the forms of wager are socially diverse.[23]

Microhistory, on the other hand, has not rejected the consideration of social differentiation in the same way as interpretive anthropology but regards it as essential to have as formal a reading as possible of actions, behaviour, social structures, roles and relationships. In other words, although customs and the use of symbols are always polysemic, nevertheless they assume more precise connotations from the mobile and dynamic social differentiations. Individuals constantly create their own identities, and groups define themselves according to conflicts and solidarities, which however cannot be assumed a priori but result from dynamics which are the object of analysis.

I would like now to look at another characteristic common to the work of microhistorians which is the problem of communication with the reader – the problem of narrative. The revival of narrative should not be seen merely in terms of the choice between qualitative, individualized history and that quantitative history whose ambition is to establish laws, regularity and formal collective behaviour. Microhistory has specifically addressed the problem of communication and has been acutely aware that historical research does not coincide solely with the communication of results in a book. This was a central point neglected in a well-known article by Stone.[24] In general the problems of proof and demonstration in history by means of the recounting of concrete instances have a close connection with techniques of exposition. This is not simply a problem of rhetoric, for the meaning of historical work cannot be reduced to rhetoric, but specifically a problem of communicating with the reader, who is never a *tabula rasa*, and therefore always poses a problem of reception.[25] It seems to me that the particular function of narrative can be summarized in two characteristics. The first is the attempt to demonstrate, by an account of solid facts, the true functioning of certain aspects of society which would be distorted by generalization and quantitative formalization used on their own, since these operations would accentuate in a functionalist way the role of systems of rules and mechanistic processes of social change. In other words, a relationship is shown between normative systems and that freedom of action created for individuals by those spaces which always exist and by the internal inconsistencies which are part of any system of norms and normative systems. The second characteristic is that of incorporating into the main body of the narrative the procedures of research itself, the documentary limitations, techniques of persuasion and interpretive constructions. This method clearly breaks with the traditional assertive, authoritarian form of discourse adopted by historians who present reality as objective. In microhistory, in contrast, the researcher's point of view becomes an intrinsic part of the account. The research process is explicitly described and the limitations of documentary evidence, the formulation of hypotheses and the lines of thought followed are no longer hidden away from the eyes of the uninitiated. The reader is involved in a sort of dialogue and participates in the whole process of constructing the historical argument. (One illuminating example of this process is Ginzburg and Prosperi's book.)[26] Henry James adopted a similar approach in his story *In The Cage*[27] which serves as an extraordinary metaphor of the historian's work. In the story James describes the whole process of interpretation of reality constructed by a telegraph operator in her confined place of work in a district of London. Her raw material is the scant, fragmentary and fallacious documentation presented by the text of daily telegrams exchanged by her aristocratic clients. The story of this evident process of making sense of the world is a metaphor for the historian's work but it also provides an example of the role which narrative can play in such a work.

The microhistorical approach addresses the problem of how we gain access to knowledge of the past by means of various clues, signs and symptoms. This is a procedure which takes the particular as its starting-point (a particular which is often highly specific and individual, and would be impossible to describe as a typical case) and proceeds to identify its meaning in the light of its own specific context.

Contextualization, however, can mean many things. The most coherent theory of context is the functionalist one whose most characteristic aspect is perhaps that of focusing on context to explain social behaviour. For functionalism, it is not so much the causes of behaviour themselves which are objects of analysis but rather the normalization of a form of behaviour within a coherent system which explains that behaviour, its functions and how it operates. The

Durkheimian model of contextualization emphasises the binding nature of some of our general concepts but the contextualization is a functionalist element even if it confines itself to underlining the fit between an institution, a form of behaviour or a concept and that system of which it is part. As Gellner points out,[28] even Wittgenstein was a 'follower and successor' of Durkheim in that even he 'supposed (that) categories were validated by being parts of a "form of life"'.

I would point out that, contrary to functionalism's emphasis on social coherence, microhistorians have concentrated on the contradictions of normative systems and therefore on the fragmentation, contradictions and plurality of viewpoints which make all systems fluid and open. Changes occur by means of the minute and endless strategies and choices operating within the interstices of contradictory normative systems. This is truly a reversal of perspective in that it accentuates the most minute and localised actions to demonstrate the gaps and spaces which the complex inconsistencies of all systems leave open. To return to the example previously mentioned, it is ultimately more functionalist to consider the meaning of cock-fighting in the context of a coherent system of Balinese culture than to consider the socially fragmented multiple meanings of cock-fighting itself as a means of interpreting Balinese culture in general with all its inconsistencies.[29]

In fact, even if we think of a repertoire of local cultures not comparable with each other and from which general, more or less abstract rules can only be deduced in a purely arbitrary fashion, it is still possible that this approach may yield a very functionalist interpretation if it takes the local culture to be one coherent, homogeneous, systematic whole. There are, therefore, two possible ways of reading social context: as a place which imputes meaning to seemingly 'strange' or 'anomalous' particulars by revealing their hidden significance and consequently their fit with a system; or, on the other hand, as a matter of discovering the social context in which an apparently anomalous or insignificant fact assumes meaning when the hidden incoherences of an apparently unified social system are revealed. The reduction of scale is an experimental operation precisely because of this fact, that it assumes that the delineations of context and its coherence are apparent and it brings out those contradictions which only appear when the scale of reference is altered. This clarification can also occur, incidentally, as Jacques Revel[30] has rightly observed, by enlarging the scale. The choice of micro dimensions arose as a direct result of the traditional preponderance of macro contextual interpretation, in view of which it was the only experimental direction possible to take.

Another concept of contextualizing is that which understands cultural context as a process of collocating an idea within the boundaries prescribed by the languages available. I am thinking here, for example, of the intellectual history of the English contextualists.[31] This theory sees context as being dictated by the language and idioms available and used by a particular group of people in a particular situation to organize, for example, their power struggles. This school of thought has had great influence on social theory itself and has initiated so many discussions that it seems to me superfluous to restate the arguments. However, microhistory's perspective is, again, different because prime importance is given to the activities, forms of behaviour and institutions which provide the framework within which idioms can be properly understood, and which permit a meaningful discussion of those concepts and beliefs which would otherwise remain hermetically closed in on themselves without adequate reference to society – even if discourse is conceptualized as action rather than reflection.

Contextualizing may have a third meaning: this consists of the formal, comparative placing of an event, form of behaviour or concept in a series of others which are similar though they may be separated in time and space. This contextualization presupposes that formalized and explicit structures are comparable but is concerned not only with grouping individual items characterized by one or more common aspects but also with classification based on 'indirect' similarities via analogy. Here, context involves not only the identification of a set of things sharing certain characteristics but can also work on the level of analogy – that is, in the area where the perfect similarity is between the relationships linking things rather than between the things themselves, which may be very diverse. The similarity is between systems of relations involving different elements. It is, so to speak, an identification of family likenesses. (I refer here in particular to Needham's position.)[32]

Microhistory has demonstrated the fallibility and incoherence of social contexts as conventionally defined: see for example the criticisms made by M. Gribaudi[33] regarding the social delimitation of working-class neighbourhoods. Gribaudi shows that solidarities may be based not so much on similarity of social position but rather on similarity of position within systems of relationships. Another example is the analysis of rules of matrimony and of the effects of consanguinity in the Como region in the seventeenth century;[34] in this analysis, a strong social contextualization and a reduction of scale bring out the importance of formal abstract rules of matrimony as a basis for social categorizations. For another example, see Ago's study of a feud.[35]

These observations pose further problems which it is necessary to consider briefly. Firstly, the problem of the contrast between individualizing and generalizing knowledge – a recurring debate among social historians. It is sufficient to recall the debate on qualitative or quantitative history of the family or, in a wider context, the crisis which has shaken a belief widespread in the sixties in the possibility of quantifying social occurrences and formulating rigorous laws of social behaviour. I want to concentrate here on one aspect only which, though unique in itself perhaps, serves to illuminate an important problem. I would like to examine what is meant by quantitative history, or rather, to examine those characteristics of quantification which were implicit in a mechanistic concept of social reality.

Microhistory tries not to sacrifice knowledge of individual elements to wider generalization, and in fact it accentuates individual lives and events. But, at the same time, it tries not to reject all forms of abstraction since minimal facts and individual cases can serve to reveal more general phenomena. In a weak science in which, if experimentation itself is not impossible, that aspect of experiment involving the ability to reproduce the causes is excluded, even the smallest dissonances prove to be indicators of meaning which can potentially assume general dimensions. Edoardo Grendi has defined this perspective as being the attention given to 'the exceptional normal'.[36] The alternatives of sacrificing the particular to the general or of concentrating only on the uniqueness of the particular is thus an inappropriate distinction. The problem is rather that of how we can elaborate a paradigm which hinges on knowledge of the particular whilst not rejecting formal description and scientific knowledge of the particular itself.[37] Nevertheless, comparisons between quantitative and qualitative, event and series, particular and general have led to a mistaken view of what the proper tools for formalization are. Social history has traditionally considered itself able to apply rigid models to history and to use a quantitative type of formalization in which the concept of causality could not be weakened by attention to personal choices, uncertainties, individual and group strategies which were held to recall a less mechanistic perspective. Because this tendency to identify formalization with quantification has been prevalent for a long time, history has lagged paradoxically behind the other social sciences. It seems to me that microhistory moves more firmly towards the non-quantitative branches of mathematics in order to furnish more realistic and less mechanistic representations, thus broadening the field of indeterminacy without necessarily rejecting formalized elaborations. Problems such as those connected with graphs of relational networks, with decision in uncertain situations, with the calculation of probability and with games and strategies have all, incredibly, been passed over in the debate about so-called quantitative history. If one decides to work with a different, more complex and realistic picture of the rationality of social actors and if one considers the fundamentally interwoven nature of social phenomena, it immediately becomes necessary to develop and use new formal tools of abstraction. The field remains wide open for historians to explore.

These, then, are the common questions and positions which characterize microhistory: the reduction of scale, the debate about rationality, the small clue as scientific paradigm, the role of the particular (not, however, in opposition to the social), the attention to reception and narrative, a specific definition of context and the rejection of relativism. These characteristic elements are in many ways similar to those outlined by Jacques Revel in a recent article on microhistory which is perhaps the most coherent attempt to date to interpret this experimental work.[38] Revel[39] defines microhistory as the attempt to study the social not as an object invested with inherent properties, but as a set of shifting interrelationships existing between constantly adapting configurations. He sees microhistory as a response to the obvious limitations of those interpretations of social history which in their quest for regularity give prominence to over-simple indicators. Microhistory has tried to construct a more fluid conceptualization, a less prejudicial classification of what constitutes the social and cultural, and a framework of analysis which rejects simplifications, dualistic hypotheses, polarizations, rigid typologies and the search for typical characteristics. 'Why make things simple when one can make them complicated?' (p. xxiv) is the slogan Revel suggests for microhistory. By this he means that the true problem for historians is to succeed in expressing the complexity of reality, even if this involves using descriptive techniques and forms of reasoning which are more intrinsically self-questioning and less assertive than any used before. The problem is also that of selecting the important areas for examination: the idea of seeing the subjects of the traditional history in one of their localized variations is analogous to the idea of reading between the lines of a particular document, or between the figures of a painting in order to discern meanings which have previously evaded explanation; or the true importance of that which previously appeared to have arisen merely from either circumstance or necessity; or the active role of the individual who had previously appeared simply passive or indifferent.

With reference to Revel's definition, I have attempted to underline more clearly the anti-relativistic thrust of microhistory and the aspirations towards formalization which characterize, or in my opinion ought to characterize, the microhistorian's work. This is important since the concepts we use in history and the social sciences are often imprecise and used metaphorically. The very concept of configuration, for example, Elias's apt, intuitive formula, seems to me to be typical in the sense that it is powerfully expressive but remains allusive and does not move towards something which, as I have attempted to show in this article, I believe it possible to express in more formal terms.

I do not know whether this presentation of microhistory is a reliable one. I wanted to present in relatively strongly characterized terms a group of people who in reality have been involved in many and various debates within Italian social history in the seventies and eighties. I should perhaps have explained more fully the various different opinions involved and the references to a historical debate ranging far beyond the Italian framework. I must, therefore, clarify matters by informing the reader that my guiding principles are strongly personal ones; this is a self-portrait rather than a group portrait. I could not have done otherwise and I hereby warn the reader that this is the case.

NOTES

1 The work centred around two publications, the *Microstorie* series published by Einaudi in Turin from 1981 and, in part, the review *Quaderni Storici*, published by Il Mulino of Bologna.

2 L. Wittgenstein, *On Certainty* (Oxford, 1969), § 625.

3 Thus I disagree with the position taken by Joan Scott ('History in Crisis? The Others' Side of the Story', in *American Historical Review* 94 (1989), pp. 680–92) who considers all avant-garde historical work to be positive. Her article ends by calling for a phase of renewal without any particular perspective: 'If the many different stories of the past, based on different historical experiences, are indeed irreconcilable, is there none the less a way to think coherently and systematically about the past? . . . These questions are answerable, but only if we accept the notion that history itself is a changing discipline' (pp. 691–2). But what answer is there beyond 'creative inquiries'?

4 F. Barth (ed.), *Scale and Social Organization* (Oslo, Bergen, Tromso, 1978), p. 273.

5 F. Venturi, 'Lumi di Venezia', *La Stampa* (Turin, 27 January 1990).

6 The full text reads: 'Anthropologists don't study villages (tribes, towns, neighborhoods . . .); they study in villages.' See C. Geertz, *The Interpretation of Cultures* (New York, 1973), p. 22.

7 G. Levi, 'Un problema di scala' in *Dieci interventi di Storia Sociale* (Turin, 1981), pp. 75–81.

8 P. Redondi, *Galileo eretico* (Turin, 1983). A translation by Raymond Rosenthal was published in London in 1988 as *Galileo Heretic*.

9 C. Ginzburg, *Indagini su Piero: Il battesimo, Il ciclo di Arezzo, La*

flagellazione di Urbino (Turin, 1981). A translation by Martin Ryle and Kate Soper was published in London in 1985 as *The Enigma of Piero: Piero della Francesca: The Baptism, The Arezzo Cycle, The Flagellation.*

10 R. Merzario, *Il paese stretto: strategie matrimoniali nella diocesi di Como secoli XVI–XVIII* (Turin, 1981).

11 F. Ramella, *Terra e telai: sistemi di parentela e manifattura nel Biellese dell'Ottocento* (Turin, 1984).

12 G. Levi, *L'eredità immateriale: carriera di un esorcista nel Piemonte del Seicento* (Turin, 1985), translated by Linda Cochrane as *Inheriting Power: the Story of an Exorcist* (Chicago and London, 1988).

13 C. Geertz, 'Thick Description: Toward an Interpretive Theory of Culture' in Geertz, *Interpretation of Cultures*, pp. 3–31.

14 J. Clifford, 'On Ethnographic Authority', *Representations* I (1983), pp. 122–39.

15 M. Heidegger, *Holzwege* (Frankfurt, 1950), translated into Italian as *Sentieri interotti* (Florence, 1968).

16 G. Vattimo, *Introduzione a Heidegger* (Bari, 1985).

17 C. Geertz, 'The Growth of Culture and the Evolution of Mind' in J. Scher (ed.), *Theories of the Mind* (Glencoe, 1962), pp. 713–40; reprinted in Geertz, *Interpretation of Cultures*, pp. 55–85.

18 C. Geertz, 'Anti Anti-Relativism', *American Anthropologist* 86 (1984), pp. 263–78.

19 M. Foucault, *Les Mots et les choses: archéologie des sciences humaines* (Paris, 1966).

20 P. Rabinow, *Reflections on Fieldwork in Morocco* (Berkeley and Los Angeles, 1977).

21 R. Darnton, *The Great Cat Massacre and other Episodes in French Cultural History* (New York, 1984). See also his paper 'The Symbolic Element in History', *Journal of Modern History* 58 (1986), pp. 218–34, and R. Chartier, 'Text, Symbols, and Frenchness', *Journal of Modern History* 57 (1985), pp. 682–95, as well as G. Levi, 'I pericoli del Geertzismo', Quaderni Storia 20 (1985) pp. 269–277.

22 C. Geertz, *Local Knowledge: Further Essays in Interpretive Anthropology* (New York, 1983), pp. 121–46.

23 C. Geertz, 'Deep Play: Notes on the Balinese Cockfight', *Daedalus* 101 (1972), pp. 1–37, reprinted in Geertz, *Interpretation of Cultures*, pp. 412–54.

24 L. Stone, 'The Revival of Narrative: Reflections on a New Old History', *Past and Present* 85 (1979), pp. 3–24.

25 I recall the controversy between A. Momigliano ('La retorica della storia e la storia della retorica: sui tropi di Hayden White' in Momigliano, *Sui fondamenti della storia antica* (Turin, 1984), pp. 464–76) and H. White (*Metahistory* (Baltimore, 1973)), in which, however, Momigliano over-emphasizes the opposition between truth and rhetoric. As I maintain in the text, the problems of argumentative theory are important in practical historiography and not, as White states, imcompatible with a realistic reference to historical facts.

26 C. Ginsburg and A. Prosperi, *Giochi di pazienza: un seminario sul* 'Beneficio di Cristo' (Turin, 1975).

27 H. James, *In the Cage* (London, 1898).

28 E. Gellner, 'Concepts and Society' in B. R. Wilson (ed.), *Rationality* (Oxford, 1970), pp. 18–49, especially p. 24.

29 Geertz, 'Deep Play'; see note 23.

30 J. Revel, 'L'histoire au ras du sol', introduction to G. Levi, *Le Pouvoir au village* (Paris, 1989), pp. i–xxxiii.

31 See J. G. A. Pocock, *The Machiavellian Moment: Florentine Political Thought and the Atlantic Republican Tradition* (Princeton, 1975) and *Virtue, Commerce, and History: Essays on Political Thought and History, chiefly in the Eighteenth Century* (Cambridge, 1985). See also Q. Skinner, 'Hermeneutics and the Role of History', *New Literary History* 7 (1975–6), pp. 209–32, and Skinner's book *The Foundations of Modern Political Thought: the Renaissance* (Cambridge, 1978).

32 R. Needham, *Reconnaissances* (Toronto, Buffalo, London, 1980).

33 M. Gribaudi, *Mondo operaio e mito operaio: spazi e percorsi sociali a Torino nel primo Novecento* (Turin, 1987).

34 Merzario, *Il paese stretto*, 1981.

35 R. Ago, *Un feudo esemplare: immobilismo padronale e astuzia contadina nel Lazio del'700* (Rome, 1988).

36 E. Grendi, 'Microanalisi e storia sociale', *Quaderni Storici* 7 (1972), pp. 506–20, and *Polanyi: dall'antropologia economica alla microanalisi storica* (Milan, 1978).

37 C. Ginzburg, 'Spie: radici di un paradigma indiziario' in A. Gargani (ed.), *Crisi della ragione* (Turin, 1979),. pp. 59–106, reprinted in Ginzburg's book *Miti Emblemi Spie: morfologia e storia* (Turin, 1986), pp. 158–209. An English translation of the book was published in London in 1990 as *Myths, Emblems, Clues*.

38 C. Ginzburg and C. Poni, 'Il nome e il come: scambio ineguale e mercato storiografico', *Quaderni Storici* 14 (1979), pp. 181–90; a brief initial manifesto which, read today, appears to have been largely superseded by subsequent work in the practical field of microhistory.

39 Revel, 'L'histoire au ras du sol' in Levi, *Le pouvoir au village*, 1989.

6

Oral History

Gwyn Prins

Historians in modern, mass-literate, industrial societies – that is, most professional historians – are generally pretty sceptical about the value of oral sources in reconstructing the past. 'In this matter, I am an almost total sceptic,' observed A. J. P. Taylor tartly. 'Old men drooling about their youth? No!' Many might now be slightly more generous, and admit oral history – history written with evidence gathered from a living person, rather than from a written document – as pleasant and helpful illustration, but few would accept that such materials can become pivotal in studying documented, modern societies. Studs Terkel's 'people's histories' of the Depression and of the Second World War can never, they think, drive major historical hypotheses about those great events.

The implied weakness of oral sources is thought to be universal and irreparable, so, for societies without written records, the conventional range of judgement is bleak. At one end, Arthur Marwick in *The Nature of History* concedes that, 'history based exclusively on non-documentary sources, as, say, the history of an African community, may be a sketchier, less satisfactory history than one drawn from documents, but is history all the same.' At the other, until there are documents, there can be no proper history. Since the beginning of history (that is, history written following Ranke's method) Africa has been seen as the ahistoric continent *par excellence*. That view has held consistently from Hegel's judgement in 1831 that 'it is no historical part of the world' to Hugh Trevor-Roper's celebrated observation in 1965, which stung the then rapidly proliferating clans of anti-colonial Africanists for a generation, that Africa had no history, merely the unrewarding gyrations of barbarous tribes.[1] Nor was this only a view of the Right or only of Africa. Indian villages, exemplifying the Asiatic mode of production, simply stewed in the sun, unproductively reproducing themselves 'untouched by the storm-clouds of the political sky', in Marx's famous phrase. Marxist supporters of anti-colonial movements have writhed upon its point ever since, trying to explain that the Old Man didn't really mean what he plainly did mean.

In both the sympathetic and hostile cases, the basic Rankean test is applied. Under the Rankean hierarchy of data, when official, written sources are available, they are to be preferred. Where they are not, one has to put up with second best, filling one's bucket further away from the pure source of official text. Oral data are, in these terms, without doubt, second best or worse, so their role is to facilitate second-best histories about communities with poor sources. On these criteria, Hegel, Trevor-Roper and Marx are merely being scrupulous.

From those who employ oral sources there have been two sorts of response to such scepticism, one prickly, the other less so. Paul Thompson, a leading figure in the oral history 'movement' (a self-description which already has an evangelistic ring), which champions the value of oral sources in modern social history as giving historical presence to those whose views and values are disenfranchised by 'history from above', wrote angrily in his manifesto, *The Voice of the Past*, that

> the opposition to oral evidence is as much founded on feeling as on principle. The older generation of historians who hold the Chairs and the purse-strings are instinctively apprehensive about the advent of a new method. It implies that they no longer command all the techniques of their profession. Hence the disparaging comments about young men tramping the streets with tape-recorders.[2]

So in the battle about oral sources in contemporary history, the intemperate language reveals that deep passions are engaged on both sides. But on the role of oral sources for the history of non-literate societies, the most distinguished exponent of oral history in Africa, Jan Vansina, freely conceded Marwick's point in *his* manifesto, *Oral Tradition as History*:

> Where there is no writing, or almost none, oral traditions must bear the brunt of historical reconstruction. They will not do this as if they were written sources. Writing is a technological miracle . . . The limitations of oral tradition must be fully appreciated so that it will not come as a disappointment that long periods of research yield a reconstruction that is still not very detailed. What one does reconstruct from oral sources may

well be of a lower order of reliability, when there are no independent sources to cross-check.[3]

Note that the agreement is limited to circumstances where oral sources have to stand alone; and since Vansina shows, both in that book and in his many monographs, that this is frequently not the case, the main thrust of his argument is, in fact, much more assertive. It is that the relationship of written to oral sources is not 'one of the diva and her understudy in the opera: when the star cannot sing, the understudy appears: when writing fails, tradition come on stage. This is wrong. [Oral sources] correct other perspectives just as much as other perspectives correct it.'

Why should the use of oral sources be so controversial? Paul Thompson has suggested that old professors don't like to learn new tricks and that they resist what they perceive to be erosion of the special status of the Rankean method. This may be true, but I suspect that there are deeper reasons, and less strident ones. Historians live in literate societies and, like many of the inhabitants of such societies, unthinkingly they tend to hold the spoken word in contempt. It is the corollary of our pride in writing and our respect for the written word. And why not? As Vansina noted, communication through symbolic, written language is a quite stupendous achievement. The literate tend to forget this. The Maoris of New Zealand provide a sad but illuminating example of a common occurrence during the expansion of Europe: non-literate people who observed, then grasped with fierce energy but failed to control this instrument of power.

The bald facts are particularly striking. In 1833, perhaps 500 Maoris could read; within a year, 10,000. In 1840, the year of the Treaty of Waitangi in which the Maori chiefs lost their land (or obtained the benefit of British annexation, depending upon your point of view), uncharacteristically for a *pakeha* (white man) at that time, a traveller expressed fears for the physical health of the Maori. Instead of exercising (as befits noble savages), they were now sedentary, having 'become readers'. In 1837 the printer William Colenso – a member of a famous missionary family – completed the first edition of a Maori New Testament and by 1845, Protestant missionaries had distributed half as many Maori New Testaments as there were Maoris. In 1849 Governor George Gray believed that a larger proportion of Maori were literate than of any European population. What was the power in writing that the Maori saw and sought so eagerly?

It was a three-fold power, but like many newly conquered and newly, partially literate poeples, the Maori only successfully seized a small part of it. The first facet of book power was totemic. Illiterate Maori took books – any books – to Church, or stuffed pages into enlarged holes in their ear-lobes. It was an attempt, commonly observed in the early stages of a colonial encounter, to obtain power by association. The second facet was manipulative. The same Colenso (using the same composing-stick with which he had set the scriptures) in 1840 set the texts of the Treaty of Waitangi. At the meeting to discuss the Treaty, he failed to persuade the Governor that while the Maori might all hear, and some might read the words of the translated English draft, they could not and did not grasp the legal meaning, or share the underlying concepts of property, or understand the consequences of signature. Don McKenzie argues that the Maori lost the more resoundingly, and for longer, in the battle over control of land precisely because their exposure to literacy in the previous decade gave the impression that they could and did accept the terms of the game set by the written register, yet were unable to manipulate it successfully.[4]

The third facet of power is formal and active. It is the power to externalize, to accumulate and to fix knowledge. This, Maoris did not acquire on a politically significant scale until the next generation. It is the very essence of the miracle of writing and, in all communities, it has been the ability to cross this threshold from passive to active, from victim of to master of the written word, that has been most revolutionary in its consequences, yet most elusive.

In the haunting cave paintings of Lascaux, in France, among the images of animals are to be seen series of paired dots. These may be the very earliest examples of symbolic communication: communication which is made by the individual, yet exists independently of him in time and space. The ability to do this is a main criterion distinguishing *Homo sapiens* – wise man – from his biological predecessors: the first great divide in human history. The Lascaux dots may be, as much as polished hand axes, the first harbingers of the neolithic revolution which is the foundation of all subsequent civilization.

In the ancient Near East, iron, wheat and domestic animals were tamed.[5] Also there occurred the principal invention which unshackled the potentials of writing. Symbol writing was critically important in enabling men to transcend the impermanence of speech, but it was awkward. It was the creation of an *alphabetic* system of writing which facilitated the eventual development of essentially literate society that first flowered in Greece in the seventh century BC. Bertrand Russell called the rise of civilization in Greece the thing which in all of history was most difficult to account for, and most surprising. It was certainly another watershed, but perhaps not as momentous as that represented by the neolithic revolution, and maybe not deserving such high language.

Jack Goody, in *The Domestication of the Savage Mind*, suggests that in seeking to understand the power of literacy, it is useful, adapting Marx's terminology, to distinguish two parts within the *mode* of communication: the means and the relations of communication, the physical and the socio-cultural dimensions respectively. Furthermore, he argues, they must always be considered together. In these terms, Greece can be put into a context.

We find ourselves in a mass literature society, possessed of an alphabetic system of writing and, looking back, we can distinguish three modes of communication. We can see:

> 1   Oral cultures where language takes a purely oral form. These are typified by local languages; they are now, and have been for a long time, relatively rare.
> 2   Written cultures where language takes a written form only, because the oral form has died out. These are typified by classical languages.
> 3   Composite cultures where language takes both oral and written forms for all or a proportion of the people. We are obliged to categorize further and to distinguish between *universally literate* cultures, such as we too easily take for granted but which are historically unusual, and *restrictedly literate* cultures where most people live on the fringes of, but under the sway of, the literate register.

Existence within a composite culture is, in fact, typical today of all the great world languages. People are either personally illiterate or semi-literate yet ruled by the book, as with nineteenth-century Maori, in much of the Islamic world, or post-literate in the new world of electronic mass communication: dominated by the radio, television and telephone. But historians are literate people, *par excellence*, and for them the written word is paramount. It sets their standards and methods. It downgrades spoken words which are rendered utilitarian and flat compared to the concentrated meaning of text. The nuances and types of oral data are not seen.

One of the effects of living in a culture dominated by the written word is, through downgrading the spoken word, to cauterize it. We may have a detailed awareness of many complex, special written languages: in English, through time, we have Chaucerian and Shakespearean modes, or the special language of the King James Bible or the Book of Common Prayer, all of which live on. In looking at an oral or composite culture, we have to make a conscious effort to try and slow down our pace of intake, and to see oral testimony as, potentially, equally complex. We must recognize the distinctions between important and banal speech, just as Thomas Hardy's Tess of the d'Urbervilles switched from Dorset dialect to standard English, according to her interlocutor, just as Caribbean Rastafarians reserve a special register for religious chanting.

One of the oldest and best-known examples of how the special languages of the oral and the written register interweave in a composite culture is the oral tradition about the Koran, the *hadith*. In a magnificent study of such a composite Islamic culture, Ernest Gellner has shown how the *baraka* (charismatic authority) of the 'saints' or Holy Men of the Atlas Mountains of Morocco derives, for their illiterate neighbours, from their oral expounding of the Islamic law, the *shari'a*. But the *shari'a* is a written law, and these Holy Men may be themselves personally illiterate. Yet they derive charisma from association with book-word power.

Traditional document-driven historians look for three qualities in their sources, none of which oral data conspicuously possesses. Therefore they are not taken seriously. They demand precision in form. It is important to see the stable nature of the evidence. A document is an artefact. There are no doubts about what the testimony is, physically: the form is fixed. It can also be tested in various ways, physically (again) but also by a battery of comparative, textual, structural and other means. This gives the second quality that is sought: precision in chronology.

Historians think in serial time, as measured by the calendar and the wrist-watch. Documents can give fine detail in this dimension and thus can permit subtle arguments derived from it. The objectivity claimed by the more traditional members of the historical profession is posited largely upon the presumed strength of deduction drawn from a close study of the logic of finely textured narrative. But, as we shall see in a moment, serial time is not the only sort of time that men use, and there are other things than change to explain.

Thirdly, once you are literate, writing is easy and it leaves a fixed trace, therefore we live in an ocean of written messages and we count on understanding the message of a text by reading additional texts. *Testis unus, testis nullus*: one witness is no witness. We demonstrate by multiplication. On each of these grounds, unsupported oral evidence ranks poorly. The form is not fixed; the chronology is frequently imprecise; the communication may frequently be unsupported. For historians who do not like oral history these compose sufficient grounds for its dismissal. But two more, relating to its objects of study, are often added. One, mentioned at the beginning of this chapter, is that oral history is self-indulgently concerned with tangential issues. The other is that it cannot be other: it is locked into the irrelevance of the small scale.

I think that the general complaint from methodological premises about precision often reflects a belief that oral data cannot explain change, and that change is what historians mainly study. But that is not wholly true; and in some circumstances, notably in non- or quasi-literate societies, continuity is much more interesting, and more difficult to explain, than change. The complaint about self-indulgence reflects either a prejudice against history from below or fear that since oral data are uttered in the scale of the individual's perceptions, the historian will be trapped in the small scale by them, possibly misled and thus be unable to extrapolate efficiently. In short, we would just get unhelpfully cluttered. Oral history tells us only trivia about important people and important things (by their own lights) about trivial people.

Is this really true? It was, of course, to blast that sort of dismissive position that the artillery of the 'oral history movement' was wheeled onto the battlefield. It may have been loaded over-enthusiastically during early firings, but the issues in dispute are real and are equally clearly linked to the functions of memory and the purposes of history in societies with different modes of communication. There are tests other than Rankean ones to be applied.

To judge these complaints and to see who is smuggling what assumptions about the historian's purposes, we must be precise in defining terms in order to avoid category mistakes. Therefore, at once, I distinguish two types and within one type, following Vansina, four different forms of oral data and we must prepare to encounter different arguments about each of them in different types of society.

What is oral evidence more precisely? At the beginning I defined it as evidence obtained from living people as opposed to inanimate sources, but that is no longer sufficiently detailed. There is oral tradition. In *De la tradition orale*, the book which, more than any other, has revolutionized our perception of oral tradition, Jan Vansina defined it as, 'oral testimony transmitted verbally *from one generation to the next, or more*' (my emphasis). Such material is the substance of what we have with which to reconstruct the past of a society with an oral culture. Oral tradition becomes less and less pronounced as a culture moves towards mass literacy, although some oral tradition can persist in a dominatingly literate environment.

The other type of oral source is personal reminiscence. This is oral evidence specific to the life experiences of the informant. Such evidence does not pass from generation to generation except in highly emaciated form, for example in private family stories. In the 1870s my maternal grandfather was working as a gardener's boy in a big house in Cornwall. The butler was a sadist who used to put kittens onto the hot kitchen range and enjoy watching their agony. Understandably, my grandfather did not forget this behaviour, and indeed, left the house to work in the tin mines because of that man. This snippet I heard from my mother. Direct personal reminiscence forms the overwhelming bulk of the oral evidence used by Paul Thompson and the oral history movement.

Oral tradition is distinguished from reminiscence in another way. The transmission of large amounts and special shapes of oral data from generation to generation requires time and considerable mental effort; so there must be some purpose. It is usually thought that the purpose is structural. Some theorists, like Durkheim, would see the purpose in the creation and transmission of oral tradition to be systematically and dependently related to the reproduction of social structure. Others see wider and more autonomous cognitive purposes. But whatever they are, before they can be considered, oral tradition must be further subdivided into four types.[6]

		Rote		Non-rote
		WORDING		
		frozen		free
FORM	frozen	POETRY (INCLUDING SONG) & LISTS		EPIC
			AND	
	free	FORMULAE (names, proverbs etc)		NARRATIVE

If an account is learned by rote, then the words belong to the tradition. If the form of the performance is fixed, then the structure belongs to the tradition. I shall take each category in turn.

Rote-learned, frozen-form materials actually present the historian with the smallest problems of checking, for rigorous textual criticism of versions of the same tradition will give a way to get at the common core of form and words. The rules of form and language can be identified. African praise poems, of which the best known are the Zulu *isibongo*, are good examples of this genre. The words, the form and the intonation are all strictly defined. Frequently, praise poems describe the relations between the ruler and the ruled: they mediate a relationship that could not be conducted in colloquial language. Their structure thus reflects their purpose. Here is an extract from a Lozi praise poem of this sort which I collected in western Zambia. It is performed in Luyana, the old language, which is about as close to the everyday language, siLozi, as Anglo-Saxon is to modern English

> Although I am near you, I cannot talk to you. But I am not concerned, for I know whence my kin comes. I come from a line of relationship which is attached to you. Every song has its origin . . .
> When the King is in Court, he is like an elephant in the thorn scrub; like a buffalo in the thick forest; like a garden of maize on a mound in the Zambezi floodplain. Rule the country well! When the country dies, you will be responsible. When it prospers, it will be proud of you and will acclaim you.

Formulaic materials are especially useful when one is trying to discover the dimensions of a popular culture. A study of proverbs is often an efficient way to begin to make such a map, both in the present of an oral or composite culture and in its past. This is because it is not easy to tamper with their wording; or if they are tampered with, it is clear that this has been done. Here is another illustration, again connected with the Lozi kingship in Zambia. The colonial century in Africa has been, whatever else, tumultuous. Great forces of change have touched Lozi society, like most others. Therefore, if one finds elements which remain constant despite such pressures, that is particularly interesting; and this example is one showing them.

In 1974 I was living in Bulozi, and used to collect proverbs in a notebook, at first mainly from curiosity. A common one refers by analogy to the Kingship. It is in Luyana.

> Nengo minya malolo wa fulanga mei matanga, musheke ni mu ku onga. (The hippopotamus [King] stirs the deepest waters of the river; the white sands of the shallows betray him.)

I found it again a few years later but in a different context: it had been turned into an antiphonal song by a healing cult, mixing modern siLozi with the ancient Luyana.

> Healer (chants): Mezi mwa nuka ki tapelo! (Water from the river is a prayer!)
> Healer (sings): Kubu, mwana lilolo (Hippo, child of the whirlpool)
> Chorus: Itumukela mwa ngala! (He surfaces in mid-stream!)

Healer: Musheke ni mu konga (The sands betray him)
Chorus: Itumukela mwa ngala!

So here we have two variants, sharing the same major theme and both firmly in the post-colonial era. The example shows clearly how crystals of wording remain unchanged within a changing kaleidoscope of structures adapted to particular purposes.

The strength of formulaic material is seen when these modern versions are placed beside the same proverb, but in the forms collected by a French missionary at the very beginning of the colonial experience, in the 1890s: 'wa fulanga meyi matungu, musheke ni mu k'onga' and 'Mbu ku mwan'a lilolo, wa twelanga matungu, musheke ni mu k'onga.'[7] Such a vivid example of persistence in the form of an oral source witnesses to its continual reproduction in popular culture; and that in turn witnesses to its continuing to possess some persisting cultural function.[8] This in turn raises an important question about selective memory in oral sources, of which more below.

Some formulaic materials are less prone to such selective memory than others. For example, one's identity within one's personal culture is often rendered and expressed publicly in a semiotic description of physical boundaries. Therefore, if decoded, the landscape of home described by a migrant can demonstrate cultural reproduction most vividly. It is shown brilliantly in another African case study. *Siyaya: the Historical Anthropology of an African Landscape* makes such a decoding and uses it to challenge the conventional presumption that migration leads to broken relationships.[9]

The main problems of use and misuse of oral tradition relate to traditions not learned by rote: epics and narratives. The fixed form of epic means that most African epic is narrative in this schematization. By 'epic', here, I mean the Homeric epic: heroic poetry composed orally, according to rules. Of course, the poems were written down subsequently, and we cannot know how far they were altered, at this point or subsequently; but the structure is strong enough to transcend that process. It is a patchwork, a rhapsody – literally 'sewn together' (from the Greek verb $\dot{\rho}\alpha\pi\tau\hat{\omega}$) – so that repetition of formulae play a part in giving the work shape, for both bard and audience. About a third of the *Iliad* consists of lines or blocks of lines which occur more than once. The same is true of the *Odyssey*. Twenty-five formulaic expressions occur in the first twenty-five lines of the *Iliad*. For example, dawn is almost always 'rosy fingered', Athena 'owl eyed' the isle of Ithaca 'sea girt', Achilles 'city-sacking' and, most famously, the sea, 'wine dark'. But it is not monotonous repetition. There are thirty-six different epithets for

Achilles, chosen and employed by firm rules.[10] Thus, out of such pieces of material, the bard stitches together a new work, although the individual patches may be old and well known. But this category and this method again raise obvious questions about the limitation upon the quantity of knowledge which oral tradition can contain or transmit. Isn't this all cripplingly limiting?

Even with a range of alternatives, such oral composition cannot advance knowledge or precision. It is shackled by the impermanence of the spoken word, and by the limited capacity of the human memory, even when aided by mnemonic devices; so oral cultures cannot innovate and must forget. This view lies at the heart of Professor Jack Goody's argument in *The Domestication of the Savage Mind*. The 'savage' mind becomes 'domesticated' when the *means* of communiction make it possible to change the *mode*:

> Writing, and more especially alphabetic literacy, made it possible to scrutinise discourse in a different way by giving oral communication a semi-permanent form; this scrutiny favoured the increase in scope of critical activity and hence of rationality, scepticism, logic. It increased the potentialities of criticism because writing laid out discourse before one's eyes in a different kind of way; at the same time it increased the potentiality for cumulative knowledge, especially knowledge of an abstract kind . . . No longer did the problem of memory storage dominate man's intellectual life. The human mind was free to study static text rather than be limited by participation in dynamic utterance.[11]

While few oral historians would quarrel with Goody's account of the intellectual liberation of writing, many, and notably Vansina in *Oral Tradition as History*, would dispute the extension of Goody's case to say that oral traditions are therefore also homeostatic: that what is inconvenient or no longer of functional significance is forgotten. He suggests that a structural amnesia afflicts oral cultures, which are therefore forced to be selective by the limitations of memory, so traditions cannot be good historical data.

In fact, such structural amnesia is rarely total. In many earlier works, culminating in his masterpiece on the pre-colonial history of equatorial central Africa entitled *Paths in the Rain-forest*,[12] Vansina shows how one can disentangle and decode the several strands of a tradition present in the last of the chain of transmission. It involves comparing variants and interlocking the oral with sources of different provenance. The technique of internal textual comparison to defeat homeostasis is well known. Islamic scholars evaluate versions of the *hadith* by assessing the value of each of the links in the chain (*isnâd*), and will not accept any tradition for which data about the *isnâd* are not extant and reasonably complete. But even if one can defeat homeostasis and establish what traditions are present in a testimony, i.e. seek precision of form, how are they to be dated?

Precision of chronology was the second of the three qualities sought by document-driven historians. It has been in the attempt to meet this requirement and thus to gain the trappings of respectability that oral data have been most seriously misused. The problem is easily illustrated.

The narrative category often contains three sorts of transmission. There are traditions of genesis, dynastic histories and accounts of social organization. Now these three sorts of narrative do not all exist within the same concepts of time, although, to complicate matters, the performance of the evidence may mix up the types of material rather like different sorts of meat in a sausage.

UNSTRUCTURED TIME

　　Traditions of genesis

'TRADITIONAL' TIME (sequenced but not serial)

　　Dynastic histories

　　　Accounts of state structure

SERIAL TIME

Edward Evans-Pritchard, the great anthropologist who studied the Nuer people of the southern Sudan before the Second World War, wrote a seminal essay describing what he called 'oecological time', that is, cyclical time where men see its passage in the turning of the seasons, not in the march of the years. Amplifying this point, the social historian E. P. Thompson argued that the shift from task-specific senses of time – a 'rice cooking' (half an hour) in Madagascar; a 'maize roasting' (fifteen minutes) in western Nigeria; a 'couple of Credos' in Catholic seventeenth-century Chile – to the general, culturally autonomous and purposeful time discipline of the clock was part of the social consciousness both engendered by and fundamental to industrial society.[13] At once, the abuses of oral data can be guessed: literate historians have tried to get serial time chonologies out of traditions which exist in 'traditional' time. There, past or present importance of the subject may affect its position. For example, very important things may be said to be very old – or very new – telescoping or elongating, depending upon the context and upon present purposes.

But the explorer historians, chasing chronological precision with the conviction and devotion of nineteenth-century gentlemen collectors, did not think of this. They took, say, a royal legend. They counted the number of kings mentioned. They hypothesized a generation span of, for example, thirty-three years. They multiplied the one by the other and, hey presto, dates for oral cultures! One historian in particular, David Henige, has probed and exploded such simplemindedness. *The Chronology of Oral Tradition*, tellingly subtitled *Quest for a Chimera*, ranges from African kingdoms to Assyrian king-lists and, as well as spreading iconoclasm and scepticism, Henige also spreads some hope.[14] For once one understands what sort of time one is dealing with, and what sort of purposes have supported the tradition in memory, one can, albeit roughly, take defensive measures. Such knowledge is almost always contextual.

One measure is more important than most. One of Henige's most important chapters is entitled 'History as present politics'. Recognition of the fact of the invention of tradition has been one of the most destructively creative insights in extra-European history of the last academic generation and in the use of this idea, for example by David Cannadine to re-examine the myths of British monarchy, we see an important methodological importation into European historiography from extra-European history, where the more severe interdisciplinary and linguistic requirements have propelled much methodological pioneering in historical studies during the last academic generation.[15]

The invention of tradition is neither surprising nor dishonest, especially not in cultures with no single criterion of truth. It is akin to the prisoner's self-defence by playing dim or dumb, vividly explored by Alexander Solzhenitsyn in *One Day in the Life of Ivan Denisovitch*. Colonial situations are similar in being also marked by extremes of power and powerlessness. In certain special circumstances, no recovery at all is possible; in totalitarian ones, it may be the very sequence and tempo of time itself which is contorted; in colonial contexts, accounts of social structure and of dynastic tradition are most commonly reinvented.

There are certain sorts of memory which may be forever irrecoverable because of the manner of their loss. Such was the case made by the Italian writer Primo Levi, a survivor of Auschwitz, with regard to the Holocaust. *The Drowned and the Saved*, his final book, is one of the finest insights into the nature of life and the manner of psychological operation of the death camps which posterity possesses. Yet in it Levi asserted the eccentricity of his own recollection and the consequently flawed nature of his interpretation. By definition, he could not recover memory from the depths where the majority drowned; from there no one returned, and he was one of the few saved. In the end, for him as for the great Freudian psychoanalyst Bruno Bettelheim, another survivor of the camps, it appears that the burden of survival was too much and both, in their old age, committed suicide. Perhaps for them, the past could be neither reinvented nor communicated. It was literally unspeakable.[16]

One step closer to us than silence stands the reconstitution of substance. The historian of the Soviet experience, Geoffrey Hosking, illustrated the totalitarian situation with a quotation from 'Armenian Radio': 'All the fundamental truths about Soviet life are illuminated by oral anecdotes, many of which originate from the mythical Armenian Radio. Thus: Armenian Radio is asked, "Is it possible to foretell the future?" Answer, "Yes, that is no problem: we know exactly what the future will be like. Our problem is with the past: that keeps changing.'[17] Since the coming of *glasnost* in the USSR, the battle for control of memory has been bitter. One faction indeed calls itself Pamyat (Memory); another, wholly opposed to the fervent Slav nationalism and anti-semitism of Pamyat, is called Memorial. Memorial was stimulated by the late Academician Andrei Sakharov as a way of rescuing the victims of Stalin from the oblivion of silence. Recovering popular memory from the Siberia of the mind has become a prominent and in no sense marginal political activity in the second Russian Revolution. Reforming forces caused a commission to report to the full Congress of People's Deputies late in 1989 on the rescue and reinterpretation of one crucial episode, the Hitler–Stalin pact.[18]

The nature of history is fought over fiercely in Britain also. In 1985, Her Majesty's Inspectorate published a view of what children should learn. The HMI 'Blue Book' synthesized much that was best of innovation in schools over the previous twenty years; work such as the Schools Council History project, which taught children aged 11 to 14 to discriminate good from bad evidence, to recognize the legitimacy of many types of sources, including the oral, to question all received truths, to empathize with the predicaments of people in the past as an essential stimulus to the historical imagination.[19] Like the modern revolutionaries in the USSR, the Inspectors understood exactly the political significance of a robust study of history and therefore placed on the back cover of the book, the following saying of Nikita Khruschchev. 'Historians are dangerous people. They are capable of upsetting everything.'

Mrs Thatcher's government abolished the Schools Council. There was an angry, protracted and unsuccessful attempt by Mrs Thatcher and the radical Right to set as the exclusive terms of the 1990 Saunders Watson

History Working Group advising the Department of Education and Science on the content of the British national curriculum its triumphalist, Whiggish, document-driven and parochial syllabus of British political and constitutional history, with an emphasis on rote learning of dates and 'facts' and an aversion to the historical imagination. Denial of the legitimacy of oral history is to be found there also.

The Working Group reported in terms similar to those of HMI in 1985, only to be abruptly overthrown by ministerial fiat when Mr Kenneth Clarke, newly installed in office, imposed the views rejected by Working Group, teaching profession and Inspectorate 'Blue Book' alike. At the time of writing (February 1991) there is confusion and resentment of such an action to be seen in the profession.[20]

These stories make two points. The Siberia of the mind is not only the terrain of dead silence but also of a living denial of legitimacy. It surrenders the voiceless to the desiccative condescension and the proscribing hegemony of present rulers. In this, the British chillingly echoes the Soviet debate. Secondly, the evidence of the fragility and, under contemporary pressure, malleability of the past is underscored. The scale of such invention can be great.

The Tiv people of central Nigeria were not gentlemen. In the early 1900s they fought off white soldiers laying telegraph lines through their land, and thereby gained a reputation for being lawless, treacherous and, of course, deeply pagan. Furthermore, they stank of anarchy, for they had no clear hierarchy of chiefs. Therefore, when in 1907 a British Resident, Charles Forbes Gordon, described their society for the first time, he saw and recorded the segmentary nature of their clans. But by the time of the First World War, the British administration in Nigeria was badly over-stretched, and found it convenient to give up looking at the Tiv as Tiv, instead bracketing them with their more numerous neighbours, the Hausa. Obligingly, Tiv headmen 'Hausaized' themselves for colonial eyes: speaking Hausa, dressing like Hausa and so on. But then in 1930/1, the Tiv were visited and studied by R. C. Abraham, a government anthropologist, and R. O. Downes, a District Officer.

The Abraham-Downes report proposed a fresh view of the Tiv. They saw the acephalous society described by Forbes Gordon in fairly hierarchical terms, reflected in a new set of tiered councils. But legitimizing these councils and their headmen cut off a younger generation of literate Tiv from potential political patronage. So they, in turn, began to champion a new cause, that of the Tor Tiv – a Tiv paramount chief to trump the councils and (coincidentally) exactly congruent with the 'normal' model of native authority held by British officers trained in Lord Lugard's school of indirect rule. Another anthropological investigation in 1940 decided that the Tiv were actually ruled by patriarchs who formed a pyramid of authority. Perhaps there really was a native paramount chief? In forty years, the perception of Tiv social structure had turned upside down. Then, in the late 1940s, came two more anthropologists, the Bohannans, and their classic study of the Tiv as a segmentary lineage society, like the one described upon first acquaintance with it, still stands.

Each European investigator sought the 'real' Tiv and each time that outsiders came up with a new image, some Tiv constituency, who saw it to be in their interests, reinvented their past to oblige. We know this story only because an historian, D. C. Dorward, realized that the investigators were interactively part of the history and because he knew that grandly invented tradition was a possibility.[21] Clearly, the defence against invented tradition is just that: to have a less trusting view of the reliability both of unsupported oral testimony and of one's academic predecessors, unless they have shown signs of being aware of the problem. Nor is the problem confined to oral history alone.

Another African example confirms Vansina's objection to the image of divas and their understudies. It shows that too trusting a view of unsupported *written* sources, combined with too much respect for historians, can be an equally misleading combination. By the application of systematic doubt, Julian Cobbing has convincingly thrown into question three central tenets of Southern African history: the popular view of the Matabele of Zimbabwe as a warrior culture, the central myth of Zimbabwean nationalism – that its direct antecedent lay in the risings of 1896 (a view importantly rooted in the views of the document-driven British historian T. O. Ranger), and, most recently, the significance and very existence of the *Mfecane* – that scattering of the peoples which was thought to have resulted from the destruction of the Zulu state in the mid-nineteenth century.[22] In the case of the risings, modern Zimbabwe being a composite culture, Ranger's nationalist interpretation has now entered the oral register of the personally illiterate and has thus become the answer given to questions about those events, overlaying any other tradition. While it may be helpful to understand the reasons why traditions are invented, it is also depressing to witness the loss of the possibility of ever constructing a reliable account of important events such as these as a result of inadequate historiographic technique. Nor is this excused by recognizing the need which such a community has for what, in his own phrase, Ranger elsewhere called 'usable history'.[23]

Recognition of the vulnerability of document-driven historians to such shipwreck lends proportion to concerns about the misuse of oral data in the quest for serial chronology. In both cases, the solution is the one with which Vansina dismissed the operatic analogy: the use of multiple, converging, independent sources. With regard to chronology, from internal analysis formal oral traditions may yield a sequenced but not necessarily closely dated history. For greater precision, one must seek correlation with external sources. Archaeological evidence, eclipses of the sun or moon or major natural disasters are common points of reference. Myths of genesis, dynastic histories, family histories of ordinary people, proverbs, praise poetry, epics and narratives may give us some access to the inside of a culture and time. When keyed to external sources, we may defend ourselves against invented tradition, give some serial time dates and in this fashion reconstruct this sort of past.

One sort of narrative remains to be considered. It is deliberately placed in a separate category because it is about the single individual and his or her experiences. Such personal reminiscence is the principal data used by historians studying societies dominated by the written word. Its reach extends from the threshold of biological possibility – about eighty years – onwards.

While it is the primary sort of oral data, reminiscence is not the only type in literate societies. Formal tradition, in the sense just discussed, persists. The classic example of this is in the work of Iona and Peter Opie. In *The Lore and Language of Schoolchildren* they establish that a playground riddle can pass intact through long chains of transmission. Because the generation of schoolchildren is shorter than that of Lozi speakers of the royal proverbs given earlier, a jingle which is transmitted across 130 years will pass through twenty generations of schoolchildren, say 300 tellers: equivalent to more than 500 years among adults.[24] This calculation makes forcefully the point that continuity, sustained by the energy of such ceaseless renewal, requires more explanation than change. Of 137 chants recorded in 1916 in Norman Douglas's *London Street Games*, the Opies found 108 in use in the 1950s. In one case, a rhyme about a grenadier, the Opies have versions which carry the stable cardinal elements back to 1725. Conversely, personal reminiscence is not absent in non-literate society; but it is its role in literate society which is of the greatest concern and interest. Is personal reminiscence just senile drooling about the good old days? Yes and no.

Much of the criticism by document-driven historians is along the lines that reminiscence by the famous is too easily open to convenient self-vindication *ex post facto* and, by the unimportant, to lapse of memory. In either case, memory is notoriously unreliable and an untrustworthy vault compared to the inanimate and unchanging records of documents over those intervening years. The first point, as shelves of political autobiography may attest, is well taken, the second not so, for documentary sources are not as unintentionally, unselfconsciously bequeathed to us as one might think.

The days when the fifth Earl of Rosebery confided his innermost thoughts to his journal, when government meant the thinking and the hand-written memoranda of a discrete and identifiable group and when the historian might, with some reasonable confidence, hope to find and read all such documents, and believe that he could believe them, ended a century ago. Since then, the volume of official paper has cascaded beyond control. There has to be selection for preservation, so the 'weeders' have also been systematically at work, and therefore what official archives contain may, either by conscious, usually mischievous, intent or by virtue of wrong choices in what to preserve and what to burn, be quite as misleading as other sources. A long-running object-lesson is provided by the contrast between the arbitrary and increasingly secretive deposition policy of British government departments and the access afforded to British matters through American archives under the Freedom of Information Act. At the time of the Falklands War in 1982, for example, papers relating to earlier discussions of the islands, and especially a Foreign Office opinion from the 1930s, which cast doubt on the solidity of the British legal claim to sovereignty, were suddenly withdrawn from public access, although not before a vigilant and, as it turned out, correctly mistrustful historian had been able to make a pencil copy of the opinion, which was subsequently released to the Press, much to Mrs Thatcher's anger.

The trial of Oliver North, President Reagan's aide and manager of the murky Iran/Nicaraguan Contra affair, provided a lurid illustration of the collapse of traditional historians' working assumptions about documents. A fascinated courtroom heard of late-night shredding sessions, of Mr North's glamorous secretary, the improbably named Fawn Hall, smuggling incriminating documents out of the Pentagon in her boots and her underclothing and of North's attempt to avoid leaving any document trail by using computer networks to send his messages. Unfortunately for him, it proved to be possible to retrieve erased messages from the computer banks. But the point is simply of the shift back to the oral, via electronic information technology, for primary decision-making. When documents do survive and can be read, they often refer back to decisions made in telephone conversations.

Occasionally, the distance between the oral original and the subsequent written official text comes to light accidentally. In Britain during the Great depression, an important committee on finance sat under the chairman-ship of Judge Macmillan. The published evidence of the committee is extensively cited in standard works on the period. One of them is Robert Skidelsky's *Politicians and the Slump*.[25] A particularly important witness before the committee was Montagu Norman, Governor of the Bank of England, but the public version of Norman's testimony was not what he actually said. Norman's oral submission was heavily reworked for the record. By accident, we know this. The Public Record Office copy of the verbatim testimony was destroyed, but another copy was kept in the Bank of England archives, where an economic historian looking for something else came across it by chance.

In the United States, the extent to which the State Department officials, whose briefs he spurned, had to rework the oral testimony of the great cold warrior and Secretary of State John Foster Dulles, is well known. It was considered impolitic for the *Congressional Record* to carry such salty judgements upon the allies of the United States as Dulles's response to the Appropriations Committee that 'the French all had mistresses and sold dirty postcards,' but that none the less 'France was a useful bit of real estate.' (His *obiter dicta* on Germany and Britain also repay discovery.)

So we could turn the tables. We could argue that in fact oral testimony, whether collected on tape (without Nixonian lacunae), or by field research among tribes of admirals and secretaries of state, is closer to the fountain-head. It is certainly vulnerable to problems as severe as those which affect modern documentary sources, but they are different. Both have in common that they may be subjected to the invention of tradition, (as the withdrawal of the Falkland Islands opinion from the PRO showed), but problems in the misuse of oral data are possibly easier to spot and to resolve.

In addition to misuse, which is avoidable, there are two common problems of source criticism that affect oral testimony, which are not. One is the unconscious influence of literary form upon oral testimony. This occurs unavoidably in composite cultures. There is the hermeneutic reinsertion of a written point of view into an illiterate person's oral testimony. This is most common in highly charged contexts, such as that of a colonial encounter, and the Zimbabwean example of the reinsertion of Ranger's interpretation into the oral culture was mentioned above. There is also a second aspect of such an influence, differently baleful, when the dominance of literary form erodes and eventually erases oral modes of recollection. The best-known examples of this are musical. Ralph Vaughan Williams, Percy Grainger and Benjamin Britten were among many composers early in the twentieth century who collected and/or used folk songs in their own work, which translated and perpetuated the original songs just at the moment of their extinction in the wild. Further, some of the most celebrated modern collectors, such as Ewan McColl, who has saved and reinvigorated a large number of Scottish and Northern English working people's work songs and ballads, were also genre composers, and their new and collected songs are not distinguished by listeners and other performers. Thus what is now heard sung in a bar in Kerry or in Galloway has almost certainly gone through the cycle of hermeneutic reinsertion. But these problems can, with forethought, be anticipated and accommodated in the critical technique; and this may be becoming relatively easier than is the case with documentary sources, as the Rankean stream becomes polluted by invention of tradition even before it springs from the ground. In the case of general recollection of the informant's life, structured by what he thinks to be important, we may have what is arguably the purest sort of record.

The biochemistry of memory is still only poorly understood. But tests on different types of memory tend to agree that long-term memory, especially in individuals who have entered that phase which psychologists call 'life review', can be remarkably precise. People acquire an 'information pool' filled by personal relationship. It is circumscribed by their social context, obviously forms personal identity and has remarkable stability. This, observes David Lowenthal, is especially true of the intense, involuntary recollections from childhood, when one sees and remembers what is there, not (as do adults) what is expected.[26] Life review is the end-product of a lifetime of reminiscence. A stable life-review narrative in the information pool is the beginning of long-term oral tradition. The fragment given earlier about my grandfather's time at the Cornish big house is one such constituent crystal of tradition.

It has been the use of just such recollection which has been the biggest contribution made so far by historians like Paul Thompson. They are social historians and they use oral data to give voice to those who are voiceless in the documentary record. Although not inherently a radicalizing instrument, oral data in contemporary society have been extensively used by historians with radical intent for, as Thompson says in the first lines of *The Voice of the Past*, 'All history ultimately depends upon its social purpose,' and oral history best reconstructs the minute particulars of the lives of ordinary people for those who wish to do this. It is in the tradition of Mayhew, who recorded the lives of the London poor in the 1850s, of Charles Booth who studied the life and labour of people in London between 1889 and 1903, and of Seebohm Rowntree's study of poverty in York in 1901. Such a purpose has been prominent in the practice of oral history from reminiscence in modern Italian history.[27]

What personal reminiscence can bring is a freshness and a wealth of detail which is not otherwise to be found. It makes possible small-scale group histories, like Bill Williams's work on Manchester Jewry, and geographically small-scale work: local histories of villages or of a few streets. It gives historians the means to write what the anthropologist Clifford Geertz has called 'thick description': richly textured accounts which have the depth and the contours to permit substantial anthropological analysis.

But ideological sympathy or potential for structural analysis apart, even if oral history by reminiscence is most powerful for social history, sceptics still have a question, which I mentioned at the beginning of this chapter. It may be helpful, it may be illustrative, it may even be historically liberating; but is it formative of explanation? Oral testimony may permit deeply moving descriptive evocation of what it is like to be a poor Mexican, through Oscar Lewis's masterpiece, *The Children of Sanchez*, but in the last analysis, surely it is trapped in the small scale; and it is not there that the propulsive forces of historians' explanatory theories are to be found.[28]

A good test of this assertion is to look at Paul Thompson's own monograph, *The Edwardians*.[29] This is an attempt to recreate the fabric and feel of life in the years immediately before the Great War. It is a period suffused with rosy romanticism in popular memory, when there was honey still for tea, when the Grantchester church clock still stood at ten to three, when God was in his Heaven and all was right with a world about to be broken into fragments by war. But, Thompson wishes to say, it simply wasn't like that for more than a very few.

The central resource of the book is a series of five vignettes of remembered Edwardian childhoods, chosen to be representative of each level of society from the very rich to the very poor. They are closely tied to the archival record by the sampling procedure which led to the selection of the individuals. They are immensely vivid, but they do not carry the main weight of Thompson's view of these years, which he sees as the Edwardian crisis: of the conservative classes over the Irish question and the profound and widespread labour unrest of 1911 to 1914. But while the vignettes provide splendid illustration, Thompson's analysis of the dimensions of inequality in the society, his view of what drove the crisis and all the larger-scale data upon which this level of the book rests come from a sensitive use of written sources.

So in this sense, I accept the critics' view. *The Edwardians* is not a vindication of the more exaggerated claims made for oral history written from personal reminiscence. But then, as we saw was the case with oral tradition, the exaggerated claims collapse. The strength of oral history is the strength of any methodologically competent history. It comes from the range and the intelligence with which many types of source are harnessed to pull together. Nor is this an obligation which lies asymmetrically upon oral historians as practitioners of a lesser art. I have observed above that the move to a post-literate, newly, globally, electronically oral and visual culture deflates the professional self-esteem of traditional document-driven historiography. All historians are equal before this challenge.

Personal reminiscence permits the historian to do two things. First, rather obviously, to be a full-range historian: one who can draw on appropriate source materials to study the whole range of scales and problems in contemporary history. No historian of modern high politics, steeped in the public records, can expect to be read with confidence if oral sources (and, one might add, photographic and film sources) have not been employed, any more than a social historian of gypsies would expect to be. As Vansina stated, the oral data serve to check other sources as they serve to check it. They also can give minute detail which is otherwise inaccessible and may thus stimulate the historian to reanalyse other data in fresh ways. That is what happened in Paul Thompson's discussion of class in *The Edwardians*. That is what happened when Mr Donald Regan, President Reagan's White House Chief of Staff, published his self-exculpatory account of his period of office and his battles with Mrs Nancy Reagan which revealed, among other concrete things, that the timing of the signature of the Intermediate Nuclear Forces Treaty at the superpower summit of December 1987 was actually governed by Mrs Reagan's personal astrologer, a fact not to be found in official papers. That is what is happening in Christopher Lee's forthcoming study of British defence policy-making since 1945.

This is a subject for which the official documentary record is, in any case, closed under the flexible British 'thirty-something' rule, whereby the government of the day may, if it so wishes, prescribe a longer period of closure for sensitive government papers – of which defence matters are the supreme example – than the normal thirty-year period. Mrs Thatcher is reported to be of the view that nothing relating to the Intelligence activities of British agents in tsarist Russia should be published, lest it give aid and comfort to enemies. She, and the 1989 amendments to the Official Secrets Act, do so wish. In Lee's case, his many years as the BBC Defence Correspondent put him in a position to know and to gain the trust of his subjects. The transcripts of his interviews with all the central actors in the piece will become themselves a vital documentary source. His book will be one that no university-bred historian could write. It will give a radically different cast to our understanding of a vital period of change in Britain's descent from power. Oral materials enter what Professor Hexter calls the 'second record' more immediately than other sorts of data. Lee's ability to track, read and interpret the 'first record' is crucially predicated upon his possession of a highly specific and unusual 'second record.'[30] This does not make him a new sort of historian; rather the opposite. Many nineteenth-century historians were amateurs in the sense that they wrote and lived principally outside Academe. In both past and present, fieldwork is an invaluable adjunct to bookwork.

Secondly, there is the converse effect. Possession of a rich and varied 'second record' – for example, through personal experience rather than via an interview – can make historians out of ordinary people. Railway historians are excellent examples of this. Adrian Vaughan worked as a signalman on Brunel's great line from London to the West Country. He lived through the period of contraction and closure in the 1960s, watched the strangulation of the old ways of working and the spurning of craft skills, was several times made redundant and then decided to record the world that he had lost. His first works, *Signalman's Morning* and *Signalman's Twilight*, were compositions of reminiscence. But as his skill as an historian developed, he deepened his analysis and has now become the author of a remarkable new biography of Brunel himself, enriched and informed by Vaughan's education on his subject's railway line.[31]

Another and final example, again originating in anger at the destruction of skills, is found in an astonishing book on architecture by a master joiner. Roger Coleman comes from a North London family of skilled artisans. He became a master joiner, but in the process observed and suffered from the 'de-skilling' of the building trades. He was angered at both the arrogance and the technical incompetence of architects whose work he had to execute, and who never thought to ask for his opinion. Thus developed the sullen battle, akin to the colonial battles over invented tradition, in which the craftsman pretended to ignorance and withdrew his co-operation and the soft-handed, book-learned architects dictated.

Was it always like this? Triggered by his 'second record', Coleman began a long investigation of art and work. In the process, like William Morris, he acquired the conventional skills of art history and criticism. But in his fiery book, *The Art of Work: an Epitaph to Skill* the seminal passages could not have been written from book learning alone. One remarkable passage asks why William of Sens was the only man injured in the accident during the restoration of Canterbury Cathedral. The answer – that he was both the chief contractor but also the most skilled artisan – shows that the division of labour was not then as it is now. It is woven into an account which passes through Coleman's recovery of the submerged culture of joiners, written out of his knowledge gained orally and in apprenticeship from old men, to an exposition, unique in my reading, of his own skills. He describes the practical procedures involved in making a new window. To learn about the marking up and use of 'rods' (lengths of wood with which the joiner transfers the exact dimensions of the hole in the brickwork to the frame of the window) sounds pedestrian, if useful. But Coleman's account surprisingly does more. Joiners' rods link together in one fraternity William of Sens, Villard de Honnecourt (the cathedral designer and builder whose medieval work-books are, in a sense, direct precursors of Coleman's own), the anonymous eighteenth-century carpenters who worked for Vanbrugh and John Wood the Younger (anonymous unless you know where to look for their hidden marks), Coleman's old craftsmen teachers and the new window in question. The description of making his contemporary window situates historically and analytically each aspect of tasks which are usually invisible, because they are undervalued.[32]

Some historians think that their job is to describe and, perhaps, to explain why things happened in the past. This is a necessary but not a sufficient remit. There are two other essential components of the historian's trade. Continuity must be explained. Historical continuity, especially in oral cultures, requires more attention than change. Tradition is a process – it only lives as it is continually reproduced. It is effervescently vital in its apparent stillness. Secondly, the historian's task is to give the reader confidence in his or her methodological competence. To show awareness of the pitfalls of invented tradition and hence in the explanations offered, the historian must also reveal what it was like to have been there – a bard in Homeric Greece; a villager in Africa before the white man came; an exhausted Victorian engine-driver; a chief of staff in Mr Reagan's White House; or if that cannot be done, to say so, and to explain why.

It is to these vital parts of the historian's task that oral history – tradition and reminiscence, past and present – with its detail, its humanity, frequently its emotion and always its well developed scepticism about the entire historiographic undertaking – is best addressed. Without access to such resources, historians in modern, mass-literate, industrial societies, that is, most professional historians, will languish in a pool of understanding circumscribed by their own culture, like abandoned lovers standing in the flickering circle of light under a single lamp-post in a dark and wind-swept street.

NOTES

1 For the view from a different route which starts from this same point, see Henk Wesseling, 'What is overseas history' p. 67–92.

2 P. Thompson, *The Voice of the Past: Oral History* (Oxford, 1978), p. 63.

3 J. Vansina, *Oral Tradition as History* (Madison, Wisconsin, 1985), p. 199.

4 D. F.McKenzie, 'The sociology of a text: oral culture, literacy and print in early New Zealand' in P. Burke and R. Porter (eds), *The Social History of Language* (Cambridge, 1987), pp. 161–97.

5 Iron was also independently tamed in Thailand and probably near the Great Lakes in Central Africa; the importance of the Near Eastern discovery lies in its combination with horse and grain.

6 This grid is borrowed from J. Vansina, 'Once upon a time: Oral traditions as history in Africa', *Daedalus* 2 (Spring 1971), pp. 442–68, on p. 451.

7 For further exposition of the visible and the hidden in Lozi history, see G. Prins, *The Hidden Hippopotamus. Reappraisal in African History: the early Colonial Experience in Western Zambia* (Cambridge, 1980).

8 For further discussion of the significance and usefulness of proverbs, see J. Obelkevich, 'Proverbs and social history', in Burke and Porter (eds), *The Social History of Language*, pp. 43–72.

9 David W. Cohen and E. S. Atieno Odhiambo, *Siyaya, the Historical Anthropology of an African Landscape* (London, 1988) and a review in *African Affairs* 188 (October 1989), pp. 588–9.

10 M. I. Finley, *The World of Odysseus*, Penguin edition, 1962), p. 34.

11 J. Goody, *The Domestication of the Savage Mind* (Cambridge, 1977), p. 37.

12 J. Vansina, *Paths in the Rain-forest* (Madison, Wisconsin, 1990).

13 E. E. Evans-Pritchard, *The Nuer* (Oxford, 1940); E. P. Thompson, 'Time, Work Discipline and Industrial Capitalism' in M. W. Flinn and T. C. Smout (eds), *Essays in Social History* (Oxford, 1974), pp. 40–1. See also Jacques Le Goff, 'Au Moyen Age: temps de l'Église et temps du marchand', *Annales*, 15 (1960), pp. 417–33.

14 D. Henige, *The Chronology of Oral Tradition: Quest for a Chimera* (Oxford, 1974).

15 D. Cannadine, 'The Context, Performance and Meaning of Ritual: the British Monarchy and the "invention of tradition"' in T. O. Ranger and E. Hobsbawm (eds), *The Invention of Tradition* (Cambridge, 1983), pp. 101–64; the same point is made by Wesseling on p. 76.

16 Primo Levi, *The Drowned and the Saved* (London, 1988); Michael Ignatieff, 'A cry for help – or of release', *Observer*, 1 April 1990 (on the suicide of Bruno Bettelheim on 13 March 1990).

17 Geoffrey A. Hosking, 'Memory in a totalitarian society: the case of the Soviet Union' in Thomas Butler (ed.), *Memory* (Oxford, 1988), p. 115.

18 'On the political and legal assessment of the Soviet–German Non-Aggression Treaty of 1939', Report to the Second Congress of People's

Deputies by Commission Chairman, Alexander Yakovlev, 23 December 1989 (Moscow, 1990).

19   *History in the Primary and Secondary Years: an HMI View* (London, 1985).
20   Martin Kettle, 'The great battle of history', *Guardian* 4 April, 1990, p. 23 (reviewing the political furore over the History Working Group Report, published after long delay on 3 April 1990).
21   D. C. Dorward, 'Ethnography and administration: the study of Anglo-Tiv "working misunderstanding"', *Journal of African History* 15 (1974), pp. 457–77.
22   J. Cobbing, 'The evolution of the Ndebele Amabutho', *Journal of African History* 15 (1974), pp. 607–31; *idem*, 'The absent priesthood: Another look at the Rhodesian Risings of 1896–7', *Journal of African History* 18 (1977), pp. 61–84; *idem*, 'The Mfecane as Alibi: Thoughts on Dithakong and Mbolompo', *Journal of African History* 29, (1988), pp. 487–519; T. O. Ranger, *Revolt in Rhodesia, 1896–7*, paperback edition (London, 1979).
23   T. O. Ranger, 'Towards a usable African past' in C. Fyfe (ed.), *African Studies since 1945: A Tribute to Basil Davidson* (London, 1976), pp. 17–30.
24   I. and P. Opie, *The Lore and Language of Schoolchildren* (Oxford, 1959), p. 8.
25   R. Skidelsky, *Politicians and the Slump: the Labour Government of 1929–31*, (London, 1967).
26   D. Lowenthal, *The Past is a Foreign Country* (Cambridge, 1985), pp. 202–3.
27   G. Levi, L. Passerini and L. Scaraffini, 'Vita quotidiana in un quartiere operaio di Torino fra le due guerre: l'opporto della storia orale', pp. 209–24; L. Bergonzini, 'Le fonti orale come verifica della testimonianze scritte in una ricerca sulla antifascismo e la resistenza bolognese', pp. 263–8, both in B. Bernardi, C. Poni and A. Triulzi (eds), *Fonti Orale: Antropologia e Storia* (Milan, 1978).
28   Oscar Lewis, *The Children of Sanchez: Autobiography of a Mexican Family* (London, 1962).
29   P. Thompson, *The Edwardians: the Remaking of British Society* (London, 1975).
30   C. R. Lee, *Whitehall Warriors: Postwar Defence Policy Decision-making*, (forthcoming).
31   A. Vaughan, *Signalman's Morning* (London, 1981) and *Signalman's Twilight* (London, 1983). Both volumes in a paperback omnibus edition (London, 1984); *idem*, *Isambard Kingdom Brunel*, forthcoming.
32   R. Coleman, *The Art of Work: An Epitaph to Skill* (London, 1988).

7

History of Reading

Robert Darnton

Ovid offers advice on how to read a love letter: "If your lover should make overtures by means of some words inscribed on tablets delivered to you by a clever servant, meditate on them carefully, weigh his phrases, and try to divine whether his love is only feigned or whether his prayers really come from a heart sincerely in love." It is extraordinary. The Roman poet might be one of us. He speaks to a problem that could arise in any age, that appears to exist outside of time. In reading about reading in *The Art of Love*, we seem to hear a voice that speaks directly to us across a distance of two thousand years.

But as we listen further, the voice sounds stranger. Ovid goes on to prescribe techniques for communicating with a lover behind a husband's back:

> It is consonant with morality and the law that an upright woman should fear her husband and be surrounded by a strict guard . . . But should you have as many guardians as Argus has eyes, you can dupe them all if your will is firm enough. For example, can anyone stop your servant and accomplice from carrying your notes in her bodice or between her foot and the sole of her sandal? Let us suppose that your guardian can see through all these ruses. Then have your confidante offer her back in place of the tablets and let her body become a living letter.[1]

The lover is expected to strip the servant girl and read her body – not exactly the kind of communication that we associate with letter-writing today. Despite its air of beguiling contemporaneity, *The Art of Love* catapults us into a world we can barely imagine. To get the message, we must know something about Roman mythology, writing techniques, and

This article is reprinted from the *Australian Journal of French Studies* 23 (1986), pp. 5–30, by kind permission.

domestic life. We must be able to picture ourselves as the wife of a Roman patrician and to appreciate the contrast between formal morality and the ways of a world given over to sophistication and cynicism at a time when the Sermon on the Mount was being preached in a barbarian tongue far beyond the Romans' range of hearing.

To read Ovid is to confront the mystery of reading itself. Both familiar and foreign, it is an activity that we share with our ancestors yet that never can be the same as what they experienced. We may enjoy the illusion of stepping outside of time in order to make contact with authors who lived centuries ago. But even if their texts have come down to us unchanged – a virtual impossibility, considering the evolution of layout and of books as physical objects – our relation to those texts cannot be the same as that of readers in the past. Reading has a history. But how can we recover it?

We could begin by searching the record for readers. Carlo Ginzburg found one, a humble miller from sixteenth-century Friuli, in the papers of the Inquisition. Probing for heresy, the inquisitor asked his victim about his reading. Menocchio replied with a string of titles and elaborate comments on each of them. By comparing the texts and the commentary, Ginzburg discovered that Menocchio had read a great deal of Biblical stories, chronicles, and travel books of the kind that existed in many patrician libraries. Menocchio did not simply receive messages transmitted down through the social order. He read aggressively, transforming the contents of the material at his disposition into a radically non-Christian view of the world. Whether that view can be traced to an ancient popular tradition, as Ginzburg claims, is a matter of debate; but Ginzburg certainly demonstrated the possibility of studying reading as an activity among the common people four centuries ago.[2]

I ran across a solidly middle-class reader in my own research on eighteenth-century France. He was a merchant from La Rochelle named Jean Ranson and an impassioned Rousseauist. Ranson did not merely read Rousseau and weep: he incorporated Rousseau's ideas in the fabric of his life as he set up business, fell in love, married, and raised his children. Reading and living run parallel as leitmotifs in a rich series of letters that Ranson wrote between 1774 and 1785 and that show how Rousseauism became absorbed in the way of life of the provincial bourgeoisie under the Old Regime. Rousseau had received a flood of letters from readers like Ranson after the publication of *La Nouvelle Héloïse*. It was, I believe, the first tidal wave of fan mail in the history of literature, although Richardson had already produced some impressive ripples in England. The mail reveals that readers responded as Ranson did everywhere in France and, furthermore, that their responses

conformed to those Rousseau had called for in the two prefaces to his
novel. He had instructed his readers how to read him. He had assigned
them roles and provided them with a strategy for taking in his novel.
The new way of reading worked so well that *La Nouvelle Héloïse*
became the greatest best-seller of the century, the most important single
source of romantic sensibility. That sensibility is now extinct. No
modern reader can weep his way through the six volumes of *La Nouvelle
Héloïse* as his predecessors did two centuries ago. But in his day,
Rousseau captivated an entire generation of readers by revolutionizing
reading itself.[3]

The examples of Menocchio and Ranson suggest that reading and
living, construing texts and making sense of life, were much more
closely related in the early modern period than they are today. But
before jumping to conclusions, we need to work through more archives,
comparing readers' accounts of their experience with the protocols of
reading in their books and, when possible, with their behaviour. It was
believed that *The Sorrows of Young Werther* touched off a wave of
suicides in Germany. Is not the *Wertherfieber* ripe for fresh examination?
The Pre-Raphaelites in England provide similar instances of life
imitating art, a theme that can be traced from *Don Quixote* to *Madam
Bovary* and *Miss Lonelyhearts*. In each case the fiction could be fleshed
out and compared with documents – actual suicide notes, diaries, and
letters to the editor. The correspondence of authors and the papers of
publishers are ideal sources of information about real readers. There are
dozens of letters from readers in the published correspondence of
Voltaire and Rousseau, and hundreds in the unpublished papers of
Balzac and Zola.[4]

In short, it should be possible to develop a history as well as a theory
of reader response. Possible, but not easy; for the documents rarely
show readers at work, fashioning meaning from texts, and the
documents are texts themselves, which also require interpretation. Few
of them are rich enough to provide even indirect access to the cognitive
and affective elements of reading, and a few exceptional cases may not
be enough for one to reconstruct the inner dimensions of that
experience. But historians of the book have already turned up a great
deal of information about the external history of reading. Having
studied it as a social phenomenon, they can answer many of the "who",
the "what", the "where", and the "when" questions, which can be of
great help in attacking the more difficult "whys" and "hows".

Studies of who read what at different times fall into two main types, the
macro- and the microanalytical. Macroanalysis has flourished above all

in France, where it feeds on a powerful tradition of quantitative social history. Henri-Jean Martin, François Furet, Robert Estivals, and Frédéric Barbier have traced the evolution of reading habits from the sixteenth century to the present, using long-term series constructed from the *dépôt légal*, registers of book privileges, and the annual *Bibliographie de la France*. One can see many intriguing phenomena in the undulations of their graphs: the decline of Latin, the rise of the novel, the general fascination with the immediate world of nature and the remote worlds of exotic countries that spread throughout the educated public between the time of Descartes and Bougainville. The Germans have constructed a still longer series of statistics, thanks to a peculiarly rich source: the catalogues of the Frankfurt and Leipzig book fairs, which extend from the mid-sixteenth to the mid-nineteenth century. (The Frankfurt catalogue was published without interruption from 1564 to 1749, and the Leipzig catalogue, which dates from 1594, can be replaced for the period after 1797 by the *Hinrichssche Verzeichnisse*.) Although the catalogues have their drawbacks, they provide a rough index to German reading since the Renaissance; and they have been mined by a succession of German book historians since Johann Goldfriedrich published his monumental *Geschichte des deutschen Buchhandels* in 1908 and 1909. The English-reading world has no comparable source; but for the period after 1557, when London began to dominate the printing industry, the papers of the London Stationers' Company have provided H. S. Bennett, W. W. Greg, and others with plenty of material to trace the evolution of the English book trade. Although the British tradition of bibliography has not favoured the compilation of statistics, there is a great deal of quantitative information in the short-title catalogues that run from 1475. Giles Barber has drawn some French-like graphs from customs records, and Robert Winans and G. Thomas Tanselle have taken the measure of early American reading by reworking Charles Evans's enormous *American Bibliography* (18,000 entries for the period 1638–1783 including unfortunately an undetermined population of "ghosts").[5]

All this compiling and computing has provided some guidelines to reading habits, but the generalizations sometimes seem too general to be satisfying. The novel, like the bourgeoisie, always seem to be rising; and the graphs drop at the expected points – most notably during the Seven Years' War at the Leipzig fair, and during World War I in France. Most of the quantifiers sort their statistics into vague categories like "arts and sciences" and "belles-lettres", which are inadequate for identifying particular phenomena like the Succession Controversy, Jansenism, the Enlightenment, or the Gothic Revival – the very subjects that have attracted the most attention among literary scholars and cultural historians. The quantitative history of books will have to refine its categories and sharpen its focus before it can have a major impact on traditional strains of scholarship.

Yet the quantifiers have uncovered some significant statistical patterns, and their achievements would look even more impressive if there were more of an effort to make comparisons from one country to another. For example, the statistics suggest that the cultural revival of Germany in the late eighteenth century was connected with an epidemic-like fever for reading, the so-called *Lesewut* or *Lesesucht*. The Leipzig catalogue did not reach the level it had attained before the Thirty Years' War until 1764, when it included 1,200 titles of newly published books. With the onset of *Sturm und Drang*, it rose to 1,600 titles in 1770; then 2,600 in 1780 and 5,000 in 1800. The French followed a different pattern. Book production grew steadily for a century after the Peace of Westphalia (1648) – a century of great literature, from Corneille to the *Encyclopédie*, which coincided with the decline in Germany. But in the next fifty years, when the German figures soared, the French increase looks relatively modest. According to Robert Estivals, requests for authorizations to publish new books (*privilèges* and *permissions tacites*) came to 729 in 1764, 896 in 1770, and only 527 in 1780; and the new titles submitted to the *dépôt légal* in 1800 totalled 700. To be sure, different kinds of documents and standards of measurement could produce different results, and the official sources exclude the enormous production of illegal French books. But whatever their deficiencies, the figures indicate a great leap forward in German literary life after a century of French domination. Germany also had more writers, although the population of the French and German speaking areas was roughly the same. A German literary almanach, *Das gelehrte Teutschland*' listed 3,000 living authors in 1772 and 4,300 in 1776. A comparable French publication, *La France littéraire*, included 1,187 authors in 1757 and 2,367 in 1769. While Voltaire and Rousseau were sinking into old age, Goethe and Schiller were riding a wave of literary creativity that was far more powerful than one might think if one considered only the conventional histories of literature.[6]

Cross-statistical comparisons also provide help in charting cultural currents. After tabulating book privileges throughout the eighteenth century, François Furet found a marked decline in the older branches of learning, especially the Humanist and classical Latin literature that had flourished a century earlier according to the statistics of Henri-Jean Martin. Newer genres such as the books classified under the rubric "sciences et arts" prevailed after 1750. Daniel Roche and Michel

Marion notice a similar tendency in surveying Parisian notarial archives. Novels, travel books, and works on natural history tended to crowd out the classics in the libraries of noblemen and wealthy bourgeois. All the studies point to a significant drop in religious literature during the eighteenth century. They confirm the quantitative research in other areas of social history – Michel Vovelle's on funeral rituals, for example, and Dominique Julia's investigation of clerical ordinations and teaching practices.[7]

The thematic surveys of German reading complement those of the French. Rudolf Jentzsch and Albert Ward found a strong drop in Latin books and a corresponding increase in novels in the fair catalogues of Leipzig and Frankfurt. By the late nineteenth century, according to Eduard Reyer and Rudolf Schenda, borrowing patterns in German, English, and American libraries had fallen into a strikingly similar pattern: seventy to eighty per cent of the books came from the category of light fiction (mostly novels); 10 per cent came from history, biography, and travel; and less than 1 per cent came from religion. In little more than two hundred years, the world of reading had been transformed. The rise of the novel had balanced a decline in religious literature, and in almost every case the turning-point could be located in the second half of the eighteenth century, especially the 1770s, the years of the *Wertherfieber*. *Die Leiden des jungen Werthers* produced an even more spectacular response in Germany than *La Nouvelle Héloïse* had done in France or *Pamela* in England. All three novels marked the triumph of a new literary sensitivity, and the last sentences of *Werther* seemed to announce the advent of a new reading public along with the death of a traditional Christian culture: "Handwerker trugen ihn. Kein Geistlicher hat ihn begleitet."[8]

Thus for all their variety and occasional contradictions, the micro-analytical studies suggest some general conclusions, something akin to Max Weber's "demystification of the world". That may seem too cosmic for comfort. Those who prefer precision may turn to microanalysis, although it usually goes to the opposite extreme – excessive detail. We have hundreds of lists of books in libraries from the Middle Ages to the present, more than anyone can bear to read. Yet most of us would agree that a catalogue of a private library can serve as a profile of a reader, even though we don't read all the books we own and we do read many books that we never purchase. To scan the catalogue of the library in Monticello is to inspect the furnishings of Jefferson's mind.[9] And the study of private libraries has the advantage of linking the "what" with the "who" of reading.

The French have taken the lead in this area, too. Daniel Mornet's essay

of 1910, "Les enseignements des bibliothèques privées", demonstrated
that the study of library catalogues could produce conclusions that
challenged some of the commonplaces of literary history. After
tabulating titles from five hundred eighteenth-century catalogues, he
found only one copy of the book that was to be the Bible of the French
Revolution, Rousseau's *Social Contract*. The libraries bulged with the
works of authors who had been completely forgotten, and they provided
no basis for connecting certain kinds of literature (the work of the
philosophes, for example) with certain classes of readers (the bourgeoisie).
Seventy years later, Mornet's work still looks impressive. But a vast
literature has grown up around it. We now have statistics on the libraries
of noblemen, magistrates, priests, academicians, burghers, artisans, and
even some domestic servants. The French scholars have studied reading
across the social strata of certain cities – the Caen of Jean-Claude
Perrot, the Paris of Michel Marion – and throughout entire regions – the
Normandy of Jean Quéniart, the Languedoc of Madeleine Ventre. For
the most part, they rely on *inventaires après décès*, notarial records of
books in the estates of the deceased. So they suffer from the bias built into
the documents, which generally neglect books of little commercial value
or limit themselves to vague statements like "a pile of books". But the
notarial eye took in a great deal in France, far more than in Germany,
where Rudolf Schenda considers inventories woefully inadequate as a
guide to the reading habits of the common people. The most thorough
German study is probably Walter Wittmann's survey of inventories from
the late eighteenth century in Frankfurt am Main. It indicated that books
were owned by 100 per cent of the higher officials, 51 per cent of the
tradesmen, 35 per cent of the master artisans, and 26 per cent of the
journeymen. Daniel Roche found a similar pattern among the common
people of Paris: only 35 per cent of the salaried workers and domestic
servants who appear in the notarial archives around 1780 owned books.
But Roche also discovered many indications of familiarity with the
written word. By 1789 almost all the domestic servants could sign their
names on the inventories. A great many owned desks, fully equipped
with writing implements and packed with family papers. Most artisans
and shopkeepers spent several years of their childhood in school. Before
1789 Paris had 500 primary schools, one for every 1,000 inhabitants, all
more or less free. Parisians were readers, Roche concludes, but reading
did not take the form of the books that show up in inventories. It involved
chapbooks, broadsides, posters, personal letters, and even the signs on
the streets. Parisians read their way through the city and through their
lives, but their ways of reading did not leave enough evidence in the
archives for the historian to follow closely on their heels.[10]

He must therefore search for other sources. Subscription lists have been a favourite, though they normally cover only rather wealthy readers. From the late seventeenth to the early nineteenth century, many books were published by subscription in Britain and contained lists of the subscribers. Researchers at the Project for Historical Biobibliography at Newcastle upon Tyne have used these lists to work toward a historical sociology of readership. Similar efforts are under way in Germany, especially among scholars of Klopstock and Wieland. Perhaps a sixth of new German books were published by subscription between 1770 and 1810, when the practice reached its peak. But even during their *Blütezeit*, the subscription lists do not provide an accurate view of readership. They left off the names of many subscribers, included others who functioned as patrons instead of as readers, and generally represented the salesmanship of a few entrepreneurs rather than the reading habits of the educated public, according to some devastating criticism that Reinhard Wittmann has directed against subscription-list research. The work of Wallace Kirsop suggests that such research may succeed better in France, where publishing by subscription also flourished in the late eighteenth century. But the French lists, like the others, generally favour the wealthiest readers and the fanciest books.[11]

The records of lending libraries offer a better opportunity to make connections between literary genres and social classes, but few of them survive. The most remarkable are the registers of borrowings from the ducal library of Wolfenbüttel, which extend from 1666 to 1928. According to Wolfgang Milde, Paul Raabe, and John McCarthy, they show a significant "democratization" of reading in the 1760s: the number of books borrowed doubled; the borrowers came from lower social strata (they included a few porters, lackeys, and lower officers in the army); and the reading matter became lighter, shifting from learned tomes to sentimental novels (imitations of *Robinson Crusoe* went over especially well). Curiously, the registers of the Bibliothèque du Roi in Paris show that it had the same number of users at this time – about fifty a year, including one Denis Diderot. The Parisians could not take the books home, but they enjoyed the hospitality of a more leisurely age. Although the librarian opened his doors to them only two mornings a week, he gave them a meal before he turned them out. Conditions are different in the Bibliothèque Nationale today. Librarians have had to accept a basic law of economics: there is no such thing as a free lunch.[12]

The microanalysts have come up with many other discoveries – so many, in fact, that they face the same problem as the macroquantifiers: how to put it all together? The disparity of the documentation – auction catalogues, notarial records, subscription lists, library registers – does not make the task easier. Differences in conclusions can be attributed to the peculiarities of the sources rather than to the behaviour of the readers. And the monographs often cancel each other out: artisans look literate here and unlettered there; travel literature seems to be popular among some groups in some places and unpopular in others. A systematic comparison of genres, milieux, times and places would like like a conspiracy of exceptions trying to disprove rules.

So far only one book historian has been hardy enough to propose a general model. Rolf Engelsing has argued that a "reading revolution" (*Leserevolution*) took place at the end of the eighteenth century. From the Middle Ages until some time after 1750, according to Engelsing, men read "intensively". They had only a few books – the Bible, an almanach, a devotional work or two – and they read them over and over again, usually aloud and in groups, so that a narrow range of traditional literature became deeply impressed on their consciousness. By 1800 men were reading "extensively". They read all kinds of material, especially periodicals and newspapers, and read it only once, then raced on to the next item. Engelsing does not produce much evidence for his hypothesis. Indeed, most of his research concerns only a small sampling of burghers in Bremen. But it has an attractive before-and-after simplicity, and it provides a handy formula for contrasting modes of reading very early and very late in European history. Its main drawback, as I see it, is its unilinear character. Reading did not evolve in one direction, extensiveness. It assumed many different forms among different social groups in different eras. Men and women have read in order to save their souls, to improve their manners, to repair their machinery, to seduce their sweethearts, to learn about current events, and simply to have fun. In many cases, especially among the publics of Richardson, Rousseau, and Goethe, the reading became more intensive, not less. But the late eighteenth century does seem to represent a turning-point, a time when more reading matter became available to a wider public, when one can see the emergence of a mass readership that would grow to giant proportions in the nineteenth century with the development of machine-made paper, steam-powered presses, linotype, and nearly universal literacy. All these changes opened up new possibilities, not by decreasing intensity but by increasing variety.[13]

I must therefore confess to some scepticism about the "reading revolution". Yet an American historian of the book, David Hall, has described a transformation in the reading habits of New Englanders between 1600 and 1850 in almost exactly the same terms as those used by Engelsing. Before 1800, New Englanders read a small corpus of venerable "steady sellers" – the Bible, almanachs, the *New England Primer*, Philip Doddridge's *Rise and Progress of Religion*, Richard Baxter's *Call to the Unconverted* – and read them over and over again, aloud, in groups, and with exceptional intensity. After 1800 they were swamped with new kinds of books – novels, newspapers, fresh and sunny varieties of children's literature – and they read through them ravenously, discarding one thing as soon as they could find another. Although Hall and Engelsing had never heard of one another, they discovered a similar pattern in two quite different areas of the Western world. Perhaps a fundamental shift in the nature of reading took place at the end of the eighteenth century. It may not have been a revolution, but it marked the end of an Old Regime – the reign of Thomas à Kempis, Johann Arndt, and John Bunyan.[14]

The "where" of reading is more important than one might think, because by placing the reader in his setting it can provide hints about the nature of his experience. In the University of Leyden there hangs a print of the university library, dated 1610. It shows the books, heavy folio volumes, chained on high shelves jutting out from the walls in a sequence determined by the rubrics of classical bibliography: *Jurisconsulti, Medici, Historici*, and so on. Students are scattered about the room, reading the books on counters built at shoulder level below the shelves. They read standing up, protected against the cold by thick cloaks and hats, one foot perched on a rail to ease the pressure on their bodies. Reading cannot have been comfortable in the age of classical humanism. In pictures done a century and a half later, *La Lecture* and *La Liseuse* by Fragonard, for example, readers recline in chaises longues or well padded armchairs with their legs propped on footstools. They are often women, wearing loose-fitting gowns known at the time as *liseuses*. They usually hold a dainty duodecimo volume in their fingers and have a far-away look in their eye. From Fragonard to Monet, who also painted a *Liseuse*, reading moves from the boudoir to the outdoors. The reader backpacks books to fields and mountain tops, where like Rousseau and Heine he can commune with nature. Nature must have seemed out of joint a few generations later in the trenches of World War I, where the young lieutenants from Göttingen and Oxford somehow found room for a few slim volumes of poetry. One of the most precious books in my own small collection is an edition of Hölderlin's *Hymnen an die Ideale der Menschheit*, inscribed "Adolf Noelle, Januar 1916, nord-Frankreich" – a gift from a German friend who was trying to explain Germany. I'm still not sure I understand, but I think the general understanding of reading would be advanced if we thought harder about its iconography and accoutrements, including furniture and dress.[15]

The human element in the setting must have affected the understanding of the texts. No doubt Greuze sentimentalized the collective character of reading in his painting of *Un père de famille qui lit la Bible à ses enfants*. Restif de la Bretonne probably did the same in the family Bible readings described in *La vie de mon père*: "Je ne saurais me rappeler, sans attendrissement, avec quelle attention cette lecture était écoutée; comme elle communiquait à toute la nombreuse famille un ton de bonhomie et de fraternité (dans la famille je comprends les domestiques). Mon père commençait toujours par ces mots: 'Recueillons-nous, mes enfants; c'est l'Esprit Saint qui va parler.'" But for all their sentimentality, such descriptions proceed from a common assumption: for the common people in early modern Europe, reading was a social activity. It took place in workshops, barns, and taverns. It was almost always oral but not necessarily edifying. Thus the peasant in the country inn described, with some rose tinting around the edges, by Christian Schubart in 1786:

> Und bricht die Abendzeit herein,
> So trink ich halt mein Schöpple Wein;
> Da liest der Herr Schulmeister mir
> Was Neues aus der Zeitung für.[16]

The most important institution of popular reading under the Old Regime was a fireside gathering known as the *veillée* in France and the *Spinnstube* in Germany. While children played, women sewed, and men repaired tools, one of the company who could decipher a text would regale them with the adventures of *Les quatre fils Aymon*, *Till Eulenspiegel*, or some other favourite from the standard repertory of the cheap, popular chapbooks. Some of these primitive paperbacks indicated that they were meant to be taken in through the ears by beginning with phrases such as, "What you are about to hear . . . " In the nineteenth century groups of artisans, especially cigar makers and tailors, took turns reading or hired a reader to keep themselves entertained while they worked. Even today many people get their news by being read to by a telecaster. Television may be less of a break with the past than is generally assumed. In any case, for most people throughout most of history, books had audiences rather than readers. They were better heard than seen.[17]

Reading was a more private experience for the minority of educated persons who could afford to buy books. But many of them joined reading clubs, *cabinets littéraires*, or *Lesegesellschaften*, where they could read almost anything they wanted, in a sociable atmosphere, for a small monthly payment. Françoise Parent-Lardeur has traced the proliferation of these clubs in Paris under the Restoration,[18] but they went back well into the eighteenth century. Provincial booksellers often turned their stock into a library and charged dues for the right to frequent it. Good light, some comfortable chairs, a few pictures on the wall, and subscriptions to a half-dozen newspapers were enough to make a club out of almost any bookshop. Thus the *cabinet littéraire* advertised by P. J. Bernard, a minor bookseller in Lunéville: "Une maison commode, grande, bien éclairée et chauffée, qui serait ouverte tous les jours, depuis neuf heures du matin jusqu'à midi et depuis une heure jusqu'à dix, offrirait dès cet instant aux amateurs deux mille volumes qui seraient augmentés de quatre cents par année." By November 1779, the club had 200 members, mostly officers from the local *gendarmerie*. For the modest sum of three livres a year, they had access to 5,000 books, thirteen journals, and special rooms set aside for conversation and writing (see appendix).

German reading clubs provided the social foundation for a distinct variety of bourgeois culture in the eighteenth century, according to Otto Dann. They sprang up at an astounding rate, especially in the northern cities. Martin Welke estimates that perhaps one of every 500 adult Germans belonged to a *Lesegesellschaft* by 1800. Marlies Prüsener has been able to identify well over 400 of the clubs and to form some idea of their reading matter. All of them had a basic supply of periodicals supplemented by uneven runs of books, usually on fairly weighty subjects like history and politics. They seem to have been a more serious version of the coffee house, itself an important institution for reading, which spread through Germany from the late seventeenth century. By 1760, Vienna had at least sixty coffee houses. They provided newspapers, journals, and endless occasions for political discussions, just as they had done in London and Amsterdam for more than a century.[19]

Thus we already know a good deal about the institutional bases of reading. We have some answers to the "who", "what", "where", and "when" questions. But the "whys" and "hows" elude us. We have not yet devised a strategy for understanding the inner process by which readers made sense of words. We do not even understand the way we read ourselves, despite the efforts of psychologists and neurologists to trace eye movements and to map the hemispheres of the brain. Is the cognitive process different for Chinese who read pictographs and for Westerners who scan lines? For Israelis who read words without vowels moving from right to left and for blind people who transmit stimuli through their fingers? For Southeast Asians whose languages lack tenses and order reality spatially and for American Indians whose languages have been reduced to writing only recently by alien scholars? For the holy man in the presence of the Word and for the consumer studying labels in a supermarket? The differences seem endless, for reading is not simply a skill but a way of making meaning, which must vary from culture to culture. It would be extravagant to expect to find a formula that could account for all those variations. But it should be possible to develop a way to study the changes in reading within our own culture. I would like to suggest five approaches to the problem.

First, I think it should be possible to learn more about the ideals and assumptions underlying reading in the past. We could study contemporary depictions of reading in fiction, autobiographies, polemical writings, letters, paintings, and prints in order to uncover some basic notions of what people thought took place when they read. Consider, for example, the great debate about the craze for reading in late eighteenth-century Germany. Those who deplored the *Lesewut* did not simply condemn its effects on morals and politics. They feared it would damage public health. In a tract of 1795, J. G. Heinzemann listed the physical consequences of excessive reading: "susceptibility to colds, headaches, weakening of the eyes, heat rashes, gout, arthritis, hemorrhoids, asthma, apoplexy, pulmonary disease, indigestion, blocking of the bowels, nervous disorder, migraines, epilepsy, hypochondria, and melancholy". On the positive side of the debate, Johann Adam Bergk accepted the premises of his opponents but disagreed with their conclusions. He took it as established that one should never read immediately after eating or while standing up. But by correct disposition of the body, one could make reading a force for good. The "art of reading" involved washing the face with cold water and taking walks in fresh air as well as concentration and meditation. No one challenged the notion that there was a physical element in reading, because no one drew a clear distinction between the physical and the moral world. Eighteenth-century readers attempted to "digest" books, to absorb them in their whole being, body and soul. The physicality of the process sometimes shows on the pages. The books in Samuel Johnson's library, now owned by Mrs Donald F. Hyde, are bent and battered, as if Johnson had wrestled his way through them.[20]

Throughout most of Western history, and especially in the sixteenth and seventeenth centuries, reading was seen above all as a spiritual exercise. But how was it performed? One could look for guidance in the manuals of Jesuits and the hermeneutical treatises of Protestants. Family Bible readings took place on both sides of the great religious divide. And as the example of Restif de la Bretonne indicates, the Bible was approached with awe, even among some Catholic peasants. Of course Boccaccio, Castiglione, Cervantes, and Rabelais had developed other uses of literacy for the elite. But for most people, reading remained a sacred activity. It put you in the presence of the Word and unlocked holy mysteries. As a working hypothesis, it seems valid to assert that the farther back in time you go the farther away you move from instrumental reading. Not only does the "how-to" book become rarer and the religious book more common, reading itself is different. In the age of Luther and Loyola, it provided access to absolute truth.

On a more mundane level, assumptions about reading could be traced through advertisements and prospectuses for books. Thus some typical remarks from an eighteenth-century prospectus taken at random from the rich collection in the Newberry Library: a bookseller is offering a quarto edition of the *Commentaires sur la coutume d'Angoumois*, an excellent work, he insists, for its typography as much as its content: "The text of the *Coutume* is printed in *gros-romain* type; the summaries that precede the commentaries are printed in *cicéro*; and the commentaries are printed in *Saint-Augustin*. The whole work is made from very beautiful paper manufactured in Angoulème."[21] No publisher would dream of mentioning paper and type in advertising a law book today. In the eighteenth century advertisers assumed that their clients cared about the physical quality of books. Buyers and sellers alike shared a typographical consciousness that is now nearly extinct.

The reports of censors also can be revealing, at least in the case of books from early modern France, where censorship was highly developed if not enormously effective. A typical travel book, *Nouveau voyage aux isles de l'Amérique* (Paris, 1722) by J.-B. Labat, contains four "approbations" printed out in full next to the privilege. One censor explains that the manuscript piqued his curiosity: "It is difficult to begin reading it without feeling that mild but avid curiosity that impels us to read further." Another recommends it for its "simple and concise style" and also for its utility: "Nothing in my opinion is so useful to travellers, to the inhabitants of that country, to tradesmen, and to those who study natural history." And a third simply found it a good read: "I had great pleasure in reading it. It contains a multitude of curious things." Censors did not simply hound out heretics and revolutionaries, as we tend to assume in looking back through time across the Inquisition and the Enlightenment. They gave the royal stamp of approval to a work, and in doing so they provided clues as to how it might be read. Their values constituted an official standard against which ordinary readings might be measured.

But how did ordinary readers read? My second suggestion for attacking that problem concerns the ways reading was learned. In studying literacy in seventeenth-century England, Margaret Spufford discovered that a great deal of learning took place outside the schoolroom, in workshops and fields where labourers taught themselves and one another. Inside the school, English children learned to read before they learned to write instead of acquiring the two skills together at the beginning of their education as they do today. They often joined the work force before the age of seven, when instructions in writing began. So literacy estimates based on the ability to write may be much too low, and the reading public may have included a great many people who could not sign their names.[22]

But "reading" for such people probably meant something quite different from what it means today. In early modern France the three Rs were learned in sequence – first reading, then writing, then arithmetic – just as in England and, it seems, all other countries in the West. The most common primers from the Old Regime – A,B,C,s like the *Croix de Jésus* and the *Croix de par Dieu* – begin as modern manuals do, with the alphabet. But the letters had different sounds. The pupil pronounced a flat vowel before each consonant, so that p came out as "eh-p" rather than "pé" as it is today. When said aloud, the letters did not link together phonetically in combinations that could be recognized by the ear as syllables of a word. Thus *p-a-t* in *pater* sounded like "ehp-ah-ent". But the phonetic fuzziness did not really matter, because the letters were meant as a visual stimulus to trigger the memory of a text that had already been learned by heart – and the text was always in Latin. The whole system was built on the premise that French children should not begin to read in French. They passed directly from the alphabet to simple syllables and then to the *Pater Noster, Ave Maria, Credo,* and *Benedicite.* Having learned to recognize these common prayers, they worked through liturgical responses printed in standard chapbooks. At this point many of them left school. They had acquired enough mastery of the printed word to fulfil the functions expected of them by the Church – that is, to participate in its rituals. But they had never read a text in a language they could understand.

Some children – we don't know how many, perhaps a minority in the seventeenth century and a majority in the eighteenth – remained in school long enough to learn to read in French. Even then, however, reading was often a matter of recognizing something already known rather than a process of acquiring new knowledge. Nearly all of the schools were run by the Church, and nearly all of the schoolbooks were religious, usually catechisms and pious textbooks like the *Escole paroissiale* by Jacques de Batencour. In the early eighteenth century the Frères des Ecoles Chrétiennes began to provide the same text to several pupils and to teach them as a group – a first step toward standardized instruction, which was to become the rule a hundred years later. At the same time, a few tutors in aristocratic households began to teach reading directly in French. They developed phonetic techniques and audio-visual aids like the pictorial flash cards of the abbé Berthaud and the *bureau typographique* of Louis Dumas. By 1789 their example had spread to some progressive primary schools. But most children still learned to read by standing before the master and reciting passages from whatever text they could get their hands on while their classmates struggled with a motley collection of booklets on the back benches. Some of these "schoolbooks" would reappear in the evening at the *veillée*, because they were popular best-sellers from the *bibliothèque bleue*. So reading around the fireside had something in common with reading in the classroom: it was a recital of a text that everyone already knew. Instead of opening up limitless vistas of new ideas, it probably remained within a closed circuit, exactly where the post-Tridentine Church wanted to keep it. "Probably", however, is the governing word in that proposition. We can only guess at the nature of early morning pedagogy by reading the few primers and the still fewer memoirs that have survived from that era. We don't know what really happened in the classroom. And whatever happened, the peasant reader-listeners may have construed their catechism as well as their adventure stories in ways that completely escape us.[23]

If the experience of the great mass of readers lies beyond the range of historical research, historians should be able to capture something of what reading meant for the few persons who left a record of it. A third approach could begin with the best known autobiographical accounts – those of Saint Augustine, Saint Theresa of Avila, Montaigne, Rousseau, and Stendhal, for example – and move on to less familiar sources. J.-M. Goulemot has used the autobiography of Jamerey-Duval to show how a peasant could read and write his way up through the ranks of the Old Regime, and Daniel Roche discovered an eighteenth-century glazier, Jacques-Louis Ménétra, who read his way around a typical tour de France. Although he did not carry many books in the sack slung over his back, Ménétra constantly exchanged letters with fellow travellers and sweethearts. He squandered a few sous on broadsides at public executions and even composed doggerel verse for the ceremonies and farces that he staged with the other workers. When he told the story of his life, he organized his narrative in picaresque fashion, combining oral tradition (folk tales and the stylized braggadocio of male bull sessions) with genres of popular literature (the novelettes of the *bibliothèque bleue*). Unlike other plebeian authors – Restif, Mercier, Rousseau,

Diderot, and Marmontel – Ménétra never won a place in the Republic of Letters. He showed that letters had a place in the culture of the common man.[24]

That place may have been marginal, but margins themselves provide clues to the experience of ordinary readers. In the sixteenth century marginal notes appeared in print in the form of glosses, which steered the reader through Humanist texts. In the eighteenth century the gloss gave way to the footnote. How did the reader follow the play between text and para-text at the bottom or side of the page? Gibbon created ironic distance by masterful deployment of footnotes. A careful study of annotated eighteenth-century copies of *The Decline and Fall of the Roman Empire* might reveal the way that distance was perceived by Gibbon's contemporaries. John Adams covered his books with scribbling. By following him through his copy of Rousseau's *Discourse on the Origin of Inequality*, one can see how radical Enlightenment philosophy looked to a retired revolutionary in the sober climate of Quincy, Massachussetts. Thus Rousseau, in the first English edition: "There was no kind of moral relation between men in this state [the state of nature]; they could not be either good or bad, and had neither vices nor virtues. It is proper, therefore, to suspend judgment about their situation . . . until we have examined whether there are more virtues or vices among civilized men." And Adams, in the margin: "Wonders upon wonders. Paradox upon paradox. What astonishing sagacity had Mr. Rousseau! Yet this eloquent coxcomb has with his affectation of singularity made men discontented with superstition and tyranny."

Christiane Berkvens-Stevelinck has found an excellent site for mapping the Republic of Letters in the marginalia of Prosper Marchand, the bibliophile of eighteenth-century Leyden. Other scholars have charted the currents of literary history by trying to reread great books as great writers have read them, using the annotations in collectors' items such as Diderot's copy of the *Encyclopédie* and Melville's copy of Emerson's essays. But the inquiry needn't be limited to great books or to books at all. Peter Burke is currently studying the graffiti of Renaissance Italy. When scribbled on the door of an enemy, they often functioned as ritual insults, which defined the lines of social conflict dividing neighbourhoods and clans. When attached to the famous statue of Pasquino in Rome, this public scribbling set the tone of a rich and intensely political street culture. A history of reading might be able to advance by great leaps from the Pasquinade and the Commedia dell'Arte to Molière, from Molière to Rousseau, and from Rousseau to Robespierre.[25]

My fourth suggestion concerns literary theory. It can, I agree, look daunting, especially to the outsider. It comes wrapped in imposing labels – structuralism, deconstruction, hermeneutics, semiotics, phenomenology –and it goes as rapidly as it comes, for the trends displace one another with bewildering speed. Through them all, however, runs a concern that could lead to some collaboration between literary critics and historians of the book – the concern for reading. Whether they unearth deep structures or tear down systems of signs, critics have increasingly treated literature as an activity rather than an established body of texts. They insist that a book's meaning is not fixed on its pages; it is contrued by its readers. So reader response has become the key point around which literary analysis turns.

In Germany, this approach has led to a revival of literary history as *Rezeptionsästhetik* under the leadership of Hans Robert Jauss and Wolfgang Iser. In France, it has taken a philosophical turn in the work of Roland Barthes, Paul Riccœur, Tzvetan Todorov, and Georges Poulet. In the United States, it is still in the melting-pot stage. Wayne Booth, Paul de Man, Jonathan Culler, Geoffrey Hartman, J. Hillis Miller, and Stanley Fish have supplied ingredients for a general theory, but no consensus has emerged from their debates. None the less, all this critical activity points toward a new textology, and all the critics share a way of working when they interpret specific texts.[26]

Consider, for example, Walter Ong's analysis of the first sentences in *A Farewell to Arms*:

> In the late summer of that year we lived in a house in a village that looked across the river and the plain to the mountains. In the bed of the river there were pebbles and boulders, dry and white in the sun, and the water was clear and swiftly moving and blue in the channels.

What year? What river? Ong asks. Hemingway does not say. By unorthodox use of the definite article – "the river" instead of "a river" – and sparse deployment of adjectives, he implies that the reader does not need a detailed description of the scene. A reminder will be enough, because the reader is deemed to have been there already. He is addressed as if he were a confidant and fellow traveller, who merely needs to be reminded in order to recollect the hard glint of the sun, the coarse taste of the wine, and the stench of the dead in World War I Italy. Should the reader object – and one can imagine many responses such as, "I am a sixty-year-old grandmother and I don't know anything about rivers in Italy" – he won't be able to "get" the book. But if he accepts the role imposed on him by the rhetoric, his fictionalized self can swell to the dimensions of the Hemingway hero; and he can go through the narrative as the author's companion in arms.[27]

Earlier rhetoric usually operated in the opposite manner. It assumed that the reader knew nothing about the story and needed to be oriented by rich descriptive passages or introductory observations. Thus the opening of *Pride and Prejudice*:

> It is a truth universally acknowledge, that a single man in possession of a good fortune must be in want of a wife.
>
> However little known the feelings or views of such a man may be on his first entering a neighbourhood, this truth is so well fixed in the minds of the surrounding families that he is considered as the rightful property of some one or other of their daughters.
>
> "My dear Mr Bennet", said his lady to him one day, "have you heard that Netherfield Park is let at last?"

This kind of narrative moves from the general to the particular. It places the indefinite article first, and helps the reader get his bearing by degrees. But it always keeps him at a distance, because he is presumed to enter the story as an outsider and to be reading for instruction, amusement, or some high moral purpose. As in the case of the Hemingway novel, he must play his role for the rhetoric to work; but the role is completely different.

Writers have devised many other ways to initiate readers into stories. A vast distance separates Melville's "Call me Ishmael" from Milton's prayer for help to "justify the ways of God to men". But every narrative presupposes a reader, and every reading begins from a protocol inscribed within the text. The text may undercut itself, and the reader may work against the grain or wring new meaning from familiar words: hence the endless possibilities of interpretation proposed by the deconstructionists and the original readings that have shaped cultural history – Rousseau's reading of *Le Misanthrope*, for example, or Kierkegaard's reading of Genesis 22. But whatever one makes of it, reading has re-emerged as the central fact of literature.

If so, the time is ripe for making a juncture between literary theory and the history of books. The theory can reveal the range in potential responses to a text – that is, to the rhetorical constraints that direct reading without determining it. The history can show what readings actually took place – that is, within the limits of an imperfect body of evidence. By paying heed to history, the literary critics may avoid the danger of anachronism; for they sometimes seem to assume that seventeenth-century Englishmen read Milton and Bunyan as if they were twentieth-century college professors. By taking account of rhetoric, the historians may find clues to behaviour that would otherwise be baffling, such as the passions aroused from *Clarissa* to *La Nouvelle Héloïse* and from *Werther* to *René*. I would therefore argue for a dual strategy, which would combine textual analysis with empirical research. In this way it should be possible to compare the implicit readers of the texts with the actual readers of the past and, by building on such comparisons, to develop a history as well as a theory of reader response.

Such a history could be reinforced by a fifth mode of analysis, one based on analytical bibliography. By studying books as physical objects, bibliographers have demonstrated that the typographical disposition of a text can to a considerable extent determine its meaning and the way it was read. In a remarkable study of Congreve, D. F. McKenzie has shown that the bawdy, neo-Elizabethan playwright known to us from the quarto editions of the late seventeenth century underwent a typographical rebirth in his old age and emerged as the stately, neo-classical author of the three-volume octavo *Works* published in 1710. Individual words rarely changed from one edition to another, but a transformation in the design of the books gave the plays an entirely new flavour. By adding scene divisions, grouping characters, relocating lines, and bringing out *liaisons des scènes*, Congreve fit his old texts into the new classical model derived from the French stage. To go from the quarto to the octavo volumes is to move from Elizabethan to Georgian England.[28]

Roger Chartier has found similar but more sociological implications in the metamorphoses of a Spanish classic, *Historia de la vida del Buscón* by Francisco de Quevedo. The novel was originally intended for a sophisticated public, both in Spain where it was first published in 1626 and in France where it came out in an elegant translation in 1633. But in the mid-seventeenth century the Oudot and Garnier houses of Troyes began to publish a series of cheap paperback editions, which made it a staple of the popular literature known as the *bibliothèque bleue* for two hundred years. The popular publishers did not hesitate to tinker with the text, but they concentrated primarily on book design, what Chartier calls the "mise en livre". They broke the story into simple units, shortening sentences, subdividing paragraphs, and multiplying the number of chapters. The new typographical structure implied a new kind of reading and a new public: humble people, who lacked the facility and the time to take in lengthy stretches of narrative. The short episodes were autonomous. They did not need to be linked by complex sub-themes and character development, because they provided just enough material to fill a *veillée*. So the book itself became a collection of fragments rather than a continuous story, and it could be put together by each reader-listener in his own way. Just how this "appropriation" took place remains a mystery, because Chartier limits his analysis to the book as a physical object. But he shows how typography opens on to sociology, how the implicit reader of the author became the implicit reader of the publisher, moving down the social ladder of the Old Regime and into the world that would be recognized in the nineteenth century as "le grand public".[29]

A few adventuresome bibliographers and book historians have begun to speculate about long-term trends in the evolution of the book. They argue that readers respond more directly to the physical organization of texts than to their surrounding social environment. So it may be possible to learn something about the remote history of reading by practising a kind of textual archeology. If we cannot know precisely how the Romans read Ovid, we can assume that like most Roman inscriptions, the verse contained no punctuation, paragraphing, or spaces between words. The units of sound and meaning probably were closer to the rhythms of speech than to the typographical units – the ens, words, and lines – of the printed page. The page itself as a unit of the book dates only from the third or fourth century AD. Before then, one had to unroll a book to read it. Once gathered pages (the *codex*) replaced the scroll (*volumen*) readers could easily move backwards and forwards through books, and texts became divided into segments that could be marked off and indexed. Yet long after books acquired their modern form, reading continued to be an oral experience, performed in public. At an indeterminate point, perhaps in some monasteries in the seventh century and certainly in the universities of the thirteenth century, men began to read silently and alone. The shift to silent reading might have involved a greater mental adjustment than the shift to the printed text, for it made reading an individual, interior experience.[30]

Printing made a difference, of course, but it probably was less revolutionary than is commonly believed. Some books had title-pages, tables of contents, indexes, pagination, and publishers who produced multiple copies from scriptoria for a large reading public before the invention of movable type. For the first half-century of its existence, the printed book continued to be an imitation of the manuscript book. No doubt it was read by the same public in the same way. But after 1500 the printed book, pamphlet, broadside, map, and poster reached new kinds of readers and stimulated new kinds of reading. Increasingly standardized in its design, cheaper in its price, and widespread in its distribution, the new book transformed the world. It did not simply supply more information. It provided a mode of understanding, a basic metaphor of making sense of life.

So it was that during the sixteenth century men took possession of the Word. During the seventeenth century they began to decode the "book of nature". And in the eighteenth century they learned to read themselves. With the help of books, Locke and Condillac studied the mind as a *tabula rasa*, and Franklin formulated an epitaph for himself:[31]

> The Body of
> B. Franklin, Printer,
> Like the cover of an old Book,
> Its Contents torn out,
> And stript of its Lettering & Gilding
> Lies here, Food for Worms.
> But the Work shall not be lost;
> For it will, as he believ'd,
> Appear once more
> In a new and more elegant Edition
> Corrected and improved
> By the Author

I don't want to make too much of the metaphor, since Franklin has already flogged it to death, but rather to return to a point so simple that it may escape our notice. Reading has a history. It was not always and everywhere the same. We may think of it as a straightforward process of lifting information from a page; but if we considered it further, we would agree that information must be sifted, sorted, and interpreted. Interpretive schemes belong to cultural configurations, which have varied enormously over time. As our ancestors lived in different mental worlds, they must have read differently, and the history of reading could be as complex as the history of thinking. It could be so complex, in fact, that the five steps suggested here may lead in disparate directions or set us circling around the problem indefinitely without penetrating to its core. There are no direct routes or short cuts, because reading is not a distinct thing, like a constitution or a social order, that can be tracked through time. It is an activity involving a peculiar relation – on the one hand the reader, on the other the text. Although readers and texts have varied according to social and technological circumstances, the history of reading should not be reduced to a chronology of those variations. It should go beyond them to confront the relational element at the heart of the matter: how did changing readerships construe shifting texts?

The question sounds abstruse, but a great deal hangs on it. Think how often reading has changed the course of history – Luther's reading of

Paul, Marx's reading of Hegel, Mao's reading of Marx. Those points
stand out in a deeper, vaster process – man's unending effort to find
meaning in the world around him and within himself. If we could
understand how he has read, we· could come closer to understanding·
how he made sense of life; and in that way, the historical way, we might
even satisfy some of our own craving for meaning.

Appendix: A Provincial *Cabinet littéraire* in 1779

The following circular letter provides a rare glimpse into a *cabinet
littéraire* or reading club in prerevolutionary France. It was addressed by
P. J. Bernard, a bookseller in Lunéville, to the officers of the local
gendarmerie in September, 1779. Bernard wanted to persuade the
gendarmes to buy membership in his *cabinet* and therefore stressed its
usefulness for military officers. But it probably resembled similar
establishments scattered throughout provincial France. The circular
comes from Bernard's dossier in the papers of the Société typographique
de Neuchâtel in the Bibliothèque publique et universitaire of Neuchâtel,
Switzerland. Its spelling has not been modernized or corrected.

A Messieurs les Gendarmes

Messieurs,

Le Sr. Bernard, propriétaire du Cabinet Littéraire de la Gendarmerie,
autorisé par Monsieur le Marquis d'Autichamp, a l'honneur de vos
représenter qu'encouragé par le suffrage de ses abonnés, il désireroit
fonder un établissement plus étendu et plus utile.

Il voudroit qu'au moyen d'un abonnement certain & invariable,
Messieurs les Gendarmes trouvassent chés lui tous les secours littéraires
qu'ils peuvent désirer. Une maison commode, grande, bien éclairée &
chauffée, qui seroit ouverte tous le jours, depuis neuf heures du matin
jusqu'à midi & depuis une heure jusqu'à dix, offriroit, dès cet instant, aux
amateurs, deux mille volumes qui seroient augmentés de quatre cens par
année. Les livres seroient à la disposition de Messieurs les Gendarmes, qui
cependant ne pourront les sortir de la bibliothèque.

Le Sr. Bernard s'engage à se procurer par chaque ordinaire:

Deux journaux de Linguet	Deux Gazettes de France
Deux Mercures	Deux Gazettes de Leyde
Deux Journaux militaires	Deux Gazettes de La Haye
Deux Journaux des affaires de	Deux Gazettes de Bruxelles
l'Amérique & de l'Angleterre	Deux Courriers du Bas Rhin
Deux Esprits des journaux	Deux Courriers de Deux-Ponts
Deux Courriers de l'Europe	Deux Bulletins

Auxquels seront joints les ouvrages & instrumens de mathématiques, les cartes géographiques, les ordonnances militaires, & tout ce qui concerne un officier.

Le Sr. Bernard aussi sensible au plaisir d'être utile qu'à son intérêt particulier, se bornera pour chaque abonnement à trois livres par an.

Voilà quel sera l'ordre de sa maison:

Une salle au rais de chaussée sera destinée pour la conversation, ainsi qu'une chambre au premier étage; & les autres seront abandonnées aux lecteurs des gazettes, des ouvrages de littérature, etc.

Il ne sera question d'aucun jeu quelconque, sous tel prétexte que ce soit.

La reconnaissance que le Sr. Bernard a vouée à la Gendarmerie, lui fait saisir tous les moyens de lui être agréable. Il se flate que Messieurs les Gendarmes voudront bien jetter sur son projet un coup d'œil favorable & le mettre à portée d'ajouter aux obligations qu'il leur a deja l'hommage d'une éternelle reconnaissance.

N.B. Le Sr. Bernard prie ceux de ces Messieurs les Gendarmes qui lui seront favorables de vouloir bien lui accorder leur signature.

NOTES

1 Ovid, *Ars Amatoria*, Book III, lines 469–72 and 613–26. I have followed the translation by J. H. Mozley in *The Art of Love and Other Poems* (London, 1929), modifying it in places with the more modern version by Héguin de Guerle, *L'Art d'aimer* (Paris, 1963). All other translations in this essay are by me.

2 Carlo Ginzburg, *The Cheese and the Worms: the Cosmos of a Sixteenth-Century Miller*, tr. Anne and John Tedeschi (Baltimore, 1980).

3 Robert Darnton, "Readers Respond to Rousseau: the Fabrication of Romantic Sensitivity" in Darnton, *The Great Cat Massacre and other Episodes of French Cultural History* (New York, 1984), pp. 215–56.

4 As instances of these themes, see Kurt Rothmann, *Erläuterungen und Dokumente. Johann Wolfgang Goethe: Die Leiden des Jungen Werthers*, (Stuttgart, 1974), and James Smith Allen, "History and the Novel: *Mentalité* in Modern Popular Fiction", *History and Theory* 22 (1983), pp. 233–52.

5 As examples of this literature, which is too vast to be cited in detail here, see Henri-Jean Martin, *Livre, pouvoirs et société à Paris au XVIIe siècle (1598–1701)* (Geneva, 1969), 2 vols.; Robert Estivals, *La Statistique bibliographique de la France sous la monarchie au XVIIIe siècle* (Paris and The Hague, 1965); Frédéric Barbier, "The Publishing Industry and Printed Output in Nineteenth-Century France" in Kenneth E. Carpenter (ed.), *Books and Society in History. Papers of the Association of College and Research Libraries Rare Books and Manuscripts Preconference, 24–28 June, 1980 Boston, Massachusetts* (New York and London, 1983), pp. 199–230;

Johan Goldfriedrich, *Geschichte des deutschen Buchhandels* (Leipzig, 1886–1913, 4 vols); Rudolf Jentzsch, *Der deutsch-lateinische Büchermarkt nach den Leipziger Ostermesskatalogen von 1740, 1770 und 1800 in seiner Gliederung und Wandlung* (Leipzig, 1912); H. S. Bennett, *English Books & Readers 1475 to 1557* (Cambridge, 1952); Bennett, *English Books & Readers 1558 to 1603* (Cambridge, 1965); Bennett, *English Books & Readers 1603 to 1640* (Cambridge, 1970); Giles Barber, "Books from the Old World and for the New: the British International Trade in Books in the Eighteenth Century" *Studies on Voltaire and the Eighteenth Century* 151 (1976), pp. 185–224; Robert B. Winans, "Bibliography and the Cultural Historian: Notes on the Eighteenth-Century Novel" in William L. Joyce, David D. Hall, Richard D. Brown, and John B. Hench (eds), *Printing and Society in Early America* (Worcester, 1983), pp. 174–85; and G. Thomas Tanselle, "Some Statistics on American Printing, 1764–1783" in Bernard Bailyn and John B. Hench (eds), *The Press & the American Revolution* (Boston, 1981), pp. 315–64.

6   Estivals, *La Statistique bibliographique*, p. 309; Paul Raabe, "Buchproduktion und Lesepublikum in Deutschland 1770–1780", *Philobiblin: eine Vierteljahrsschrift für Buch- und Graphiksammler* 21 (1977), pp. 2–16. The comparative statistics on writers are based on my own calculations.

7   François Furet, "La 'librairie' du royaume de France au 18ᵉ siècle" in Furet et al., *Livre et société dans la France du XVIIIᵉ siècle* (Paris, 1965), pp. 3–32; Daniel Roche, "Noblesses et culture dans la France du XVIIIᵉ: les lectures de la noblesse", in *Buch und Sammler. Private und öffentliche Bibliotheken im 18. Jahrhundert. Colloquium der Arbeitsstelle 18. Jahrhundert Gesamthochschule Wuppertal Universität Münster vom 26.–28. September 1977* (Heidelberg, 1979), pp. 9–27; Michel Marion, *Recherches sur les bibliothèques privées à Paris au milieu du XVIIIᵉ siècle (1750–1759)* (Paris, 1978); Michel Vovelle, *Piété baroque et déchristianisation en Provence au XVIIIᵉ siècle. Les attitudes devant la mort d'après les clauses des testaments* (Paris, 1973).

8   Jentzsch, *Der deutsch-lateinische Büchermarkt*; Albert Ward, *Book Production, Fiction, and the German Reading Public 1740–1800* (Oxford, 1974); Rudolf Schenda, *Volk ohne Buch. Studien zur Sozialgeschichte der populären Lesestoffe 1700–1910* (Frankfurt am Main, 1970), p. 467.

9   For Jefferson's model of a minimal library for an educated but not especially scholarly gentleman, see Arthur Pierce Middleton, *A Virginia Gentleman's Library* (Williamsburg, 1952).

10 Daniel Mornet, "Les Enseignements des bibliothèques privées (1750–1780)", *Revue d'histoire littéraire de la France* 17 (1910), pp. 449–96. For an overview of the French literature with bibliographical references, see Henri-Jean Martin and Roger Chartier (eds), *Histoire de l'édition française* (Paris, 1982–), of which the first two volumes covering the period up to 1830 have appeared. Walter Wittmann's study and related works are discussed in Schenda, *Volk ohne Buch*, pp. 461–7. On the Parisian common reader, see Daniel Roche, *Le Peuple de Paris. Essai sur la culture populaire au XVIIIᵉ siècle* (Paris, 1981), pp. 204–41.

11   Reinhard Wittmann, *Buchmarkt und Lektüre im 18. und 19. Jahrhundert. Beiträge zum literarischen Leben 1750–1880* (Tübingen, 1982), pp. 46–68; Wallace Kirsop, "Les mécanismes éditoriaux" in *Histoire de l'édition française* (Paris, 1984), vol. II, pp. 31–2.

12   John A. McCarthy, "Lektüre und Lesertypologie im 18. Jahrhundert (1730–1770). Ein Beitrag zur Lesergeschichte am Beispiel Wolfenbüttels" *Internationales Archiv für Sozialgeschichte der deutschen Literatur* 8 (1983), pp. 35–82.

13   Rolf Engelsing, "Die Perioden der Lesergechichte in der Neuzeit. Das statistische Ausmass und die soziokulturelle Bedeutung der Lektüre", *Archiv für Geschichte des Buchswesens* 10 (1969), cols 944–1002 and Engelsing, *Der Bürger als Leser. Lesergeschichte in Deutschland 1500–1800* (Stuttgart, 1974).

14   David Hall, "The Uses of Literacy in New England, 1600–1850" in *Printing and Society in Early America*, pp. 1–47.

15   For similar observations on the setting of reading, see Roger Chartier and Daniel Roche, "Les pratiques urbaines de l'imprimé", in *Histoire de l'édition française*, vol. II, pp. 403–29.

16   Restif de la Bretonne, *La vie de mon père*, Ottawa, 1949, pp. 216–17. Schubart's poem is quoted in Schenda, *Volk ohne Buch*, p. 465, and can be translated: "When the evening time comes round, / I always drink my glass of wine. / Then the schoolmaster reads to me / Something new out of the newspaper."

17   On chapbooks and their public use in France, see Charles Nisard, *Histoire des livres populaires ou de la littérature du colportage* (Paris, 1854, 2 vols); Robert Mandrou, *De la culture populaire aux 17ᵉ et 18ᵉ siècles: la bibliothèque bleue de Troyes* (Paris, 1964); and for examples of more recent scholarship the series "Bibliothèque bleue" edited by Daniel Roche and published by Editions Montalba. The best account of popular literature in Germany is still Schenda, *Volk ohne Buch*, although its interpretation has been challenged by some more recent work, notably Reinhart Siegert, *Aufklärung und Volkslektüre exemplarisch dargestellt an Rudolph Zacharias Becker und seinem "Noth- und Hülfsbüchlein"* (Frankfurt am Main, 1978). As an example of workers reading to each other, see Samuel Gompers, *Seventy Years of Life and Labor. An Autobiography* (New York, 1925), pp. 80–1.

18   Françoise Parent-Lardeur, *Les cabinets de lecture. La lecture publique à Paris sous la Restauration* (Paris, 1982).

19   The studies by Dann, Welke, and Prüsener, along with other interesting research, are collected in Otto Dann (ed.), *Lesegesellschaften und bürgerliche Emanzipation: ein europäischer Vergleich* (Munich, 1981).

20   Heinzemann's remarks are quoted in Helmut Kreuzer, "Gefährliche Lesesucht? Bemerkungen zu politischer Lektürekritik im ausgehenden 18. Jahrhundert" in Rainer Gruenter (ed.), *Leser und Lesen im 18. Jahrhundert. Colloquium der Arbeitsstelle Achtzehntes Jahrhundert Gesamthochschule Wuppertal, 24.–26. Oktober 1975* (Heidelberg, 1977). Bergk's observations are scattered throughout his treatise, *Die Kunst Bücher zu Lesen* (Jena,

1799), which also contains some typical remarks about the importance of "digesting" books: see its title-page and p. 302.

21 Newberry Library, Case Wing Z 45.18 ser.la, no 31.

22 Margaret Spufford, "First Steps in Literacy: The Reading and Writing Experiences of the Humblest seventeenth-century Autobiographers", *Social History* 4 (1979), pp. 407–35 and Spufford, *Small Books and Pleasant Histories. Popular Fiction and its Readership in Seventeenth-century England* (Athens, Georgia, 1981). On popular reading in nineteenth- and twentieth-century England, see R. K. Webb, *The British Working Class Reader* (London, 1955), and Richard D. Altick, *The English Common Reader: A Social History of the Mass Reading Public 1800–1900* (Chicago, 1957).

23 This discussion is based on the research of Dominique Julia, notably his "Livres de classe et usages pédagogiques" in *Histoire de l'édition française*, vol. II, pp. 468–97. See also Jean Hébrard, "Didactique de la lettre et soumission au sens. Note sur l'histoire des pédagogies de la lecture" in *Les textes du Centre Alfred Binet: L'enfant et l'écrit* 3 (1983), pp. 15–30.

24 Jean-Marie Goulemot (ed.), Valentin Jamerey-Duval, *Mémoires. Enfance et éducation d'un paysan au XVIIIe siècle* (Paris, 1981); Daniel Roche (ed.), *Journal de ma vie. Jacques-Louis Ménétra compagnon vitrier au 18e siècle* (Paris, 1982).

25 Adams' margin notes are quoted in Zoltán Haraszti, *John Adams & the Prophets of Progress* (Cambridge, Mass., 1952), p. 85. On glosses and footnotes, see Lawrence Lipking, "The Marginal Gloss", *Critical Inquiry* 3 (1977), pp. 620–31 and G. W. Bowersock, "The Art of the Footnote", *The American Scholar* 53 (1983–84), pp. 54–62. On the Prosper Marchand manuscripts, see the two articles by Christiane Berkvens-Stevelinck, "L'Apport de Prosper Marchand au 'système des libraires de Paris'" and "Prosper Marchand, 'trait d'union' entre auteur et éditeur" in *De gulden Passer* 56 (1978), pp. 21–63 and 65–99.

26 For surveys and bibliographies of reader-response criticism, see Susan R. Suleiman and Inge Crosman (eds), *The Reader in the Text: Essays on Audience and Interpretation* (Princeton, 1980), and Jane P. Tompkins (ed.), *Reader-Response Criticism: From Formalism to Post-Structuralism* (Baltimore, 1980). One of the most influential works from this strain of criticism is Wolfgang Iser, *The Implied Reader: Patterns of Communication in Prose Fiction from Bunyan to Beckett* (Baltimore, 1974).

27 Walter J. Ong, "The Writer's Audience Is Always a Fiction", *PMLA* 90 (1975), pp. 9–21.

28 D. F. McKenzie, "Typography and Meaning: The Case of William Congreve", in Giles Barber and Bernhard Fabian (eds), *Buch und Buchhandel in Europa im achtzehnten Jahrhundert* (Hamburg, 1981), pp. 81–126.

29 Roger Chartier, *Figures de la gueuserie* (Paris, 1982). See also the general reflections of Chartier in his essay, "Une histoire de la lecture est-elle possible? Du livre au lire: quelques hypothèses", to appear in the transactions of the Colloque de Saint-Maximin, October 1982.

30   Paul Saenger, "Manières de lire médiévales", *Histoire de l'édition française*, vol. I, pp. 131–41 and Saenger, "From Oral Reading to Silent Reading", *Viator* 13 (1982), pp. 367–414. Of course one can find exceptional cases of individuals who read silently long before the seventh century, the most famous being Saint Ambrose as described in the *Confessions* of Saint Augustine. For further discussion of reading and the early history of the book, see Henri-Jean Martin, "Pour une histoire de la lecture", *Revue française d'histoire du livre*, new series, no 16 (1977), pp. 583–610.

31   On the long-term history of the notion of the world as a book to be read, see Hans Blumenberg, *Die Lesbarkeit der Welt* (Frankfurt am Main, 1981). Franklin's epitaph does not actually appear on his gravestone. He probably wrote it in 1728, when he was a young printer and a wit in the Junto club: see *The Papers of Benjamin Franklin*, Leonard W. Labaree, ed., New Haven, 1959–, vol. 1, pp. 109–11. The phrasing differs slightly in each of the three autograph texts.

8

History of Images

Ivan Gaskell

Visual Material

Although historians use source material of many kinds their training generally leads them to be most at ease with written documents. Consequently they are often ill-equipped to deal with visual material and many use images simply illustratively in ways which can appear naïve, trite or ignorant to people professionally concerned with visual problems. Of course, this is far from invariably the case. Some historians have made valuable contributions to our vision of the past – and of the place of visual material within it – by using images in a sophisticated, specifically historical, manner. None the less, the historian's point of view is scarcely taken into account when images are debated in a wider context. This need not continue to be the case if historians are apprised of some of the concerns which dominate the thoughts and practice of those who deal with visual material. This is what I hope to do in the present chapter in the context of a discussion of a selection of recent work in an awesomely large field of enquiry.

In order to avoid possible misunderstandings I shall define my use of terms before going any further. By history I mean the discourse made by historians rather than 'the past'. By art I mean those artefacts and, on occasion, the concepts associated with them produced by those designated as artists, either by themselves, their contemporaries or retrospectively by others. (Also included should be those means developed by artists to evade art as artefact, notable amongst them being performance art, though this will not be discussed here.) Yet my discussion is not limited to art, although I know no single term to describe the wide range of visual material to which I wish to refer. It includes art as just defined but also, first, those constituents of the

human-made visual environment which are or have been valued for
reasons other than their ostensible practical purpose (if they have one),
whether by design from the outset (for instance, the chair not simply
designed to be sat upon), or retrospectively (the 'found object' or
'collectable' invested with new significance by designation); secondly,
those constituents of the human-made visual environment which are
primarily communicative, including graphic design and photography. I
will term this somewhat nebulous mass – which includes art – 'visual
material'.

art as inclusive term.

   This chapter is headed 'History of Images' rather than 'History of Art'
for the very reason that I wish to consider issues concerning visual
material beyond the boundaries of art as well as within it. Indeed, the
distinction between art and other visual material suggests not only
questions of terminology, but also the relative status or privilege of
different kinds of material. Art history is largely concerned with art
alone and the perception of qualitative hierarchies within it, though this
discriminatory aspect of the discipline has been increasingly questioned
by some practitioners in recent years. Both the history of art, though,
and other forms of study of visual material are largely and legitimately
ahistorical. (In the present context it seems worth making the point that
the history of art is not a sub-discipline of history.)

   Furthermore, much interpretative work concerned with art and other
visual material does not take written form, or written form alone.
Indeed, many of those most intimately involved with the consideration
of visual material distrust, or even reject, academic discourse and the
implicit claim of interpretative precedence often allowed it. The
presentation and implied interpretation of such material by museums
and galleries, in exhibitions and within art itself are equally if not more
important.

   In occidental culture three interlinked institutions are central to the
definition by practice of what constitutes visual material and – equally
importantly – its internal boundaries and hierarchies. These institutions
are: first, dealers, sale-room staff and collectors; second, museum and
public gallery staff and, behind them, public funding bureaucrats; third,
academic art historians, editors and (as junior partners) critics.
Although some members of each individual group may claim to remain
aloof from the others, there is considerable exchange between the three
at many levels, from that of ideas and assumptions to that of money.
Indeed, the first two are clearly interdependent (for instance, the
exhibition sponsor can glide between them). Just outside this central
triad, having a limited bearing upon it, may be placed artists and art-
school teachers. Their practice has next to no immediate effect on the

discussion of premodern visual material within this triad and in one sense only a limited effect on discussion of contemporary issues. What artists do can very easily be ignored and they cannot have an effective independent voice, for their work and to an extent they themselves are treated as the property of the members of the triad.

An analysis of received opinion underlying the hierarchical constitution of 'visual material' is difficult to formulate owing to the complexity of the material and the lack of true consensus. However, what follows may serve as a broad outline guide. Within this vast body of material the primary distinction is between 'art' and 'other'. Within 'art' there is a distinction based on classically-derived Renaissance humanist criteria between ' fine art' (as an expression of individual human invention) and decorative or applied art, terms which have been partially superseded by 'design' when referring to the modern era.

Standing to one side is an activity the status of which has changed somewhat so as to become ambiguous: architecture. Italian Renaissance writers such as Leon Battista Alberti and Giorgio Vasari followed the Roman architect and theorist Vitruvius in conceiving of architecture as the pinnacle of the visual arts, owing to its combination of functional and abstract constituents giving scope for individual inventiveness. In many subsequent art historical analyses the emphasis is placed less upon the practical or social function of buildings than upon invention by treating structures and their related plans almost exclusively as vehicles of individual artistic expression, an approach also ultimately derived from Vitruvius (*De architectura*, II, ii). On the other hand, the current practice of architecture is generally seen as the preserve of a separate profession whose members and whose critics tend to treat the definition of the relationship between practical and expressive considerations ambiguously. There is a tendency to treat the current practice of architecture not as a fine art (as it may have been conceived when Michelangelo alternately carved statues, painted pictures and designed buildings), but as design on a grand scale, though retaining vestiges of the prestige of its earlier associations preserved in part by the work of art historians who write on architecture.

Also between 'art' and 'other' in a position of curiously unresolved status, though in a quite different way from that of architecture, stands photography. Although the range of images which can be produced by this technique is in one sense not very great, its spectrum of cultural significance is considerable, being treated at one end as a transparent means of conveying information and at the other as an opaque art medium. The cultural impact of photography over the last hundred and fifty years, both in itself and in the form of the moving visual image to which it has also given rise, has been immense, completely changing the visual environment and means of exchange of information of a large part of the population of the globe. Photography has subtly, radically and directly transformed the discipline of art history and the practice of all the members of the triad defined above, regardless of whether their objects of concern were created before or after its invention. Almost all make daily use of it, whether as illustrations, aids to memory, or as substitutes for objects depicted by its means. However, most members of these professions have avoided explicitly considering the consequences of photography as it affects their own work, as well as on a larger scale.

The category inadequately designated above as 'other' is in practice largely defined by museums and commerce. A concern for the local past has long made local museums depositories of objects. Obsolete domestic items evoking past practices, routines and even social relationships came to be displayed in addition to the works of art, archaeology and natural history which characterized the local museums founded in Britain in the years following the Museums Act of 1845. A greater concern with 'popular culture' since the 1970s has vested these artefacts with an enhanced, more strictly historically orientated significance owing to changes in display techniques. The entire area was promoted from the fringes of folklore studies to take its place within a revivified study of popular culture closely related to concurrent developments in historical writing represented in Britain by Peter Burke's *Popular Culture in Early Modern Europe* (1978). The new status accorded to the study of the material remains of non-élite sections of past societies is epitomized in display terms by the lavish construction of the Musée National des Arts et des Traditions Populaires in Paris. While vitrines contain agricultural implements or craft tools displaying regional variation and the value of anonymous craftsmanship, the print room is a repository of the predominantly anonymous broadsheet and catchpenny prints which were produced for popular consumption from the sixteenth century onwards.

The engagement of commerce with this wide variety of 'other' visual material is certainly not defined by a scholarly participation in debates concerning the cultural significance of such objects. Indeed, the impact of commerce on this area of the visual environment and on people's perception of the past is probably more considerable than that of the scholarship of museum staff and social historians. Even the leading auction houses have taken considerable pains to develop the area known as 'collectables' (paste pot lids, cigarette cards, toys etc.). This area sees the intersection of various concerns. First, it appeals to a sense of ordering and it serves as a recreational equivalent to commercial techniques of auditing and exchange; but, unlike the collector's business interests, it promises eventual completion and closure. Stamp-collecting is its paradigm. Second, 'collectables' appeal to another commercial impulse: the accrual of value by the completion of defined sets and the expectation of a return on investment. Thirdly, collecting is postulated on the implicit notion that knowledge concerning the objects is ostensibly finite: the possibility of interpretation does not enter the mental set. I once visited a Palladian country house in which many of the rooms were devoid of furniture and decoration, but the floors were entirely covered with teapots. Teapots, each one different, were placed edge to edge in corridors and on parts of staircases, making them impassable. To the owner this was not an arrangement expressing or inviting interpretation, but simply a matter of convenience. Fourthly – and most importantly for the historian – collecting of this kind implies a particular relationship with the past. Two of its elements are nostalgia based on an object's perceived synecdochical qualities (a Matchbox toy evoking a 1950s childhood, for example) and the supposed adherence of an immutable quality owing to personal contact with a celebrated or revered person or persons (a pair of boots owned by Elvis Presley or the first Duke of Wellington, for example). Indeed, when this attitude redolent of sympathetic magic is institutionalized, as it is in an increasingly widespread manner, we may wonder whether a distinction can be drawn between, say, Graceland and Apsley House, since both imply a profoundly unanalytical attitude to a past dominated by great men whose essence can be known through the perusal of the objects with which they surrounded themselves.

Having made some inroads into the vast mass of visual material ('art', matter of unresolved status, such as architecture and photography, and the 'other', including certain categories of artefact and 'collectables') arrival at the conjunction of all these phenomena in the institutionalized presentation of heroes (Presley as 'the King', Wellington as 'the Iron Duke') may be the point at which to address the problem of how knowledge about visual material can be established so that it can be deployed for various purposes (entertainment, propaganda, making money and relating the present to the past). I will attempt to explore only three of the various aspects of speculation with reference to selected recent work: authorship, canonicity and interpretation.

Authorship

To seek to establish authorship is not simply a consequence of art market values, as some sceptics maintain (that is, a painting by Van Gogh will be worth incomparably more than a painting which looks as though it is by Van Gogh, but is not). Rather, it is a consequence of the conception of the artist and his (and very occasionally her) perceived relationship with art in the occidental tradition. As a corollary, the authorship of visual material not considered to be art (artisanal or industrial products) is generally held to be of little consequence, although the growth of 'design' as a strategy for subsuming the immediately exploitable elements of 'art' for directly commercial purposes is leading to a partial transfer of the prerogative of the artist to the designer. Here, however, there is hardly the scope for contention to be found in the field of art, especially its subgroup premodern (or 'old master') painting and drawing.

Connoisseurship – the technique by which authorship of individual works of art is generally proposed – is 'the id of the art-historical ego', as Gary Schwartz expressed it in a recent critique.[1] Many art historians who are far from radical in their opinions acknowledge the intellectually insecure basis of connoisseurship and concentrate on other areas of enquiry (iconography, patronage). Connoisseurship's apologists cannot help but reveal its internal contradictions. In 1985 the London auction house Sotheby's and Cambridge University's Fitzwilliam Museum, collaborated to produce the 'First Sotheby Fitzwilliam Exhibition'. Its subject was *The Achievement of a Connoisseur: Philip Pouncey*, who, during a long career, has worked in both museums and the trade, primarily concerned with Italian Renaissance drawings. Describing Pouncey's work in the introduction to the accompanying catalogue,[2] John Gere described Pouncey's 'clarity, accuracy, concision and exactness of expression, attention to shades of meaning, the distinction between hypothesis and fact and the relevant and irrelevant, and the expression of assent and dissent' in graduated terms'. He continues, 'Mr Pouncey is a scholar . . . for whom . . . accuracy is not a virtue but a duty.' Over the page, though, Gere reveals the bizarre double standards of connoisseurship, stating 'It is one thing to make a satisfactory attribution, but quite another to explain it satisfactorily' and he further describes Pouncey's use of gesture in response to this problem: 'Unforgettable, even after thirty years, was his way of demonstrating the "Correggiosity" of no. 19 in the present exhibition by throwing himself into the pose of the St Sebastian in the drawing.' For many art historians the inarticulateness which allows pantomime and – more seriously – 'brief annotations on the mounts of drawings' to be the connoisseur's main mode of expression (described by Gere as 'the tangible monument of his [Pouncey's] most remarkable life-work') is inextricably bound up with authoritarianism, for it eschews rational argument and appeals to personal reputation. Many find difficulty in accepting pure assertion as scholarship. As a consequence a number of radical art historians and theorists openly denigrate connoisseurship as an inherently right-wing, blinkered activity which simply bolsters the art market and fosters the evasion of major issues by concentrating on discrete, insignificant minutiae. In return, many connoisseurs have scant regard for art historians whose speculations concern issues other than authorship. An ideological polarization exists.

Connoisseurship deserves closer examination rather than dismissal. Gere, in the introduction cited above, gives an excellent definition of the traditional conception of connoisseurship which is worth quoting in full. (I number Gere's criteria for ease of subsequent reference.)

Connoisseurship, in the technical sense of identifying the authors of works of art, is not exactly a science, in the sense of being a rational system of inference from verifiable data; nor is it exactly an art. It stands somewhere between the two, and it calls for a particular combination of qualities of mind, some more scientific than artistic and others more artistic than scientific: [1] a visual memory for compositions and details of compositions, [2] exhaustive knowledge of the school or period in question, [3] awareness of all the possible answers, [4] a sense of artistic quality, [5] a capacity for assessing evidence, and [6] a power of empathy with the creative process of each individual artist and [7] a positive conception of him as an individual artistic personality.

If one accepts that connoisseurship is necessary activity (which I do, though as a means to a variety of ends, not an end in itself) criteria numbers 1, 2 and 5 seem uncontentious. Number 3, however, is a rational impossibility as expressed and I hope I do Gere no disservice by suggesting that the quality I understand him as wishing to convey is actually comprehended as far as rationally possible by his first two criteria. Number 4 may be thought to beg various vital questions, but might none the less be accepted in the present circumstances. The real problems lie in numbers 6 and 7, the latter especially being basic to connoisseurship as generally conceived. The notion that each individual artist inevitably betrays him- or herself in a unique manner by unconscious stylistic traits which the connoisseur can recognize forms the very basis of connoisseurship. Gere admits that 'the connoisseurship of Italian drawings is based almost entirely on internal, stylistic evidence': therefore only refinement of and the discussion of perceived inconsistencies within a set of circularly defined arguments is open to the participant. It is essentially a closed, self-confirming system and therefore not demonstrably anything other than a fiction. (I am not denying, however, that a fiction can express a truth.) Furthermore, the contention behind criteria numbers 6 and 7 is itself not demonstrable. The stylistic parameters within which an individual artist works may conceivably be considerably wider than would permit the sustenance of a connoisseurship system based on the ostensible differentiation between inexplicable niceties. Various groupings of works can be made on the basis of observed similarities and differences, but this itself provides neither necessary nor sufficient cause to attribute those which exhibit similar characteristics to the same artist. To do so is to subscribe to an unacknowledged arbitrary system not necessarily corresponding to actuality. This may turn out to be unavoidable; but I propose first, that the status of such a system should be acknowledged by its practitioners, second, that any claims regarding its relationship to the world should be scrutinized with care in individual instances and third, that recent research concerning perception and cognition should be taken into account.

Great efforts are currently being made to evade this problem while not explicitly acknowledging that it exists. While remaining silent about the myth of the refined and sophisticated 'eye' which functions in a manner explicitly acknowledged to be something close to intuition, the new connoisseurs place their faith in technical and scientific examination. This has been made possible by developments in conservation practice and the application of scientific techniques to the analysis of the components of works of art, especially oil paintings. The problem of this kind which has probably gained most public attention in recent years concerns not an art object as such, but an item of visual material the uncertain status of which as either a real relic or as a man-made image has been of widespread interest: the Turin Shroud. In 1988 fragments were analysed in three laboratories in Switzerland, Britain and the USA simultaneously by carbon dating techniques, the results suggesting that the material was of late medieval, rather than palaeo-Christian origin. This experience may remind us that the centuries-old practice of the examination and subsequent certification or rejection of purported relics by ecclesiastical officials might well be regarded as the intellectual antecedent of present-day connoisseurship.

Amongst current connoisseurship projects proper, the Rembrandt

Research Project is pre-eminent. For more than twenty years a small group of Dutch scholars, working collaboratively, has examined paintings attributed to Rembrandt van Rijn and has amassed considerable quantities of technical information. A chronological catalogue of accepted works (with a consideration of doubtful and some previously accepted works rejected by the team) is in the course of publication.[3] However, the basic premise of the entire project itself seems increasingly questionable; that is, the assumption that it is both desirable and possible to define a corpus of work produced by Rembrandt himself distinct from that of his pupils, assistants, followers and contemporary imitators. Interestingly, both the desirability and the viability seem considerably less secure now than they must have done to the Project's initiators, largely and inadvertently thanks to the work of the team itself. The question has now become: if the 'Rembrandt' is the product of a workshop comprising a fluctuating membership in which Rembrandt himself is the only constant, is it even appropriate to attempt to identify paintings by Rembrandt alone, even if this were possible, given the limitations of connoisseurship techniques which in this instance can only rely on internal stylistic and technical evidence? We are, however, culturally reluctant to relinquish or at least to qualify the conception of the artist as an essentially individual creator whose unique activity ('the creative process') and character ('artistic personality') can be discerned by the empathetic observer (compare Gere's criteria numbers 6 and 7 above).

Much technical examination is actually a heightened pursuit of the artist's ostensibly unique traces: his touch, his personal abbreviations. Although the place of a work within wider categories, such as approximate date and likely place of production, may usefully be established, results usually sanction only negative rather than positive statements ('analysis has shown that no materials that are anachronistic for a seventeenth-century picture are employed'). Comparative analysis can establish patterns of workshop practice. For instance, a canvas without a distinctive double ground discernible in paint layer cross-sections made for microscopic examination is unlikely to have been prepared in Rembrandt's workshop. All the techniques available, from autoradiography to X-ray diffraction analysis, can be and are used to establish parameters within which works can be discussed by legitimate processes of comparison and exclusion. None the less, the principal aim in the interpretation of such results by art historians and curators remains the establishment of, or disqualification from, the corpus of an individual artist. The process for making connoisseurship decisions remains fundamentally unaltered, the only difference being that more data is at the connoisseur's disposal. The significance of this, however, is rarely precise enough for his or her requirements.

At present the use of technical analysis is escalating without due consideration of the epistemological implications. Some of the published working hypotheses of the Rembrandt Research Project have recently been placed in doubt as a result of the technical and scientific examination of the Rembrandt holdings of the National Gallery, London: the most thorough examination of a group of works associated with the Rembrandt workshop yet undertaken.[4] Its implication was that the extensive and detailed technical information used by the Rembrandt Research Project is actually inadequate. If so, where does one stop and at what point can decisions be made? Neutron activation autoradiography (which effectively reveals the disposition of individual paint constituents in a series of radiographic images) was a technique unavailable to the National Gallery team, yet a number of paintings attributed to Rembrandt sufficient to provide comparative material have been analysed in this manner. Would similar examination of the National Gallery paintings upset its newly published attributive hypotheses? Or should, rather, the limitations of connoisseurship – however extensive the technical data at the connoisseur's disposal – be examined and the entire project of attributive speculation pursued thereafter on a new basis, a basis in which hypothesis is recognized for what it is and opinion is not presented as secure knowledge?

The problem of the epistemological status of knowledge derived from connoisseurship becomes most acute when that necessarily insecure information is employed in the construction of complex art historical arguments in conjunction with knowledge established by more trustworthy processes (for instance, inferences drawn from mutually corroborative sources). If the evidence of connoisseurship is made to bear a weight equal to that sustained by more securely established evidence in such structures, those structures must be weak. The quality of the nature of the evidence, rather than the quality of the evidence in individual circumstances alone, must be taken into account. By this reckoning connoisseurship evidence by its very nature cannot be as persuasive as some other forms of evidence. To acknowledge this would not lead to the dismissal or exclusion of connoisseurship evidence, rather to its proper, circumspect use.

Questions of the relative weight of different kinds of evidence do not arise in the same way when considering forms of argument in which connoisseurship alone is involved. Yet to acknowledge the epistemological limitations of connoisseurship would hardly serve the vested interests of the art world. A shift of emphasis is unlikely because works of art function as individual objects (rather than as indeterminate components) in the determining context: the market and its dependent partner, the museum. Within this context it is highly desirable that the status of each individual object should not be in doubt. As a consequence, lack of knowledge is regularly compensated for by the presentation of opinion bolstered by reputation and authority in the guise of secure knowledge. An admission of ignorance is all too often seen as culpable failure, an attitude which colours practice in the field. (Only those to whom great authority has accrued can get away with occasional admissions of ignorance: judiciously made such admissions actually confirm those positions of great authority.) Too much is at stake for participants to acknowledge this state of affairs: status, prestige (both individual and institutional) and, above all, money. As in any other capitalist market, confidence and credulity go hand in hand. Those whose principal medium of exchange is the idea rather than the dollar are at a considerable disadvantage.

From the point of view of those concerned with the relationship between the present and the past, we should note that the definition of past practice established by connoisseurship alone must be counted a fiction, however persuasive when well argued. We should also note that those art-historical arguments which place too great a weight on connoisseurship must be treated with great caution, for they are likely to contain weak elements, if not outright flaws. One of the consequences of an acceptance of this argument will probably be that the question of individual authorship will become less pressing than before. Yet, if we accept that changes in artists' practice result at least in part from intentionally motivated choices made by individuals which are subsequently spread by 'influence' (which can comprehend imitation and emulation), the question of individual authorship will not be entirely superseded.

Canonicity

The rhetorically exaggerated differentiation between knowledge and opinion in the previous section is, of course, far from adequate for the analysis of critical and historical procedure where the consideration of visual material is concerned. Disentangling knowledge from opinion is not a simple matter, as Frank Kermode argued in *Forms of Attention* (1985) when examining the formation and perpetuation of canons in both literature and the visual arts. He demonstrated that ill-informed opinion and fashion, rather than fine critical judgement, can create the circumstances in which an artist can be 'rediscovered' and his work admitted to the canon of material subject to repeated scholarly and critical re-examination. Kermode described the case of Sandro Botticelli, whose paintings were largely ignored between the sixteenth and later nineteenth centuries. He cogently argued that neither the interest of Herbert Horne, who did much to define the corpus of Botticelli's paintings by connoisseurship and archival research,[5] nor Aby Warburg, who examined aspects of Botticelli's work in the context of his own systematic theories of cultural history,[6] would have been aroused had there not been a popular cultural shift which accommodated a taste for work attributed to Botticelli. Both Horne and Warburg were in effect swimming with the *fin-de-siècle* tide. The consequence was that Botticelli's work was (in general terms) adequately distinguished from that of his contemporaries, pupils and imitators and an 'artistic personality' defined.[7]

Those paintings designated Botticelli's masterpieces, notably the *Birth of Venus* and the *Primavera* ('Spring') (both in the Galleria degli Uffizi, Florence) have joined the totemic group of massively reproduced images familiar to a wide public through many forms of reproduction. The *Primavera* has been apotheosed as the definitive 'greatest treasure' of the Uffizi Gallery, its central female figures appearing on the cover of the visitors' handbook published in numerous languages. A lengthy and extensive restoration of this painting was completed in 1982. It was re-presented to the public as the climax of the exhibition *Metodo e scienza. Operatività e ricerca nel restauro* (Palazzo Vecchio, Florence, 1982–3) when it was exhibited by itself in a dark room, dramatically lit like a cinema screen, a calculatedly awe-inspiring spectacle. The entry in the catalogue accompanying this exhibition (pp. 207–50) was the longest yet devoted in this form of publication to the technical description of a single painting. We have seen that technical information is employed in the service of connoisseurship. However, the presentation to the public of technical findings, while ostensibly demystificatory, is (amongst other things) a principal modern means of enhancing the mystique and status of a work of art by publicly according it special treatment. Whereas two hundred years ago visitors to the Uffizi expected to admire the *Venus de' Medici* as its 'greatest treasure', the Botticelli Room has now taken the place of the Tribuna (notwithstanding its recent historicist restoration) as the ultimate goal of popular artistic pilgrimage, the *Primavera* its designated centrepiece. This is at least in part a perfectly calculated development in which the gallery staff knowingly play a leading role.[8]

We can see, therefore, that several complex intersecting issues are raised when canonicity is considered. Two of these are intimately entangled with the debt of art history to its acknowledged founding text: Giorgio Vasari's *Lives of the Artists*.[9] They are, first, its coincidence with literary studies in predominantly treating the life work of an individual as the basic unit for consideration. As we have seen, this approach is sustained by the underlying assumptions of much connoisseurship. Second, the canon based on authorship is perpetuated, amongst other means, by writing in Vasari's mode. The canon is also subject to modification: Vasari himself set the precedent in the second edition of his *Lives*. Artists are added as their careers develop, with or without national bias (by van Mander, Bellori, de Piles . . .). Artists, or the 'schools' into which they are grouped, are occasionally dropped (like Guido Reni and the seventeenth-century Bolognese) or discovered (like Botticelli, or more recently, Caravaggio). These changes affect and are affected by shifts in the art institutions: the market and the museum. One way of treating these shifts and gauging the disparities at any one time between scholarly attitudes to 'the canon' and a wider, public state of affairs (as expressed primarily by collecting) is the area of scholarship which has grown considerably in recent years: the history of taste.

The leading exponent of the history of taste is Francis Haskell. Haskell's *Rediscoveries in Art. Some Aspects of Taste, Fashion and Collecting in England and France* (1976) and (with Nicholas Penny) *Taste and the Antique. The Lure of Classical Sculpture, 1500–1900* (1981) have helped to engender an awareness that canons of perceived artistic excellence are historically contingent and are determined by a variety of factors, some of which are not necessarily primarily to do with artistic issues. Haskell deals with the life of objects subsequent to the circumstances of their creation (the concern of retrieval art history, to be discussed below) and anterior to their possible active effects in the present (the stuff of criticism). Yet far from simply enhancing an historical attitude to the circumstances in which art functions, this work has helped to effect a thorough critical reappraisal of the presentation of the art of the past in the museum. This development in the public art institutions can be seen as an inherently and at times explicitly non-Modernist approach to canonicity. For instance, it would be difficult to imagine the revival of serious interest in nineteenth-century French academic art without the work of, amongst others, Francis Haskell and Albert Boime,[10] which has culminated in the elaboration of a non-Modernist nineteenth century in the new Musée d'Orsay in Paris. The teleology which sustained the Modernist project (lending retrospective critical privilege to Courbet, Manet, the Impressionists and Cézanne) is no longer unwaveringly upheld. For a new generation of gallery visitors the names of Couture, Gérôme and Bouguereau may achieve canonical status.

The growth of the history of taste has also helped to sanction a regressive attititude to collections. Museum trustees and staff are less willing to argue against the acceptance of gifts or bequests of collections with the condition attached that they should only be displayed intact, rather than dispersed amongst the museum's holdings as the staff see fit. Steps have been taken to attempt to return collections open to the public in their original settings to their original arrangements. Perhaps the most successful example in Britain is the Wallace Collection in London, which is in any case a 'dead' collection: nothing can be added or taken away, even temporarily as loans. Too uncritical an approach to this matter, though, can lead to a lack of critical awareness of the social function of collections as monuments to a supposedly great man (or occasionally woman), and I believe it is the duty of curators to treat this as an issue in its own right, or at least to recognize its problematic nature. The subordination of the individual work of art to an overall scheme is inherent in any gallery arrangement, but when that arrangement is chosen because of its illumination of an individual's taste in an uncritical manner and is instituted as a permanent, not a temporary, arrangement, a petrifying authoritarianism seems inherent in the project.

The position is even worse when the supposed restoration of original arrangements takes place within a changing collection and moreover is faked. The most outstanding example of this treatment is the new refurbishment of the National Gallery of Scotland, Edinburgh, which was berated by Caroline Elam in an editorial in the conservative art journal, the *Burlington Magazine*.[11] The ostensible motive of restoring nineteenth-century authenticity is belied by the artificial archaizing of the 1970s mezzanine extension with, in Elam's accurate description, 'marbled skirting, dados, cornices, pseudo-Victorian carpet, fringed corduroy ottomans and violently coloured Lyons silk wall-coverings . . . draining colour even from the Van Goghs'. She observed that in the main galleries a double or triple hang means that 'field glasses are needed for skied pictures'. Concluding, Elam suggested that 'the current vogue for authentic decor and historicising picture hanging is just one manifestation of the contemporary uncertainty about aesthetic values as we approach the second millennium.'

The growth of the history of taste implies a new attitude to canonicity paradoxically uniting a new critical – some would say uncritical – eclecticism which implicitly challenges the teleological art-historical canon and an attitude which can foster an authoritarian petrification of individual collections to produce an alternative criterion of canonicity, the collection itself. Other forces are also at work modifying or undermining both the canon and the notion of canonicity. Some of these are centred upon notions of interpretation, meaning and intention.

Interpretation

From the authorially defined canon and the canon defined by collection I now turn to pictorial meaning and interpretation. Here again we shall confront some now familiar themes. 'If historicism prevails,' wrote Caroline Elam in her *Burlington Magazine* editorial mentioned above, 'the individual work of art is locked in its period, and cannot break out to meet the contemporary eye.' The direct presentation of visual material is increasingly affected by the application of 'history of taste' criteria. However, in academic discourse this has little place; rather the battle lines are (broadly) between historical retrieval (the attempt to interpret visual material as it might have been when it was first made, whether by the maker, his contemporaries, or both) and direct critical engagement of several, often mutually irreconcilable kinds. These include first, the approach which admits the possibility of direct, intuitive access to the 'artistic personality' and the 'creative process' (which we have already encountered in the section on connoisseurship); second, a theoretically engaged, post-structuralist concern with visual hermeneutics; and third, an approach which stresses the essential continuity of art so that the art of any period in the past cannot be understood beyond the context of its relation to current practice in art and by extension in any visual medium.

These interpretational conflicts have been increasingly politicized in recent years. In an impassioned article entitled 'The Death of British Art History'[12] the academic art historian Michael Rosenthal reviewed the political overtones of certain recent art world events in the context of a denunciation of British academics for their failure to engage in broadly based cultural and political debate. Rosenthal re-examined the furore in 1982 over the Tate Gallery's exhibition of the work of the eighteenth-century British landscape painter, Richard Wilson. An attempt was made discreetly in the exhibition itself and in a thorough, scholarly manner in the accompanying catalogue by David Solkin to locate Wilson's ideal landscapes within the social and cultural context of their creation and initial consumption.[13] This was denounced in several influential organs, including a *Daily Telegraph* leader, as Marxist subversion. Two years previously the literary scholar John Barrell had published a similarly questioning historical examination of eighteenth-century paintings of rural subjects in *The Dark Side of the Landscape. The Rural Poor in English Painting 1730–1840* (1980). Barrell examined the ideology implicit in the representation of rural labourers in the paintings of Thomas Gainsborough, George Morland and John Constable, suggesting that their condition is shown to be natural rather than socially determined. He opposed a nostalgic mythology with an appeal to history, arguing that 'we should look twice at a notion of nature by which it seems "natural" that some men should work while others do not.'[14] Being simply an academic text and, furthermore, not especially well-informed about the role of artistic tradition in the generation of imagery, Barrell's book could be ignored by the trade and gallery establishment. We can acknowledge with Michael Rosenthal that academic writing is, after all, a socially marginal activity in Great Britain. Neil McWilliam and Alex Potts perceptively explained why Solkin's contribution to social art history was not similarly simply ignored:[15] Solkin had broken the rules by infiltrating the institution of the 'prestigious old master exhibition held at a major national gallery'. McWilliam and Potts went on: 'Even rather faded cultural treasures, such as the English enjoyment of landscape, and the supposed taste and refinement of the Georgian era, had to be defended if challenged on territory where they still seemed vaguely credible.'

The historical approach to visual material is not confined to the ascription of ideological significance, such as was discerned, rightly or wrongly, by Barrell and Solkin. Significance at the time of production goes beyond an often unconscious conformity with the socio-political ideology of the consumer to encompass modes of perception which are not liable to provoke politically motivated attention in the present day. Their elucidation has a long and distinguished historiography, which was examined in a broader art-historical context by Michael Podro in *The Critical Historians of Art* (1982). One of the foremost practitioners of this kind of retrieval art history is Michael Baxandall, whose book *Painting and Experience in Fifteenth Century Italy* (1972) is tellingly subtitled *A Primer in the Social History of Pictorial Style*. Baxandall sought to go beyond simple iconographical analysis. He wrote: 'Some of the mental equipment a man orders his visual experience with is variable, and much of this variable equipment is culturally relative, in the sense of being determined by the society which has influenced his experience.' The historian's task, therefore, is to recover the 'period eye': the culturally specific way of seeing peculiar to, say, early sixteenth-century south German limewood sculptors and their clients, as Baxandall attempted in *The Limewood Sculptors of Renaissance*

Germany (1980). Other scholars have applied their own versions of Baxandall's approach to other visual cultures, one of the most controversial being Svetlana Alpers's examination of Dutch art in the seventeenth century, *The Art of Describing* (1983). Alpers argued that it was characteristic of the Dutch in the seventeenth century to seek to know the world taxonomically by accurate pictorial description comprehending mapping, microscopy and the realistic representational transcription of observed reality. This, she argued, should take precedence over any allusion or allegory in the interpretation of Dutch visual material, a view which provoked a vigorous debate with other scholars in the field.[16] This debate demonstrated that speculation on superseded cognitive processes can be more controversial than seeking to elucidate the original pictorial meaning of individual works by comparing visual images with each other and with contemporary texts, a procedure which is now art-historically orthodox amongst academics, even if not amongst museum and art-market staff.

All these forms of retrieval art history are currently under attack from three notable directions. Some of those who are interested in visual hermeneutics question the notion that cultural significance can be encoded in visual material and subsequently decoded by a later interpreter to produce an adequate 'meaning'. Hans Belting, for instance, in *Das Ende der Kunstgeschichte?* (1983) noted how this ostensibly symmetrical process of encoding and decoding degenerates into the 'humanist parlour game' of Renaissance iconology, whereby pictorial images are held to be interpretable by reference to ostensibly equivalent literary texts (often programmes devised by humanist scholars for translation into pictorial terms in decorative schemes). Furthermore, the model of pictorial interpretation derived from Erwin Panofsky's distinction between the pre-iconographic, iconographic and iconological levels[17] was long ago theoretically superseded by the realization that denotation is ultimately indistinguishable from connotation and that even the simplest meaning (the image of a pipe to signify 'pipe', for instance) is culturally contingent. (See, for example, the opening section of Roland Barthes, *S/Z*, 1970 and Michel Foucault, *Ceci n'est pas une pipe*, 1973.) Perhaps the most interesting position now adopted is that the visual material of the past, specifically its art, can only be adequately interpreted by the creation of new visual material – art as part of a field of representational behaviour – which is rigorously conceptually disciplined. The cultural theorist and the artist can become one and the same (for example, Victor Burgin, an artist, theoretical writer and academic whose work was aptly described by Chris Miller as 'ideological counter-abuse of "appropriated imagery" from advertizing'[18] and whose publications include *Between*, 1986 and *The End of Art Theory. Criticism and Postmodernity*, 1986).

A certain questioning of retrieval art history comes from more orthodox, art-historical sources too; amongst them Michael Baxandall. In *Patterns of Intention. On the Historical Explanation of Pictures* (1985) Baxandall describes Giorgio Vasari's use of what is probably an historical fiction in order to make a purely critical point about the appearance of drapery in paintings by Piero della Francesca:

> Piero was very fond of making clay models which he would drape with wet cloths arranged in very many folds and then use for drawing and similar purposes.' . . . Any attentive reader of Vasari learns to recognize this sort of remark as Vasari chancing his inferential arm: it is unlikely he had the sort of evidence for this practice that would let us nowadays feel happy about making the statement so firmly. This does not matter. Vasari's own generic character places his remark for what it is – a critical truth, so to speak, as one sees when one matches it with, say, the white middle angel in the *Baptism of Christ* – and no reader of Vasari's own time would have had a false sense of its historicity. Indeed, Vasari's nimbleness between the critical and the historical is enviable; but we live in more muscle-bound times in these matters and if I said such a thing about Piero so flatly now you would be entitled to expect me to have actual collateral of a kind I could not produce. (p.117)

In his essay on connoisseurship Gary Schwartz remarked that 'Art historians, trained from the start to toggle back and forth between historical and ahistorical approaches to art, never seem to notice the basic contradiction between them.'[19] One might infer from Baxandall's text that this contradiction can be reconciled by acknowledging that historical veracity is contingent and that the application of historical criteria to the study of visual material produces fictions which are not necessarily epistemologically distinguishable from ahistorical critical commentaries. Placing discussion of art within an historical framework, therefore, is no more than what Baxandall terms a 'special taste': historical retrieval and critical appraisal are inherently no better than one another; indeed, insofar as historical retrieval is based on contingent criteria, it is nothing other than a special form of critical appraisal. One might therefore suggest that criticism which openly engages with current cultural and social concerns and which does not claim unprovable access to universal and perpetual 'truths' may be less likely to mislead viewers and readers than might ostensibly purely historical accounts. Perhaps we can only ever know the art of the present, some of which is what survives from the past, providing only the most tenuous and untrustworthy access to that past. The meaning of visual material changes; interpretations differ across chronological and cultural boundaries: those which we know can only ever be the ones we generate ourselves.

Considerably more worrying than doubts expressed and prompted by historically inclined art historians are the attempts to interpret the past as either readily accessible via the instant emotional response to visual material, or via the 'heritage industry' in which the 'instant emotional response' is often exploited. The most trenchant critique of the growth of 'heritage' as a social and increasingly political factor in recent years is Robert Hewison's *The Heritage Industry. Britain in a Climate of Decline* (1987). I will mention only two points raised by Hewison's book: 'heritage' is profoundly unanalytical and it implies that history, as a process of change, is – or should be – over. The production of a population capable of viewing the past only in terms of nostalgia and patriotism helps to ensure political docility.

The material of heritage is 'treasure' and its paradigm is the country house. The country house is invested not only with a social, but with an aesthetic mystique. For instance, 'The country house as a collective work of art is one of Britain's most important contributions to western civilisation' is found on the back cover of the catalogue accompanying the huge exhibition, *The Treasure Houses of Britain. Five Hundred Years of Private Patronage and Art Collecting* (National Gallery of Art, Washington DC, 1985–6). This exhibition was described in the *Economist* as 'a shameless sales pitch for the British heritage'.[20] Others seek to solicit money less directly: by inspiring sympathy by suggesting that the country house is an institution under threat, often in thinly-veiled political terms. The opening words of the first essay in the catalogue accompanying the exhibition concerning the National Heritage Memorial Fund held at the British Museum in 1988–9, *Treasures for the Nation. Conserving our Heritage* are: 'Hardly a week passes when one does not see the auctioneer's notice of the impending sale and dissolution of some big estate.' Continuing to quote W. G. Hoskins, Marcus Binney goes on, 'The house is seized by the demolition contractors, its park invaded and churned up' and so on. This mythology of destruction sponsored by museum grandees such as Roy Strong (in the exhibition and its catalogue *The Destruction of the Country House*, Victoria & Albert Museum, London, 1974) and politicians such as Patrick Cormack (*Heritage in Danger*, 1976) provides a convenient smokescreen behind which power and privilege continue to operate. In *The Latest Country Houses* (1984) John Martin Robinson disclosed that more than two hundred new country houses have been built in Britain since the Second World War. It is simply politically prudent (and might bring tax advantages) for those who enjoy private wealth to play the role of guardians of a 'national heritage', part of which is displayed to the public as the epitome of good taste and an unvaryingly 'good' past which should be preserved uncritically for evermore. There is no interpretation, merely accumulation which sanctions a social and aesthetic *status quo*.

Photography is the visual medium in which past events are often held to be most accessible via the instant emotional response. This is because the photograph bears a material, causal relation to its subject. Part of our response is to the photograph as a real trace of an event. The apologists of photojournalism go so far as to suggest that the information about any given event conveyed by a photograph gives us vital knowledge of it. Indeed, the recent past is increasingly known by means of partly fortuitous, instantaneous images. As the newspaper editor Harold Evans expressed it, 'Our impressions of major and complex events may be permanently fashioned by a single news photograph' – an observation quoted on the introductory panel in the exhibition *Eyewitness. 30 Years of World Press Photography* at the National Museum of Photography, Film and Television, Bradford (1989). However, certain points are now obvious and have been rehearsed repeatedly, not least in the permanent displays of that museum: the arrested instant need tell the observer little or nothing of an event that takes place in time; photographs are subject to many forms of manipulation (the excision of figures; cropping and toning to affect the observer's interpretation) and readily legible meaning is often only generated by combination with a caption. Different captions for the same photograph often produce radically different or even contradictory meanings. The certain information provided by a photograph may be of tangential use in an analytical account of a past event, yet by preserving a detail which might otherwise be ignored, new lines of not necessarily strictly historical curiosity about the past may be opened up. Why, for instance, did the woman who administered the presidential oath to Lyndon Johnson on board Airforce One on 22 November 1963 after the assassination of John F. Kennedy, place her thumb on the little finger of the hand in which he held the Bible, as is to be seen in Cecil Stoughton's photograph of the event?

One of the most interesting current areas of discussion about press and documentary photography concerns the role of the photographer in the events he or she depicts. It can be argued that the notion of the 'innocent eye' is no longer tenable and that the camera is always an intrusive presence. A photograph such as Sadayuki Mikami's of grieving relatives of passengers killed on board Korean Airlines flight 007, made in September 1983 on a boat where the aeroplane plunged into the sea, might be interpreted as taking intrusion as its subject: lenses are thrust towards the faces of the weeping relatives, including, by implication, that of the maker of this photograph. Is a bayonet thrust into a victim's stomach because a photographer (Michel Laureat) is present, or would it have happened in any case; or has the presence of a photographer deterred would-be assailants from thrusting other bayonets into other stomachs? Whatever the answer in any given instance, it is difficult not to regard the photographer as a participant.

History

From the foregoing the reader may infer that I do not believe that the historian is best placed to deal with visual imagery: he or she is naturally enough primarily occupied with interpreting the past, not with current visual practice and critical issues. However, historians have raised issues regarding visual material in worthwhile ways which can remind those of us who are primarily concerned with criticism and current cultural matters that all material from the past is potentially admissible as evidence for the historian.

Bob Scribner's *For the Sake of Simple Folk. Popular Propaganda for the German Reformation* (1981) is an example of the refreshing levelling effect an historian's gaze can bring to a mass of material – early sixteenth-century German woodcuts – which art historians cannot help but treat in an hierarchical manner according to perceived artistic merit. Scribner attempted to elucidate the iconographic and formal conventions which allowed pictorial propaganda for and against religious reform to be understood by ordinary people. In turn the imagery is taken to reveal their range of cultural understanding and the notions within it (the Antichrist, the world turned upside-down) to which reformers could appeal. It is appropriate for him to treat works by Dürer and the Cranachs in the same terms as prints by their contemporaries which art historians might dismiss as coarse and of little intrinsic interest; although when the success of imagery is assessed (in terms of the imitation or emulation of motifs and visual devices) quality, artistry and the role of existing visual tradition ought also to be considered, as should different probable markets for images of different quality.

A second example of a book in which an historian makes sophisticated use of visual material is Simon Schama's *The Embarrassment of Riches. An Interpretation of Dutch Culture in the Golden Age* (1987). In his description of middle-class Dutch social habits and beliefs concerning national identity, domestic probity, the duties of women and domestic servants and the rearing of children Schama presses a vast range of material into service, including poetry, chorography, travellers' accounts, notarial documents, court records, prints and paintings. In doing so he has shown an awareness of current art-historical debates concerning the interpretation of Dutch art and produced what I have described elsewhere as 'a masterly re-ordering of nineteenth-century anecdotal antiquarianism along anthropological lines in the light of modern historical and art-historical scholarship'.[21]

While I sincerely hope that historians will increasingly turn their attention to visual material, I regret that few to date have shown sufficient awareness of the issues necessarily involved or the particular skills needed to cope with such material. The contribution to the study of visual material which the historian is probably best equipped to make is the discussion of its production and consumption as social, economic and political activities. One area in which historians have already made considerable headway concerns a special form of image consumption: deliberate destruction, or iconoclasm. For most art historians iconoclasm will remain marginal because the objects do not survive or are damaged curiosities.[22] This, though, does not deter the historian of religion or the social historian. In the study of Reformation iconoclasm social historians have seized the initiative, for this is an activity in which not only élite theory, but non-literate, popular notions (notably concerning image magic) and behaviour (related to carnival or festivity) often appear to be accessible. This has led to a tendency to treat iconoclasm as an unvarying phenomenon, attention being given to factors common to various instances rather than to differences between them. Now social historians are increasingly turning to what has been called micropolitics, or the study of individual events, in the light of which they are learning to modify theoretical frameworks allowing a greater attention to nuances. This is to be seen, for instance, in the work of Lee Wandel on iconoclasm in Zurich, which she presented at a symposium held at the Herzog August Bibliothek, Wolfenbüttel, in 1986.[23] This symposium also marked a readiness to bring together specialists from different disciplines – literary, social, religious and art historians – to discuss the phenomenon of iconoclasm from complementary standpoints.

A less dramatic though no less rewarding example of what the historian can do to place visual material in a socio-economic context of production and consumption is provided by the work of the economist John Michael Montias. His study, *Artists and Artisans in Delft. A Socio-Economic Study of the Seventeenth Century* (1982) reminds readers that fine-art painting was a matter of class-determined financial opportunity, both for purchaser and practitioner. As well as tracing the fortunes of Delft's painters, Montias described the proto-industrial capitalist organization of its printers and faienciers. In contrast to practitioners of the latter two crafts the painters needed little in the way of capital investment; yet rather than being an open profession, Montias found that the expense of the six-year apprenticeship effectively limited entrants to the children of only the most prosperous craftsmen, notaries, lawyers and of painters themselves. Children sponsored by the Orphan Chamber, by contrast, were more likely to be apprenticed to a faiencier and, although in the same guild as the painters, would be unlikely to rise out of the ranks of a nascent proletariat.

In conclusion, therefore, we can see that no one profession has, or in my opinion should have, a monopoly over the interpretation of visual material, including the history of images. If historians have much to learn in this area they have important points to teach too. Far worse inadequacies have been descried in the practice of those who deal professionally with art. Art historians have grown used to being told that many of them have not yet got to grips with the questions raised by semiotics, mass communication and media theory, let alone with informing themselves of how to go about coping with photography, performance art, film, television and video. The art historian and the curator, for instance, can appear to take refuge in seemingly more immediate problems: the refinement, further application and transmission of tried analytical techniques, including connoisseurship, the refinement of canons and different forms of pictorial interpretation. Although taking a critical stance, I do not believe that we should simply be impatient with those who practise these skills. They do not serve the market and the museum alone. Certain questions which may be raised in the light of contemporary (and unanticipated future) concerns may be answerable only with their help.

Meanwhile, for the moment we live in a mental climate of fragmentation, of the desystematization of knowledge described by Jean Baudrillard,[24] in which versions of the past are constantly recycled, potentially permanently present, re-usable interchangeably as information bites. Our relationship with the past is no longer primarily defined by history, rather by a variety of practice, much of it visually based, subject to analysis in terms of 'visuality' and the 'expanded gaze',[25] in which historians (and most art historians) generally feel far from at home: advertising, television, photojournalism, architecture and certain areas of art. The keywords now are 'fragment' and 'ruin',[26] neither of them mentioned in the cultural primer of the mid-1970s, Raymond Williams's *Keywords. A Vocabulary of Culture and Society* (1976). And the attentive reader will notice that throughout this chapter I have not used the term 'postmodern' even once.

NOTES

I should like to thank Patricia Rubin for her perceptive comments on an earlier draft of this essay.

1 'Connoisseurship: the penalty of ahistoricism', *International Journal of Museum Management and Curatorship* 7 (1988), pp. 261–8.

2 *The Achievement of a Connoisseur. Philip Pouncy. Italian Old Master Drawings*, by Julien Stock and David Scrase (Fitzwilliam Museum, Cambridge, 1985) (unpaginated).

3 J. Bruyn, B. Haak, S. H. Levie, P. J. J. van Thiel and E. van de Wetering, *A Corpus of Rembrandt Paintings*, vol. 1 *1625–1631* (1982), vol. 2 *1631–1634* (1986), vol. 3 *1634–1639* (1989).

4 *Art in the Making. Rembrandt*, by David Bomford, Christopher Brown and Ashok Roy (National Gallery, London, 1988–9).

5 *Alessandro Filipepi called Sandro Botticelli, Painter of Florence* (1908); new edition with an introduction by John Pope-Hennessy (1980).

6 *Sandro Botticelli's 'Geburt der Venus' und 'Frühling'. Eine Untersuchung über die Vorstellungen von der Antike in der italienischen Frührenaissance* (1893).

7 Ronald Lightbown, *Sandro Botticelli: Life and Works and Complete Catalogue*, 2 vols (1978) is now the standard text.

8 This was made clear during the round table discussion amongst the directors of several major European and American galleries and other scholars with which the conference in 1982 on the history and future of the Uffizi concluded. An edited transcript was subsequently published in *Gli Uffizi. Quattro secoli di una galleria*, edited by Paola Barocchi and Giovanna Ragioneri (1983), vol. 2, pp. 557–635.

9 Primarily in its second edition, *Le vite de' più eccellenti pittori, scultori ed architettori* (1568).

10 Albert Boime, *The Academy and French Painting in the Nineteenth Century* (1971); idem, *Thomas Couture and the Eclectic Vision* (1980).

11 'The hanging's too good for them', *Burlington Magazine* 131 (1989), pp. 3–4.

12 *Art Monthly*, no. 125 (April 1989), pp. 3–8.

13 *Richard Wilson. The Landscape of Reaction*, by David Solkin (Tate Gallery, London, 1982).

14 p. 164.

15 In the new introductory section to their article 'The Landscape of Reaction: Richard Wilson (1713?–1782) and his Critics' in *The New Art History*, edited by A. L. Rees and Frances Borzello (1986), pp. 106–19 (originally published in *History Workshop* 16, (1983), pp. 171–5.

16 For the hostile reaction to Alpers by the leading Dutch iconologist, Ed de

Jongh, see his review in *Simiolus* 14 (1984), pp. 51–9. My own review was judged by others to be sympathetic to Alpers, but is actually critical, though not along 'party lines': *Oxford Art Journal* 7 no. 1 (1984), pp. 57–60. For an overview, see Egbert Haverkamp-Begemann, 'The state of research in northern baroque art', *Art Bulletin* 69 (1987), pp. 510–19, especially pp. 510–11.

17 Erwin Panofsky, 'Introductory' in *Studies in Iconology. Humanistic Themes in the Art of the Renaissance* (1939) and the same author's 'Iconography and Iconology: an Introduction to the Study of Renaissance Art' in *Meaning in the Visual Arts* (1955). The 'pre-iconographic' concerns the viewer's recognition of an object or act represented; the 'iconographic' the place of a representation within a set of conventions to produce recognizable specific significance (for example, saints' individual attributes); the 'iconological' concerns the artist's innovatory or unique handling of subject matter within culturally contingent parameters to generate implicit significance requiring an imaginative response from the viewer for its elucidation.

18 *European Photography* 8 no. 3 (1987), p. 47.

19 G. Schwartz, 'Connoisseurship' (1988), p. 265.

20 Quoted by Robert Hewison, *The Heritage Industry* (1987), p. 52.

21 *Burlington Magazine* 130 (1988), pp. 636–7.

22 An exception is David Freedberg; for example, his *Iconoclasts and their Motives* (1985).

23 'Iconoclasts in Zurich' in *Bilder und Bildersturm im Spätmittelalter und in der frühen Neuzeit*, ed. Bob Scribner and Martin Warnke (*Wolfenbütteler Forschungen* 46, (1990), pp. 125–41.

24 'La précession des simulacres', *Simulacres et Simulation* (1981).

25 For instance, Norman Bryson, 'The gaze in the expanded field' in *Vision and Visuality*, ed. Hal Foster (1988).

26 For instance, Douglas Crimp, 'On the Museum's Ruins' in *Postmodern Culture*, ed. Hal Foster (1985) and Arthur Kroker and David Cook, *The Postmodern Scene. Excremental Culture and Hyper-Aesthetics* (1986): 'Excurses on the (Post) Nouveau. The body in ruins . . . science in ruins . . . theory in ruins . . . philosophy in ruins . . . history in ruins . . .

9

History of Political Thought

Richard Tuck

In the course of the 1960s a number of historians of political thought (by a pleasing and convenient coincidence, many of them connected with the University of Cambridge) published reflections of a general character on their professional activity. Three of these essays have achieved some lasting reputation – John Pocock's 'The History of Political Thought: A Methodological Enquiry',[1] John Dunn's 'The Identity of the History of Ideas'[2] and Quentin Skinner's 'Meaning and Understanding in the History of Ideas'.[3] And of these three, it was Skinner's which occasioned most discussion, partly because of its much greater length and comprehensiveness, but largely because, unlike Pocock and Dunn, he made his targets very precise and gave names to them. The principal target, and the one which subsequent writers were most eager to defend, was described by Skinner in the following passage.

I turn first to consider the methodology dictated by the claim that the *text* itself should form the self-sufficient object of inquiry and understanding. For it is this assumption which continues to govern the largest number of studies, to raise the widest philosophical issues, and to give rise to the largest number of confusions. This apppoach itself is logically tied, in the history of ideas no less than in more strictly literary studies, to a particular form of justification for conducting the study itself. The whole point, it is characteristically said, of studying past works of philosophy (or literature) must be that they contain (in a favoured phrase) "timeless elements", in the form of "universal ideas", even a "dateless wisdom' with "univeral application".

Now the historian who adopts such a view has already committed himself, in effect, on the question of how best to gain an understanding of such "classic texts". For if the whole point of such a study is conceived in terms of recovering the "timeless questions and answers" posed in the "great books", and so of demonstrating their continuing "relevance", it must be not merely possible, but essential, for the historian to concentrate simply on what each of the classic writers has *said* about each of these "fundamental concepts" and "abiding questions". The aim, in short, must be to provide a "re-appraisal of the classic writings, quite apart from the context of historical development, as perennially important attempts to set down universal propositions about political reality". For to suggest instead that a knowledge of the social context is a necessary condition for an understanding of the classic texts is equivalent to denying that they do contain any elements of timeless and perennial interest, and is thus equivalent to removing the whole point of studying what they said. (p. 30)

An array of (mainly American) political scientists were listed in the footnotes to this passage: Peter Merkl, Hans J. Morgenthau, Mulford Q. Sibley, Willim T. Bluhm, G. E. G. Catlin, Andrew Hacker, R. G. McCloskey, Karl Jaspers, Leonard Nelson, Charles R. N. McCoy, Leo Strauss and Joseph Cropsey.[4]

Although Dunn did not issue any comparable list of people, it is clear that he had had the their kind of approach in mind when in the previous year he had complained that

> few branches of the history of ideas have been written as the history of an activity. Complicated structures of ideas, arranged in a manner approximating as close as may be (frequently closer than the evidence permits) to deductive systems have been examined at different points in time and their morphology traced over the centuries. Reified reconstructions of a great man's more accessible notions have been compared with those of other great men; hence the weird tendency of much writing, in the history of political thought more especially, to be made up of what propositions in what great books remind the author of what propositions in what other great books . . . (p. 15).

As an alternative to this, both Skinner and Dunn emphasized that the proper way to read an historical text is as an historical product, in which the actual intentions of the author (in so far as they can reasonably be reconstructed) should be our principal guide as to why the text took the particular form it did (though of course neither of them supposed that intention was a *sufficient* guide – failure needs recognition and explanation too).

Though an argument of this sort had not been Pocock's primary intention, his essay of six years earlier could be recruited into this cause, and Skinner has always generously acknowledged Pocock's influence, along with that of R. G. Collingwood, Alasdair Macintyre and Peter

Laslett. Pocock's essay was in effect an appeal within the profession of the history of ideas to take seriously as the material to be understood and explained the whole set of writings or other products on politics available from a particular society – what he called the 'stereotypes' and 'languages', and what he has subsequently termed 'paradigms'. His own work, *The Ancient Constitution and the Feudal Law* (1957) had been a dazzling illustration of what he meant – that major political philosophers could only be read against a rather minutely specified and historically particular background of linguistic practices (in this case, the practice of historical assumptions within the common-law tradition), and that only in such a way could their originality or conventionality be apprehended. It was true, Pocock acknowledged, that

> as the language employed in political discussion comes to be of increasing theoretical generality, so the persuasive success of the thinker's arguments comes to rest less on his success in invoking traditional symbols than on the rational coherence of the statements he is taken to be making in some field of political discourse where statements of wide theoretical generality are taken to be possible. Here, sooner or later, our historian must abandon his role of a student of thought as the language of a society, and become a student of thought as philosophy – i.e. in its capacity for making intelligible general statements . . . [But because the historian had approached his philosopher *via* a study of the wider language, he] can now consider the level of abstraction on which the thinker's language tends to make him operate, and the level of abstraction on which the thinker's preoccupations tend to make him use his language. He can now give some precision of meaning to the vague phrase – every thinker operates within a tradition; he can study the demands which thinker and tradition make upon each other. (pp. 200–1)

This story about the 1960s has now been told many times; students have available copious summaries of the issues involved in this methodological contest of the faculties.[5] There have been many slightly peevish responses to Dunn, Pocock and Skinner, and some defensive rejoinders from the principals themselves. But to those of us from a rather younger generation, for whom this struggle had the curiously remote quality that the affairs of elder brothers always possess, the puzzle was always to understand what the point had been of a *non*-historical (in Dunn's sense) study of the history of ideas. It was obvious to us that (as Collingwood had put it devastatingly thirty years earlier), if one wanted to understand the history of something, one had actually to do the relevant work of investigating evidence and working out what the people concerned were up to.

"'Sblood!' says Hamlet, "do you think I am easier to be played on than a
pipe?" Those eminent philosophers, Rosencrantz and Guildenstern, think
tout bonnement that they can discover what the *Parmenides* is about by
merely reading it; but if you took them to the south gate of Housesteads
and said, "Please distinguish the various periods of construction here, and
explain what purpose the builders of each period had in mind", they would
protest "Believe me, I cannot". Do they think the *Parmenides* is easier to
understand than a rotten little Roman fort? 'Sblood!⁶

If this was so obvious in 1939, why did it need saying again, albeit with a
different set of philosophical considerations, in 1969?

Of the commentators on these issues, only Gunnell has dealt with this
question, seeing it (rightly) as a question about the character of mid-
twentieth-century political science. But the particular answer which
Gunnell gave to the question was less plausible, and I shall suggest a
different one. As part of his treatment of the matter, Gunnell sketched a
history in which the development of 'behaviourism' in political science
during the 1950s and 1960s led to attacks on the writing of the history of
political thought as an activity of little importance. Gunnell cited David
Easton in 1951 complaining that traditional Western political thinking
had been replaced by investigations into the history of political thought,
an activity which lived 'parasitically' on past ideas and no longer sought
either to provide a proper empirical political science or to construct 'a
valuational frame of reference' (p. 4).

'Behaviourism' here stood[7] for a wide notion of an empirical political
science, marked by (often quantitative) studies of general quasi-
scientific laws of human behaviour, and a strict divorce between facts
and values - 'ethical evaluation and empirical explanation involve two
kinds of proposition that, for the sake of clarity, should be kept
analytically distinct' (Gunnell, p. 7). Gunnell took the principal point of
Easton's critique of the history of political thought to be an implicit call
for empirical political science to become the dominant mode of thinking
about politics; he conjectured that 'the response of historians of political
theory to the challenge by behaviourists regarding the importance of
studying the tradition was not merely to reaffirm that it is relevant for
both political science and politics but to maintain that it was now
absolutely crucial' (p. 26). The idea of a great tradition of political
debate in Western Europe now became, Gunnell argued, the *locus* for a
critique of the kind of modern attitude represented by Easton and
company; their repudiation of the history of political thought was made
into an historic antagonism between a way of thinking about politics
expressible only in the language of the civilization captured in the classic

texts from Plato to Marx, and a way of thinking expressed in the pseudo-science of systems analysis or whatever 'behaviouralist' theory was in favour. Writers such as Strauss, Voegelin or Arendt were Gunnell's prime examples of theorists who espoused this idea of the tradition – and of course in at least Strauss's case the existence of this tradition and the irreducibility of its content to some straightforwardly objective and modern set of utterances was indeed central to a political vision.

Gunnell thus explained the movement which Skinner, Dunn and Pocock attacked as a response to the hostility of post-war political science to the writing of histories of political thought, and as an assertion of the continued relevance of a non-quantitative, non-behaviourist political science. There were however two problems about Gunnell's account. The first was that he assumed that it was this idea of a 'tradition' which was the prime target of Skinner and the others, and he consequently criticized their remarks on methodology as a failure to see the point of the critique of modernity and modern political science implicit in the writings of people like Strauss (p. 24). In fact, as we have seen, though their remarks were applicable to Strauss or Arendt, the actual objects of their explicit criticism were more commonly the mundane figures of the 1960s who wrote on the history of political thought from a conventional political scientific viewpoint, such as Merkl and Hacker.

The second problem about Gunnell's account was that he himself recognized and fully documented the fact that the kind of writing on the history of political thought which Easton attacked was itself the child of a positivist and virtually 'behaviourist' view of politics going back at least to the beginning of the twentieth century. There are a number of striking instances of this, one of the best being the work of George Catlin (one of the authors singled out for attack by Skinner in 1969), who wrote both a history of the political philosophers[8] and also some startlingly positivist works on the possibility of a genuinely 'scientific' study of politics. Consequently, as Gunnell conceded, 'it is difficult to discern in this literature, up through the late 1940s, the source of Easton's portrayal of either the character of scholarship in the history of political theory or the intentions and concerns that gave rise to it' (p. 21); which leaves both the supposed behaviourist onslaught on the history of political thought in the 1950s, and the retaliatory insistence on a great tradition by anti-positivists, looking rather pointless.

Gunnell's mistake, and the mistake made by many writers on these issues, was not to take seriously the claims by behaviourists such as Easton that the study of politics had to involve both facts and values, but that these belong to two logically distinct realms – the fact-value distinction which goes back (in its strong form) to Kant and which is an essential foundation for the modern human sciences. It is true that most human scientists took their quotidian professional practice to be the exploration of the 'fact' side of this distinction, but they all acknowledged in their more reflective moments that political 'values' had also to be generated in some way. The combination of this acknowledgement with a very feeble attempt actually to consider how values might appear or be justified, is the most striking feature of Anglo-American (and particularly American) political science in the first half of the twentieth century. We might describe it as Kantianism without Kant's ethical theory, though the participants themselves[9] more often described it as Humeanism – that is, an acceptance of the logical distinction between empirical and evaluative statements, but a rejection of the transcendental deduction of morality actually to be found in the *Groundwork of the Metaphysics of Morals*.

Most commonly, these human scientists assumed that in some more or less unspecified way 'the citizenry' would decide.

> "Beauty is in the eye of the beholder" is an aphorism reminding us that judgements of better or worse involve *subjective* valuations. But this does not deny that one person's nose may be *objectively* shorter than another's. Similarly, there are elements of valid reality in a given economic situation, however hard it may be to recognise and isolate them. There is not one theory of economics for Republicans and one for Democrats, one for workers and one for employers, one for the Russians and still another for the Chinese. On many basic principles concerning prices and employment, most – not all! – economists are in fairly close agreement.
>
> This statement does not mean that economists agree closely in the *policy* field. Economist A may be for full employment at any cost. Economist B may not consider it of as vital importance as price stability. Basic questions concerning right and wrong goals to be pursued cannot be settled by mere science as such. They belong in the realm of ethics and "value judgements." The citizenry must ultimately decide such issues. What the expert can do is point out the feasible alternatives and the true costs that may be involved in the different decisions. But still the mind must render to the heart that which is in the heart's domain. For, as Pascal said, the heart has reasons that reason will never know.[10]

This remarkable passage illustrates that early twentieth-century human scientists thought of values as essentially matters of the heart rather than the reason – that there could not be a systematic and rational basis for them. But all men would possess them, and as 'citizens' would use them in their decisions. Given this view, it was obviously of some practical importance that the citizenry would not pluck its values at random from the air, now it could not derive them from a transcendental deduction; and the principal purpose of studying the history of political thought, as textbook after textbook made clear, was to provide the reader (who, being normally an American college student, was seen above all as a future citizen) with a set of possible political attitudes which he would not have been able to generate himself (they were the work of 'genius'), but which he could respond to and choose between in a measured and well-governed way.

Indeed, it is striking how many of these textbooks were very loath to commit themselves to any claim about the truth or falsehood of the political theories they were considering: Sabine said expressly that 'taken as a whole a political theory can hardly be said to be true'.[11] The authors they considered were not in general supposed to have provided insights into a true theory (and in this respect these early twentieth-century historians of political thought differed from their contemporary historians of natural science), but to have constituted the sources of a specifically Western tradition of political thought in which the reader was taken to participate as he reflected on the range of ideas depicted in the textbook.[12]

It is important to recognize that this view denied the existence of genuinely universal or objectively true political theories, but asserted the universality or at least relevance of the issues which the great texts were dealing with – it was this which constituted their continued utility. We must distinguish this attitude from that of writers like Strauss or Hans Morgenthau, who insisted (explicitly against their colleagues in the American politics departments) that there are truths of political theory 'regardless of time and place'.[13] Each view implied that the texts alone were to be studied, since they represented the response by 'great minds' to a set of perennial problems, as familiar to the American college student of the 1950s as to the citizen of the Greek polis; but one view took a rather neutral approach to the merits of the various answers, anxious only to place them in the broad ethical culture of the West, while the other view had a clear answer of its own to the perennial problems. In general, the latter approach was likely to be less interested in the history of political theory, for it possessed a trans-historical criterion of moral rectitude (and Morgenthau was thus very critical of the discipline.[14] Strauss, however, was a special case, because of his belief (which I have already remarked on) that this criterion was only available to people who had immersed themselves in the study of the tradition and its texts.

The first of these two views was, by the standards of a longer-term political culture, a curiously disengaged and mandarin approach to the role of values in political life, and it was presumably its unsatisfying character to which Easton was drawing attention in his 1951 article.[15] The idea was that a disparate set of values could be inculcated into the citizenry through an education in a particular set of plausible and not too exotic texts, which differed among themselves in an intellectually stimulating way. This disparate set could then be reconciled within the society by some kind of institutional process, in which the citizens would decide on the principles by which their society was to be governed. Most of the authors of the 'great texts' themselves would have thought this was an absurd view to take of political principles, but it took a clear demonstration from within the fortress of the modern human sciences that it was absurd to convince Anglo-American political scientists. This demonstration was provided by Kenneth Arrow[16] (ironically, in the same year as Easton's article, 1951) with his famous 'theorem' in which he proved that there was no neutral, procedural method of integrating individual values into a set of social principles which did not infringe some absolutely obvious and basic assumptions which almost all citizens would be likely to make (such as that no one member of the city should be a dictator over the rest). The implication of Arrow's work was that those who believed that in some way a neutral bureaucracy of political scientific experts could look to its citizenry for an effective decision on the values to be implemented in the political process could now be seen as whistling in the dark.

Arrow's work, which became particularly influential after the revised second edition of *Collective Choice and Individual Values* appeared in 1963, impressed the hardest of the 'hard' political scientists by its methodological rigour, and convinced them that their vague assumptions about the social character of values should be revised. In doing so, it fitted into a gathering view in the mid-1960s (particularly in America) that political philosophy of an apparently traditional kind ought once again to be written. I think it is not a coincidence that the most prominent exponent of a new political philosophy, John Rawls, should regard himself and be widely regarded as a kind of Kantian – for the most likely route to take out of the crude Kantianism of America in the first part of this century was *via* the construction of a new and sophisticated Kantianism. But if a plurality of indeterminately founded values no longer made any sense in the ethical landscape of American political science, then the traditional role of the history of political thought in that culture was undermined. It was this which Dunn and Skinner sensed at the end of the 1960s, and their polemic against the traditional history of political thought went along with a clear sense that a modern and systematic political philosophy was at least possible. Skinner said precisely this:[17]

> All I wish to insist is that whenever it is claimed that the point of the historical study of such questions is that we may learn directly from the answers, it will be found that what counts as an answer will usually look, in a different culture or period, so different in itself that it can hardly be in the least useful even to go on thinking of the relevant questions as being 'the same' in the required sense at all. More crudely: we must learn to do our own thinking for ourselves.

The 'new' history of political thought was thus the counterpart of the 'new' political philosophy of the English-speaking world in the 1970s and 1980s: it had transferred the burden of educating citizens into political values down the corridor of the academy and into the rooms of philosophers who were once, again, ready to take it up.

Ironically (in view of Gunnell's theory that Strauss, Voegelin or Arendt were the prime targets of this new history), writers such as Strauss and his followers were, as we have seen, better placed to resist this abdication than the allies of the positivists such as Merkl. The claim that there is, as a matter of fact, a single true political philosophy to be extracted only through esoteric readings of the great texts (the claim most memorably asociated with Strauss), is not *logically* impossible (any more than the claim that there is an infallible source of moral doctrine to be found on the right bank of the Tiber). In a sense, Strauss and Rawls were both trying to provide their readers with a single, valid political philosophy, though they were using very different methods to generate it. The institutional survival of Straussianism in North American political science departments is thus by no means surprising.

It should be said that the ideal of a new political philosophy which would provide modern America (and, by implication, similarly situated societies) with a coherent set of values is looking much less plausible in 1990 than in 1970. Twenty years of impressive philosophical activity has served largely to emphasise the disparate nature of modern values, despite some stunning complacency about this on the part of some liberal theorists. The hunt is on once again, as it was before Arrow's work, for a theory which will accommodate radical pluralism of values (though no one now supposes that 'the citizenry' will or should decide the matter). In this context, it would not be surprising if people came to believe that reflection on an existing political literature was the way to think about political values and to bring the variegated population of a liberal society into some broad intellectual equilibrium; indeed, that is more or less what Richard Rorty proposes (though the relevant literature for him is much wider than that covered by Sabine). Though the rhetoric with which Rorty talks about 'ironism' is (appropriately) different from the bashful relativism of writers like Sabine, it is not clear that there is as great an intellectual gulf as he might suppose.[18]

The story which I have been telling is avowedly one about English-language theorists, and the decline of English-language political-theory in the early twentieth century and its revival in the late 1960s plays a crucial part in it. The issues in debate in the different intellectual traditions of France or Germany played (at first) very little part in these arguments of the 1960s, and Skinner, Dunn and Pocock have always been mildly resistant to any attempt to link their work to that of theorists such as Hirsch (who drew on these debates) or Koselleck. The principal reason for this has been that, from their point of view, the important point to establish is the methodological similarity between the history of ideas and the history of other human activities. It was this which lay at the heart of Skinner's repeated attempts to analyse political theoretic utterances as 'speech acts', and thereby to treat them in the same way as more mundane historians treated other kinds of 'act'. The wider question of how we can have an historical understanding of human activity in general has not been their central concern.

On the Continent, however, this was the key issue, and the fact that human history consisted both of act and utterance was usually taken for granted. Dilthey, for example, in *The Construction of the Historical World in the Human Studies*, made it clear that 'understanding' and 'interpretation', the principal subjects of the hermeneutic tradition, are concerned with three kinds of 'expression': 'concepts, judgements and larger thought-structures', 'actions' and 'emotive expressions'.[19] His lead (or more properly Hegel's) was followed by all the participants in the German debates over hermeneutics. The English methodological debate thus stood at an angle to the Continental one, for Skinner's assimilation of utterance to action could find a home in (say) *either* Habermas's camp, *or* Gadamer's. Indeed, with its explicit references back to Collingwood, it represented an open retrieval of an older English respect for German hermeneutics.

For this reason, as David Hollinger has recently observed,[20] criticism of Skinner from a post-structuralist point of view (such as the Derridaist complaints of David Harlan[21]) misses the point, for if we must have a deconstructed history of ideas, we must by the same token have a deconstructed history of *everything*, and Skinner would presumably be happy with that conclusion, assuming the premiss to be true – something about which his methodology is, strictly speaking, neutral. His professional practice, on the other hand, and some of his express remarks, suggest that he endorses at least the possibility of acquiring some kind of genuine understanding of what historical agents are up to; or that an understanding of this kind is such a deep procedural asumption for having any doings with any other human beings (the view *inter alia* of writers like Davidson) that to question its genuineness is simply to take the type of radically sceptical view which no one can actually live by.[22]

We can now see why the history of political thought that has actually been written against this methodological background has often appeared to its detractors to be much less original and startling than they have expected from the methodological manifestos. Any evidence which a reasonable historian would accept as part of an explanation of why an historical agent did something will be acceptable to a modern historian of political thought, and there will often be no clear and single method for determining what counts as relevant evidence. A good example of this is provided by an issue with which historians of political thought are commonly called to deal – the question of whether or not there is a substantial difference between works produced by the same author at different times in his life. This is the problem of the so-called *coupure epistemologique* in the Althusserian accounts of Marx; it is the problem of the relationship between Machiavelli's *Prince* and his *Discourses*, between the various redactions of Hobbes's political theory, between Locke's earlier and later writings on toleration, between Plato's *Republic* and the *Laws*, and so on (as this list illustrates, there is scarcely a major political theorist about whom this is not a significant problem).

Clearly, some readings of the texts in question will reconcile them, and others will require them to be kept separate. The prospect of reconciliation may in itself seem to be part of the justification for a particular reading, but so may the prospect of separation – for example, it might explain why an author should have approached the same material twice. There is no *a priori* presumption either way (and in this respect consistency between texts may be thought of as different from consistency *within* a text, where some people have supposed that the burden of proof is on those who think that a text is internally inconsistent). But it is hard to see what could be adequate as an *a posteriori* argument. Neither internal nor external evidence is likely to clinch the matter. What counts as internal evidence will change if interpretative charity requires us to assume consistency between the works, while external evidence, in the absence of a clear, unequivocal and trustworthy statement by the author himself about the relationship between the works (and I know of no such statement by any great theorist), is not going to overturn any plausible reading of them.

No theory about how to interpret texts will cover this case, since what is at stake here is the very identity of a text. In one possible view, the text is the complete set of utterances by an author on a topic (particularly if – as was true for example of Machiavelli – the works in question were at one point circulated by the author together), and in another view the text is each named and separately bound work. In yet another view, the text is each utterance taken separately. Why should a work written over many years (like *Capital*) be seen as more of a unity than several separate pieces written in a shorter space of time (like Mill's essays on Liberty and Utilitarianism)?

The point of these observations is not to call into question the possibility of intelligent and sensitive writing of the history of political thought, but to emphasize that in the end there will have to be some judgement by the historian about how to tell his particular story, and what seems plausible as a way for a human being in those circumstances to behave, which cannot be decisively vindicated against a range of other, different judgements. The intellectual qualities which made for a good historian before 1969 are those which made for one after 1969, and it should not have been surprising that the better histories of political thought produced in the 1970s and 1980s have worn their methodological commitments (on the whole) fairly lightly. What was not taken lightly, however, was the conviction that what they were writing was history, and not the exposition of a set of values for the citizenry of the late twentieth century.

NOTES

1 In *Philosophy, Politics and Society*, series II, ed. Peter Laslett and W. G. Runciman (Oxford, 1962), pp. 183–202.
2 In *Philosophy* 43 (1968), pp. 85–104; reprinted in Dunn's *Political Obligation in its Historical Context* (Cambridge, 1980;, pp. 13–28.
3 In *History and Theory* 8 (1969), pp. 3–53; reprinted in James Tully (ed.), *Meaning and Context* (Oxford, 1988), pp. 26–67.
4 Ibid., pp. 291–2.
5 The best ones are John Gunnell, *Political Theory: Tradition and Interpretation* (Cambridge, Mass., 1979), Conal Condren, *The Status and Appraisal of Classic Texts* (Princeton, NJ, 1985) and James Tully (ed.), *Meaning and Context* (Oxford, 1988).
6 R. G. Collingwood, *An Autobiography* (Oxford, 1970), pp. 39–40.

7   As Easton himself acknowledged: see David Easton, *A Framework of Political Analysis* (Englewood Cliffs, NJ, 1965), pp. 19–22.

8   George Catlin, *A History of the Political Philosophers* (London, 1950).

9   George Sabine, *A History of Political Thought* (3rd ed., London, 1983), p. v.

10 Paul Samuelson, *Economics* (Englewood Cliffs, NJ, 1976), pp. 7–8; a textbook largely composed in the 1950s and 1960s.

11 Sabine, *Philosophical Theory*, p. v.

12 This seems, for example, to have been Peter Merkl's view – see his remarks in *Political Continuity and Change* (New York, 1967), pp. 26–56.

13 Hans Morgenthau, *Dilemmas of Politics* (Chicago, 1958), p. 39.

14 Ibid., p. 24.

15 David Easton, 'The Decline of Modern Political Theory', *Journal of Politics* 13 (1951), pp. 36–58.

16 Kenneth Arrow, *Social Choice and Individual Values* (London, 1951).

17 In Tully, *Meaning and Context*, p. 66.

18 See particularly Richard Rorty, *Contingency, Irony, and Solidarity* (Cambridge, 1989), pp. 80–1.

19 W. Dilthey, *Selected Writings*, ed.H. P. Rickman (Cambridge, 1976), p. 219.

20 'The Return of the Prodigal: The Persistence of Historical Knowing', *American Historical Review* 94 (1989), pp. 610–21.

21 'Intellectual History and the Return of Literature', *American Historical Review* 94 (1989), pp. 581–609.

22 Quentin Skinner, 'A Reply to my Critics' in Tully, *Meaning and Context*, especially pp. 238 and 246–8.

10

History of the Body

Roy Porter

I said, 'we were not stocks and stones – 'tis very well. I should have added, nor are we angels, I wish we were, – but men cloathed with bodies, and governed by our imaginations.

Laurence Sterne, Tristram Shandy

Resurrecting the Body

In a provocative book,[1] Leo Steinberg has drawn attention to two facts. First, in a tradition of painting flourishing through the Renaissance, Christ was commonly depicted touching, or otherwise other ways drawing attention to, his penis. Second, art historians have consistently ignored this striking mode of depiction. Steinberg explains the doctrinal significance of the gesture: it was designed to signal the humanity of the Son, that He was begotten not created. But he is no less interested in exploring the art historians' blind spot. The sexuality of Christ's body has, as it were, become 'invisible', because scholars typically work within interpretative traditions for which meanings that are mental, spiritual and ideal assume an automatic priority over matters purely material, corporeal and sensual.

Steinberg's point applies more widely. Until recently, the history of the body has been generally neglected, and it is not hard to see why. On the one hand the Classical, and, on the other, the Judaeo-Christian components of our cultural heritage each advanced a fundamentally dualistic vision of man, understood as an often uneasy alliance of mind and body, psyche and soma; and both traditions, in their different ways and for different reasons, have elevated the mind or soul and disparaged the body.[2] This is a totally familiar aspect of the metaphysics of our civilization, needing no elaboration here. It runs deep and exerts pervasive power: even writers who have sought to rescue the body from neglect or disrepute have nevertheless commonly perpetuated the old hierarchies. Thus, as my epigraph suggests, in the mid-eighteenth century Laurence Sterne could vindicate 'men' against the aspersion of not being purely spiritual ('angels'), but only to the extent of saying that men are beings '*cloathed* in bodies' – a formula which preserves the traditional dualism and leaves the body somehow secondary and almost accidental.[3] Sterne does not say that men *are* their bodies, in the way in which today's feminists can speak of *Our Bodies, Our Selves*.[4]

The implication of this last remark is that attempts are afoot nowadays to demolish the old cultural hierarchies which privileged mind over body and, by force of analogy, sanctioned whole systems of ruler-ruled power relations. This demystifying process is surely occurring, and it is easy to point to the profound cultural shifts over the last generation which have subverted the traditional puritan-cum-Platonist distrust of the body:[5] the sexual revolution and 'permissiveness' in general, consumer capitalism, the critiques mounted both by the 'counter-culture' of the sixties and the feminism of the seventies, and so forth.[6] This cultural revolution has clearly been influential – as the case of Steinberg's book suggests – in redirecting scholarly attention as well, away from well-established idealist sub-disciplines such as the history of ideas, and towards the exploration of 'material culture', one limb of which is the history of the body.

This new enterprise has benefited from numerous stimuli. Thanks to its intrinsic materialism, Marxism has provided a fruitful matrix, and works in this tradition such as Mikhail Bakhtin's *Rabelais and His World* have offered influential models of the body seen as a focus for popular resistance and criticism of official meanings.[7] With its ambitions to construct a total history, and sympathies for the project of a biologically grounded scientific history *Annaliste* scholarship has promoted research into all dimensions of material life from the cradle to the grave.[8] Cultural anthropology, in both theory and practice, has afforded historians languages for discussing the symbolic meanings of the body, in particular as contextualized within systems of social exchange;[9] and in a rather similar way, sociology,[10] and medical sociology above all,[11] have encouraged historians to treat the body as the crossroads between self and society. Academic feminism has pointed to customarily neglected or suppressed questions of the gendering of experience.[12] And not least, the massive growth of historical demography over the last generation has impressed upon us the stark vital statistics of 'birth, copulation and death', to be regarded as the key to understanding all aspects of class, culture and consciousness.[13]

We clearly cannot expect, however, to toss all these ingredients mindlessly together into a scholarly mixing-bowl and find a history of the body automatically emerging as a perfect dish. The nature and contents of the history of the body, and the methods whereby it should be pursued, are themselves bones of contention.

Approaches

Scholars have warned that it would be grossly simplistic to assume that the human body has timelessly existed as an unproblematic natural object with universal needs and wants, variously affected by culture and society (in one age, 'repressed', in another, 'liberated', etc.). Such a crass nature/culture division would obviously be unhelpful; and it would be misconceived – and ironical! – to give the old mind/body dualism a new lease of life by attempting to study the ('biological') history of the body independently of ('cultural') considerations of experience and expression in language and ideology.[14]

The point is well made. Clearly we must look at the body as it has been experienced and expressed within particular cultural systems, both private and public, which themselves have changed over time.[15] If (to make a rather Berkeleyan point) bodies are present to us only through perceiving them, then the history of bodies must incorporate the history of their perceptions. But, it could surely be argued, if this is so, does not that mean that the history of the body after all forms a project in the history of ideas or *l'histoire des mentalités* – one concerned with representations of the body as distinct (say) from representations of work or power. Indeed, attempts have been made to construe the history of the body essentially as the explication of its 'representations' in 'discourse', using post-structuralist and deconstructionist techniques of textual analysis.[16] I believe, however, that there is a real danger in driving this theorized repudiation of vulgar positivism too far.

Some of the most scintillating explorations of the anatomy of the body have been the work of literary critics and like-minded scholars engaged in discourse analysis and textual deconstruction, teasing out shifting 'representations' of the embodied self. But the gay abandonment of empiricism for theory and hermeneutics has pitfalls of its own, in particular the risk of decontextualized extrapolations, derived from uncritical use of unrepresentative bodies of evidence. An instance of a work caught in this trap is Francis Barker's *The Tremulous Private Body*, a bold attempt, spanning five centuries, to interpret the body's history – indeed its 'dissolution'.[17] Through a 'deconstructionist' reading of what seems like a purely random sample of key texts selected from high culture (*Hamlet*, Rembrandt's *Anatomy Lesson*, Pepys's *Diary*, etc.), Barker advances the generalization that the body, which had once been a public object, became privatized – indeed the site of narcissistic shame – within bourgeois culture. Indeed, he claims, the body 'disappeared' altogether as an instrument of eroticism, being displaced by the 'book'. These are mighty conclusions indeed to derive from a few texts scrutinized in glorious isolation from consideration of the texture of history at large. Moreover, Barker has such faith in his method of hermetic, textual, close reading that he systematically ignores the researches of other scholars – an idiosyncrasy which, as J. R. R. Christie has shown, amongst other things, makes a nonsense of his account of Rembrandt's painting.[18]

Other recent interpretations of the history of the body drawing principally upon the precepts of textual analysis seem equally open to objection. *The Female Body in Western Culture*, a volume of essays ranging from 'Genesis to Gertrude Stein', gives pride of place to what the editor calls '(Re)writing the Body', and stresses how the body must be seen as not just a 'flesh and blood' object but a 'symbolic construct'.[19] Well and good. But too many of its contributors proceed on the assumption which underpins Barker's book that the subtle elucidation of a small corpus of classic texts will afford privileged insights into the problems and paradoxes of experience at large. This is a dubious, not to say arrogant, assumption. Thus an essay 'Speaking Silences: Women's Suicide' leaps from examining what certain novelists tell us of the bodily consciousness of their suicidal heroines to offering general conclusions about female suicide experience in reality, taking no account of a substantial body of empirical research into the testimonies of authentic female suicides which actually contradict the findings offered.[20]

No more satisfactory an instance of this genre is Elaine Scarry's *The Body in Pain* (modestly subtitled *The Making and Unmaking of the World*).[21] Combining philosophical with literary analysis, Scarry examines intellectual, artistic, and cultural representations of physically located pain from the Bible, through Marx, to the present. The drift of her substantial text is to establish that it is of the essence of pain to be 'inexpressible'. We are offered this conclusion not merely as a novel interpretation, but as a privileged insight into 'a realm of human experience that is known to all but understood by only a few'. Yet Scarry's rarefied elitism is surely contradicted by the actual accounts of pain (which, far from being 'inexpressible', are often expressed with exactitude and eloquence) that ordinary people in the past have left us in great abundance. Of course, to someone aspiring to the higher intellectual exegesis, empirical research may, like the body itself, seem gross and banausic. To historians actually concerned with how real people felt pain, however, a work such as Barbara Duden's *Geschichte unter der Haut* – a pioneering analysis of the sickness experiences of nearly two thousand women in early eighteenth-century Germany, as preserved through the medical records kept by their physician, Dr Storch – offers an illuminating start.[22]

It is right for sensitive scholars to insist upon the conceptual complexity of the history of the body. But it is at least as important to avoid floating off into the stratosphere of discourse analysis, and neglecting the more everyday and tangible materials available. And in fact we need not be so dismissive about the possibilities of investigating the history of the body through the use of mundane empirical methods. Clearly on many issues our information is irremediably scanty. What coital positions did people use in the sixteenth century, or the eighteenth?[23] We hardly know. The first-hand written record of diaries and letters is largely silent – and where it is eloquent, it is probably unrepresentative; and there are obvious reasons for healthy scepticism towards using the testimony of such sources as pornographic prints or advice manuals.[24] Moreover, even when we have copious sources available to us, these require subtle interpretation, and may then still mystify. When we read in hospital admission registers that women were commonly admitted to infirmaries in the eighteenth and nineteenth centuries suffering from 'hysteria', it is often unclear what precisely, if anything, was physically amiss; they may have been experiencing partial paralysis, somatic or psychosomatic; they may chiefly have been simply overworked and underfed ('hysteria', despite the common stereotype, was a condition as much of the poor as of the rich). This may prove an instance in which the disease label served as little more than an administrative password to secure admission. It would be a hazardous enterprise to expect our records of medical diagnosis to provide us with a reliable, objective, epidemiological history of diseases.[25]

Such difficulties notwithstanding, an enormous quantity of sufficiently dependable information survives to permit the construction of credible profiles of the vital statistics of bodies in the past. Most fundamentally there are, of course, registers of baptisms and burials for many parts of Europe from early modern times onwards, from which scholars have devised techniques of deriving reliable indices of changing birth and death rates, fecundity, fertility, disease-related mortality crises and so forth; poor law and hospital records likewise open up windows on the history of strength and sickness and the toll taken by toil.[26] But, in addition, particular archives survive which afford extremely delicate indicators.

For example, abundant admissions ledgers exist for orphanages and schools, and recruiting records for the army and navy, over a span of several centuries. Between them, they give us access to the age and height of some tens of thousands of individuals. Those surviving from England have been processed to provide a collective profile of the age/height ratio of boys and young men changing over the generations. On the basis of controlled interrogation of such body data, extrapolations can be made about changes in food intake, both qualitative and quantitative, gradients of fitness, and so forth. Physique may prove a more trustworthy index than wages for assessing changes in the real standard of living.[27]

Likewise, we possess a photographic record now stretching back almost a century and a half of people's physical appearances. Once again, there is no need to belabour the misinterpretations which would result from a naive reliance on the veracity of visual images; of course the camera lies, or, more precisely, photographs are not snapshots of reality but, like paintings, form cultural artefacts conveying complicated coded conventional signs to primed 'readers'.[28]

But this caveat applies to some photographs more than to others. Posed portraits capture how people wish to be remembered, all scrubbed and dolled up in their Sunday best. But Victorian photographers were also fond of taking casual 'documentary' street snapshots, and these caught people in their everyday movements, gestures, and as a result, recorded such aspects as body language and social space more informatively than any printed text. The photographic archive reveals and confirms a great deal about both the physical transformations of the human condition in modern times (ageing, deformities, malnutrition, etc.), and what Goffman has called the 'presentation of self' (body language, gestures, and the appropriation of physical space).[29] Photographs remain oddly underexploited as a historical resource.

Pursuing the history of the body is thus not merely a matter of crunching vital statistics about physiques, nor just a set of methods for decoding 'representations'. Rather it is a call to make sense of the interplay between the two. When in the world we have lost the rich looked down on the poor, that gesture was both physical and symbolic: the 'grandees' (above all, their 'highnesses') were typically centimetres taller – an advantage further enhanced by the imposing accoutrements – dress and address – with which they could afford to adorn their bodies.

Given the abundance of evidence available, we remain remarkably ignorant about how individuals and social groups have experienced, controlled and projected their embodied selves. How have people made sense of the mysterious link between 'self' and its extensions? How have they managed the body as an intermediary between self and society?

Certain intellectual traditions could prove fruitful in promoting such explorations.

Sociologists of the body still find Weber's work valuable, for one of the enduring strengths of his account of the Protestant ethic lies in revealing how what we might take as rather abstract ('disembodied') doctrinal commitments (questions of salvation and justification) become internalized in such a way as to have profound implications for personal body control and discipline.[30] Psychohistory in the Freudian mould has pointed, on the other hand, to a quite reversed chain of consequences, showing how attitudes towards the world at large are commonly projections of the ways people handle their own body functions, thus revealing the inner struggles between consciousness – above all, the unconscious – and its physical expression. Even if much psychohistory remains vitiated by dogmatic Oedipal reductionism and is grossly speculative, its thematic integration of inner and outer, private and public, is highly suggestive.[31]

Moreover certain other approaches within sociology seem particularly worth historians' attention. Phenomenology and ethnomethodology have both provided programmes for the analysis of interpersonal 'close encounters' which (unlike, say, Parsonian functionalism) pay due attention to the play of the body as an organ of communication: we talk with our bodies. And brave attempts have been made to apply such methods to systematic and public presentations of social selves in specific historical communities, as for example in Rhys Isaac's analysis of life-styles in colonial Virginia.[32] Even so, the research front at present is at best spotty. A few particular areas have received attention, but mostly we are in the dark.

In the core of this paper I shall focus upon certain particular problem areas, to highlight potentially fruitful fields for a history of the body and to evaluate the implications of current research.

Body and Mind

Of cardinal importance is a grasp of the subordinate place ascribed to the body within the religious, moral and social value systems of traditional European culture. Long before Descartes, a fundamental dualism pervaded the Western *mentalité*: being human meant being an embodied mind or, in Sir Thomas Browne's formulation, 'amphibious'. It is a dualism which many thinkers found paradoxical and mystifying, because of the radical incomprehensibility of the intersections between mind and flesh. Nevertheless, such dualism has been a force profoundly

Photocopy
it
d 10/11

**The National Collection
of Modern Art in
the North of England**

Tate liverpool

A New Spring Season of Talks and Lectures at Tate Gallery Liverpool

WEDNESDAY LECTURES
Home and Away: Internationalism and British Art 1900-1990
Wednesdays 6.30 - 8.00pm

6 March   **Terry Eagleton 'Opening Lecture'**
13 March Patrick Wright 'The Imploding Nation: Englishness since W.W.II'
20 March Nikos Papastergiadis 'The Home in Modernity'
27 March Gillian Rose 'Engendering Body Spaces'
3 April   Lubaina Himid 'The Owl and the Pussycat: Advice for
                Collectors at the Turn of the Century'

Presenting a variety of approaches on *Home and Away* this lecture series
inaugurates a new programme of interdisciplinary talks. Approaches include
cultural geography, politics of race and sociology. The opportunity to discuss the
issues raised will follow the lectures. Drinks will be available.

Tickets cost £2.50 (£1.50 conc.) or £10.00 (£4.00 conc.) for the series and can be
obtained from the Tate Gallery bookshop or on the door. Places are limited and it
is advisable to book in advance.

ARTISTS' TALKS
Saturdays 1pm (Free)

2 March   **Alison Wilding** - *Home and Away* - **CANCELLED**
23 March   Dorothy Cross - *Home and Away*
13 April   *New Contemporaries 96* exhibitors

Enjoy stimulating discussion of work currently on show with artists from *Home
and Away* and *New Contemporaries 96*. All the talks take place in the gallery
alongside the artists' work and there will be time for questions from the audience.

For information and booking ring the Education Secretary on 0151 709 3223

TATE GALLERY LIVERPOOL
Albert Dock, Liverpool L3 4BB
Tel: 0151 709 3223
Fax: 0151 709 3122

shaping linguistic usage, classificatory schemes, ethics and value systems. Mind and body have traditionally been assigned distinct attributes and connotations. Mind is canonically superior to matter. Ontologically therefore, the mind, will, consciousness or self have been designated as the guardians and governors of the body, and the body should be their servant. Yet this schema has a crucial corollary: when, like an unruly servant, the body rebels, it is not the offending fists, feet or fingers which are necessarily held culpable, but the nobler faculties whose duty was properly to have controlled them. It is a fact which creates profound tensions for all systems of personal control (e.g., regimes of education or punishment).[33]

In major respects, this hierarchical subordination of body to mind systematically degrades the body; its appetites and desires are seen as blind, wilful, anarchic or (within Christianity) radically sinful; it may be regarded as the prison of the soul. Thus the body readily offends, committing evil or criminal acts . Yet because of its very nature (being imperfect, even beast-like), it may, paradoxically, be readily excused (the weakness of the flesh). The mind (self, will, or soul) by contrast, because of its nobler office, is duty-bound to rise above such disorder, such internal 'civil war'; if implicated, the will, ideally free and noble, seems all the more guilty of offence. The question of precisely how to ascribe honour and blame, duties and responsibilities, respectively to mind and body has been crucial to the evaluation of man as a rational and moral being within systems of theology, ethics, politics and jurisprudence, both theoretical and practical.[34]

In the seventeenth century a woman suffers delusions; her behaviour is erratic and bizarre. Contemporaries agree that she is sick, indeed that she is stricken with melancholy or lunacy. But what kind of an affliction is that? It could be a disorder of her mind. In that case it would probably be seen as some form of demonic possession.[35] But the notion of such a Satanic invasion was clearly dangerous (in the case of a suspected witch it could require a trial, or more generally, imply damnation). There was thus good reason to advance a counter-diagnosis: the 'madness' might instead be seen as somatic in origin, the product perhaps of a head wound or of an intestinal malaise (melancholy = literally an excess of 'black bile'). It was, of course, in its own way humiliating to be diagnosed as disordered in the guts (Swift, Pope and other satirists lampooned the *soi-disant* genius poets of their day as not being truly possessed of afflatus but merely suffering from flatulence); but, unlike Satanic possession, somatic disease had the escape clause of not automatically endangering one's spiritual destiny, one's immortal soul. In discussing such issues, perceptive historians of insanity such as

Michael MacDonald have demonstrated the dangers of anachronism. What to twentieth century minds might well be a sign of a 'sick mind', and thus part of the province of psychiatry, could have been read as a 'physical distemper' three hundred years ago; the boundaries of the body are fluid.[36]

Questions of the relative responsibility of body and soul bedevilled attempts to explain and contain disorder. At witch trials in the sixteenth and seventeenth centuries, it was crucial to determine whether possession phenomena were due to disease, deceit, or to Satan. And the tendency, strongly supported by the medical profession, was increasingly to emphasize organic causes for what we would now always call 'mental illness'. The will was thereby granted an alibi, and the body when sick was more readily excused, precisely because it was 'lower' than the mind would have been.

A couple of centuries later, perceptions of the relative responsibilities of mind and body had notably changed. By Victorian times, both laymen and practitioners were more inclined directly to ascribe 'mental disorder' to derangement of the consciousness. With the decline in literal belief in Satan and hellfire, and the termination of witch trials – in short, with a certain degree of secularization – to venture such a diagnosis no longer raised such spectres. Indeed, the emergence of psychotherapies created a new prognostic optimism: diseases of the mind could be treated and cured (so progressive psychiatrists claimed) more readily than those of the body. Obviously the new tendency to blame insanity on disorders of consciousness could carry with it distinctive forms of stigma and censure (everyone had a duty to govern his mind). Yet a new sympathy grew up alongside. Extremely individualistic, high-pressure societies (it was explained) created great expectations and taxing responsibilities; high living in high society generated high anxiety. Thus, under appropriate circumstances, mental disorders, or, as they were latterly called, nervous breakdowns, could carry social exemption, and command sympathy, or even distinction. Thus the passage of a couple of centuries witnessed profound shifts in mappings of mind and body and their relations' regroupings with enormous implications for policy and therapy.

We must not conflate these shifts in explanations with the positive progress of medical science: no scientific breakthroughs 'proved' the respective roles of mind and body in directing action. They should rather be seen as marks of cultural reorientations which rethought the attributes of mind and body. This point, which applies to wider cultural revisions, is equally germane to the problem of interpreting particular episodes.

Take Freud. In his early psychiatric practice, Freud concluded that many of his neurotic female patients had been sexually assaulted as children; this was what they told him. For complicated reasons, some professional, some personal, Freud abandoned this interpretation, adopting instead the view that the women's stories were not after all memories but rather fantasies, rooted in the unconscious, about traumatic events which had never in reality taken place. By thus developing a theory of repressed desires, Freud gave birth to psycho-analysis. Thus Freud switched from an essentially somatic explanation (real assault) of the aetiology of mental disturbance, to one located merely 'in the mind'; and proposed an equally psychiatric treatment, the 'talking cure'. The vast majority of commentators from Ernest Jones onwards have praised Freud for his supposedly profound insight in directing attention away from the life of the body to that of the consciousness. We may, however, see this praise as reflecting the ingrained privileging of the intellectual over the physical. The interpretation of Freud's switch in explanations is altogether a more complicated matter.[37]

Thus mind/body relations are not a 'given' but culture-dependent. This relativism is exemplified by a noteworthy cross-cultural distinction between the Western experience and the Chinese in the attribution of illness, which has been drawn by the historian and medical anthropologist, Arthur Kleinman. A twentieth-century American feels 'depressed'; he consults not a general physician but a psychotherapist; he is diagnosed as suffering from a psychiatric disorder, some form of neurosis; the therapist investigates his life history to restore him to happiness. The equivalent person in China, by contrast, ascribes a comparable malaise to a physical disorder and cause. His physician confirms that his malady is organic (it may be called 'neurasthenia'), and prescribes medicines. Designated a victim of somatic disease, the Chinaman is permitted to assume the 'sick role', and can thereby command sympathy and attention. By contrast, had he, like his American counterpart, pleaded some form of mental disorder, it would have been a terrible, debilitating admission of character defect and deviancy, which would have brought with it stigma and disadvantage.[38]

In other words, as Kleinman's discussion of the rival somatic and psychiatric constructs of 'mental disorder' demonstrates, the 'body' cannot be treated by the historian as a biological given, but must be regarded as mediated through cultural sign systems. The apportionment of function and responsibility between body and mind, body and soul, differs notably according to century, class, circumstances and culture, and societies often possess a plurality of competing meanings. Assessing the individual case is a matter for negotiation.

A great deal has hinged upon such attributions, for example in the practical matter of legal culpability. Historians of forensic medicine, such as Roger Smith, have elucidated the dilemmas. A blow from one man kills another. Is the proprietor of that body to be held responsible? Yes, if his 'mind' directed the blow, that is, if there was *mens rea*, a guilty intention; no, an eighteenth- or nineteenth-century court would have found, if he were out of his mind, perhaps itself as a consequence of somatic disease.

If, however, responsibility is sustained, how is redress to be exacted? Till within the last couple of centuries, it was principally directed against the body, through corporal or capital punishment. Once again, however, shifting value systems intervened; especially from the late eighteenth century, penal reformers argued that it was 'nobler' or more 'humane' not to punish the body but to correct or reform the mind: in Mably's terms, 'punishment should strike the soul rather than the body'. As Michel Foucault and Michael Ignatieff have particularly emphasised, the therapeutic intention underpinning modern penology marks yet another instance of the shifting status of the body – one which by sparing the flesh serves only to reiterate its inferiority.[39]

Take another example. A man is killed, not by a blow from another but by a micro-organism spread by a carrier. Is the carrier to be held morally or criminally responsible for the danger or disaster his body brought about? It has proved an immensely complicated issue, central to the politics of the regulation of high-density populations by medical bureaucracies ever since the bubonic plague epidemics of the Middle Ages. What is perhaps remarkable, however, as has been stressed by recent historians of public health, is how little the juridico-political systems of the West have held individuals responsible for the health havoc wreaked by their bodies. Despite the emergence of increasingly 'policed' welfare societies over the last two centuries, questions of health have been left surprisingly to private and confidential contractual relationships between the individual and his physician. (Samuel Butler's Utopia, *Erewhon*, in which it is a crime to be sick – though criminality is excused as a disease – affords a startling contrast.) Despite the 'medicalization of life', health compulsions have been few. For example, legally enforceable smallpox vaccination was briefly introduced into Victorian England, but, meeting fierce opposition, the legislation was watered down; the same is true for compulsory treatment for venereal disease.[40] This solution surely embodies a sense of that inalienable, individual proprietorship of the body stoutly advanced in the secularizing formulations of liberal political philosophy from the seventeenth century onwards. Policies and platitudes in law enforcement, political philosophy, and social administration will often be fully grasped only if their rootedness in doctrines about the ownership and privacy of the body are first understood.[41]

Policing the Body

There is a deep-seated cultural stereotype – rapturous in Rabelais,[42] reviling within Christian theology – which pictures the body as an anarch, a lord of misrule, emblematic of excess in food, drink, sex, violence – the embodiment of the principle which Freud later intellectualized as the 'id'. Historians have recently been exploring the attempts of dominant social groups to restrict, repress and reform the mayhem of the body. These strategies have obviously taken distinct forms.

Scholars have focused their attention primarily on reforms which are self-inflicted, implementing aspirations towards better self-control, associated with household education and discipline. Manuals for proper behaviour, both religious and civil, pouring off the printing presses from the sixteenth century, set great store by the submission and obedience of the body, and on the cultivation of manners, decency and decorum. Foucault has argued that the growing concern with good health and long life arising out of the Enlightenment affords a further symptom.[43] Vigarello has stressed the importance of enculturing the anarchic body through hygiene, cleanliness and dress, and Norbert Elias in particular has studied 'the civilizing process' visible in the development of body controls (clean bodies, clean habits, clean talk, clean minds). Moreover Schama's investigation of purity and body discipline amongst Dutch Calvinists illuminates the effectiveness (both social and psychological) of such strategies in creating a *cordon sanitaire* against moral and religious threats – both popery and pollution – seen to be dirty, dangerous, and contaminating.[44]

Talk of decency, delicacy, and prudery automatically suggests the Victorians, but Victorianism long antedated those who bear its name. Thomas Bowdler was a Georgian, it was Wesley who placed cleanliness next to Godliness, and the proper comportment of the body in a polite society was never so much bruited as in the age of Addison, Steele and Mandeville. In works such as *The Virgin Unmask'd* Mandeville teasingly explored the ambivalent meanings of bodily repression, in which veiling the flesh could be more titillating than revealing it.[45]

Physical self-control has typically gone hand-in-glove with the desire to police the bodies of others, so as to secure better social and moral-religious order. Notable historians of early modern France, such as Muchembled, Flandrin and Delumeau, have laid special stress upon the attempts of religious and civil authorities to regulate the bodies of the common people through persuasion, prescription and ultimately physical coercion.[46] Muchembled above all has argued that within traditional quasi-pagan peasant culture, the body enjoyed high status as a potent instrument, and that its parts and products blood, faeces, the penis and the womb – possessed magical powers. If vulnerable to famine, disease and death, the body was also the Dionysian life-force behind riot and orgiastic excess. This carnival counter-culture of the body was, however, increasingly subjected to systematic surveillance and effective repression, through the instruments of witch trials, church courts, and confession intensified by the Counter-Reformation, and the instilling of a new sexual morality underlining marriage and legitimacy.

Early modern England also witnessed parallel movements, led by Puritans, for the religious reformation of morals and manners.[47] They may have met with some success. Historical demographers have demonstrated that bastardy figures were notably lower in Stuart times than they later became in the more secular environment of the first industrial nation, possibly suggesting that moral discipline was effective.[48] Georgian England witnessed further assaults upon an anarchic body-culture with the regulation of blood sports and prize-fighting, and a new disapproval of duelling, and with the attempts of capitalist employers to drum regular work and time discipline into their work-force.[49]

Plebeian bodies had traditionally been on the receiving end of physical coercion: the whip, the pillory, the gallows. But, as Foucault particularly stressed, the people's bodies also became subjected to, and, it was hoped, regenerated by, a new political technology of the body – the routines of the factory floor, the drills of the school, the fatigues of the parade ground, the punishments of the reformatory. From swaddling and toilet training in the domestic family, through schooling, to the army or the factory floor, the state laboured to manufacture docile subjects and an obedient work-force via the systematic disciplining of people's bodies.[50] Only recently, historians of the present century have suggested, has the logic of capitalism somewhat relaxed this relentless so-called 'Protestant' emphasis on the disciplined body and on a 'this-worldly asceticism'; the imperative has recently switched from the iron-disciplined machine-like productive 'hand' to the body as consumer, brimful of wants and needs, whose desires are to be inflamed and encouraged.[51]

Focusing attention on the problem of the body – its dangers and its disciplines, its potential for pollution yet its productive powers – helps to make sense of numerous disparate developments too often studied in isolation and anachronistically through the blinkers of modern disciplines. As Catherine Gallagher has argued, we misunderstand Malthus if, for instance, we treat him simply as the founding father of modern demography.[52] Indeed he posed a dramatically new conundrum about the moral well-being of bodies politic. Traditionally the healthy body was the guarantor of the healthy state: it produced, it reproduced. But, counter-suggested Malthus, the healthy body, because of its high reproductive powers, might actually prove the state's enemy. Thus the body private and the body public might be at odds. Or, as E. P. Thompson emphasized, we miss half the significance of the quest for time discipline in factories if we see it only in terms of economic rationality and heroic captains of industry: rather it was part of a much wider attempt to govern the people through control of their bodies.[53]

Similarly, a history of education which exclusively concentrates on the achievement of skills such as reading and writing will miss one of the prime functions of the ragged, charity or elementary school in the past: instilling physical obedience, or education as a process of breaking children in.[54] Likewise, it would be blinkered to assess the goals of sanitarians and hygienists solely in terms of miasmas and drains: their concerns were no less with moral filth and the regulation of sexual contagion and contamination.[55] In the same way, the rituals of medicine at the bedside or in the hospital cannot be explained wholly by the attainments of medical science. Broader questions of bodily taboos and decorum also dictated the nature and limits of diagnostic examinations, surgical treatment and the emergence of new interventionist and gender-sensitive specialties such as man-midwifery.[56]

These wider issues show why the politics of the body demand attention in their own right; such issues are too often neglected if we pursue historical demography, the history of education, the history of medicine, and so forth through an isolated and narrow tunnel vision.

It remains unclear, however, how accurate a picture is given by historians such as Muchembled who have seen popular cultures of the body being successfully suppressed in the name of the panoptic, therapeutic state and the dictates of capitalist rationality. Aspirations may well have vastly outstripped achievements. Elite culture does not so much seem to have crushed popular culture as separated itself from it, developing its own distinct, dematerializing, expressive, body language, rituals and refinements.[57] Folklore popular sexual mores (e.g. the tradition of premarital intercourse followed by marriage on pregnancy) and grass-roots medical magic proved immensely resilient against indoctrination and infiltration from above.

And not least, the politics of controlling body behaviour in the teeth of the threats posed by epidemic disease and 'dangerous sexualities' were immensely complex. In England, the aspirations of the public health and hygiene movement of the early Victorian period, associated with utilitarianism and Edwin Chadwick, were direct and statist. No such alliance between central government and mains drainage can be found, however, in Paris. But even in England, the enterprise of policing bodies by state medicine quickly foundered, wrecked on the rocks of competing political lobbies, including purity and feminist groups furious at the attempts of male legislators to control female bodies through the traditional double standard. Overall the superficially attractive notion that the growth of state power has been directed towards the social subordination of the body turns out to be naive and unconvincing.[58]

Sex, Gender and the Body

If European society over *la longue durée* was a patriarchy, and still bears at least its scars, how far was patriarchy itself a direct symptom or consequence of the differentiation between male and female bodies – a difference, that is, not simply biological, but as constituted within social realities? Was the reason for the traditional subordination of women to men primarily and essentially *physical* – because the endless pregnancies which selfish husbands forced upon them in the days before effective contraception, shackled them to children and household, to premature ageing, exhaustion and frequently to death from the diseases of childbirth; and which furthermore trapped them in a women-only ghetto culture stained by menstrual blood and the pollutions of parturition? Thus Edward Shorter has argued in his *History of Women's Bodies*,[59] concluding that women have finally, over the last century, been emancipated from their primary biological chains by the coming of safe child-bearing, contraception and legalized abortion, all of which, by giving women control over their own fertility, have paved the way for the 'modern family', the 'egalitarian family' and even the post-family society.

What cannot be doubted is that traditional male doctors, theologians and philosophers ascribed the subordination of women to their inferior biological status within the scheme of Creation. According to Aristotle and his followers, women were defective or monstrous males, beings in whom the genitalia (designed to be on the outside of the body) had failed, for want of heat and strength, to be extruded. With their cooler and weaker nature, and their genitals trapped internally, women were equipped essentially for child-bearing rather than for a life of reason and activity within the civic forum. Women were private creatures, men public.[60]

Thomas Laqueur has argued that this bio-medical conceptualization of women's nature was eroded and replaced towards the close of the eighteenth century.[61] The female gender ceased to be seen as literally an inferior version of the male, becoming regarded instead as essentially different, but complementary. Physiologists newly argued that the female sexual reproductive apparatus was radically distinct from that of men, a view confirmed by the discovery of the functions of the ovaries and the nature of the menstrual cycle. This in turn indicated that there was no good biological reason why women should be actively sexual (i.e., erotic) beings at all: contrary to Classical medical dogma, no sexual stimulus was needed for women to conceive: they merely had to serve as semen receptacles. The passive, desexualized, 'Victorian' woman was born (though, *pace* Laqueur, it must be stressed that Peter Gay and other historians have been arguing that Victorian women were not in that sense 'Victorian' at all; it would be a gross mistake to confuse certain prescriptions for proper female behaviour with the reality).[62]

Laqueur seeks to relate this 'making of the modern body' to women's changing place in society. Desexualized, the lady became the angel in the house, docile, frail, passionless; and his account thus dovetails nicely with recent analyses of the emergence of 'separate spheres' for male and female household roles.[63] Arguing that science does not emerge from a pure logic of discovery but gives articulate form to socio-ideological pressures, Laqueur denies that the new gender image was the product of autonomous scientific inquiry. But a chicken-and-egg conundrum thus emerges. Do we accept (as Laqueur's argument implies and much feminist scholarship suggests) that cultural forces – that is, patriarchalist ideology, translated into institutional power – were primarily responsible for locking women in dolls' houses? If that is so, it becomes a matter of urgency to demonstrate why the years just before and just after 1800 should be thought to be pivotal in transforming women's social position.

Or should we rather, following Shorter, subscribe to a more 'materialist' account, in which *biological* fetters (multiple pregnancies, etc.) principally explain women's age-old servitude, and biomedical breakthroughs (contraception, abortion, etc.) are credited with doing more for women's emancipation than the agitation of feminists? But if (with Shorter) we accept the bio-medical dynamo of history, how can we explain why the ghost of patriarchy continues to rule the roost, even today, once biological emancipation has (supposedly) been achieved?

The answer perhaps is that we need not impale ourselves on the horns of a false dichotomy: the notion that explanations for gender identity must be either simply socio-cultural or simply bio-scientific. An escape route is indeed signposted by accounts, by Foucault and others, of the transformation of discourse about sex during the nineteenth century.[64] Foucault rightly stressed that the popular notion that sex, allegedly so openly discussed during the 'free' eighteenth century,[65] was silenced in the furtive nineteenth is quite false. No century had seen such extensive, almost obsessive, discussion of sex. But the focus of attention shifted.

Earlier treatments, such as that found in the popular handbook, *Aristotle's Master-piece*, regarded sexual congress essentially as the action of bodies, in accord with the urges and appetites of nature, primarily designed to secure the perpetuation of the species.[66] Nineteenth-century sexual discourse, by contrast, paid extraordinary attention to sexual disorders, abnormality and deviance. Above all, it elaborated a psychopathology of sexual perversions, linking these with practices such as masturbation and conditions such as hysteria. Sex was thus psychiatrized in the 'space' of a new theoretical construction, 'sexuality'.[67]

This analysis illuminates and helps resolve the dilemma raised by the divergent analyses of Shorter and Laqueur. For it would seem that when addressing changing conceptions of women in the nineteenth century, our attention should be focused neither literally on the bio-medical history of their bodies, nor principally upon changing pressures within marriage and the family, but rather upon the development of a new metaphysic of the feminine. This found a matrix in a psycho-physiology of motherhood, and was intimately associated with what Elaine Showalter has rightly named 'the female malady' (which was, in the extreme case, the malady of being female).[68] This new discourse, eventually enshrined in Freudian psychoanalytic theory, actually recuperated the old biologism ('anatomy is destiny'), but masked it in new fancy dress (penis envy was, after all, just in the mind). Not least, in the case of Freud himself, it aspired to the liberation of women (though not from men, but from their own neuroses).[69] This is why, despite Shorter's eupeptic tone, 'biological' emancipation has been of somewhat flimsy significance to women this century, in view of the emergence of other disciplines – the varieties of psychoanalysis which offer new rationalizations for the inferiority (neuroses) of women.[70]

An Agenda

I have just examined three key areas in which our knowledge of the body, both in reality and in representations, is critical to wider interpretations of social change. In each, the historiographical debate is already raging. By way of coda to this skimming survey, I shall point to seven other branches of the history of the body which deserve close attention, mentioning in the references signal work which has already appeared.

1 *The Body as Human Condition* The religions, philosophies and literatures of the world chorus a commentary upon the human condition, upon birth, copulation and death.[71] But how specifically and directly do the prevailing religious doctrines or artistic tempers of particular times relate to (reflect? compensate for?) the actual experiences of embodied living?[72] Was, for example, the death-obsessed culture of what Huizinga called 'the waning of the Middle Ages' a reflex response to the realities of the epidemics of bubonic plague which swept Europe in the fourteenth century? or, following Camporesi, might we better see the macabre elements of late medieval Christianity – the fascination with Christ nailed to the cross, the incorruptible bodies of saints and so forth – as an expression of a pulsating love of life and engrossment with the flesh? Or, to take a later period, is there a genuine link – as Imhof suggests – between the recent assurance of a more secure and protracted temporal existence and, on the other hand, a declining belief in personal immortality? To use Imhof's formulation, life expectation, which was once infinite, is now reduced to a matter of three score years and ten.[73]

2 *The Form of the Body* In art, creative writing, science and medicine, but no less in proverbs,[74] clichés and metaphors, the body takes on a visual, or visualized form. Thin or fat, beautiful or ugly; the mirror of the universe, the paragon of the animals, the quintessence of dust – every picture tells its story and incorporates a value system. Few historians have as yet paid much attention to language (as contained for example in living and dead metaphors) as a vehicle for hidden messages about the body. Fewer still general historians, as opposed to specialist historians of art, have pondered deeply about the significance of real visual images of bodies (in portraits, in funeral effigies – 'anatomies' – or even in snapshot albums) as historical evidence. All too often historians use visual evidence as mere 'illustrations' rather than as explicanda. Better integration of written and visual sources is a high priority.[75]

3   *The Anatomy of the Body* Bodies are objects for the external gaze; they face the outside world. But they are also subjective, integral to the internal self. Oddly, however, most accounts of the history of the self,[76] of character and personal psychology have very little to say about how people have made sense of, and related themselves to, their own bodies. We need to know much more about how particular individuals and cultures in general have ascribed meaning to their limbs and organs, their constitutions, their flesh. What is the emotional and existential topography of skin and bones? What did people mean when they talked, literally and figuratively, of their blood,[77] their head or their heart, their bowels, their spirits and their humours? How did these organs and functions embody emotions, experiences and desires? How did private and public meanings, subjective and medical connotations, interrelate? When did one feel old or young (or indeed young at heart), and what did the succession of such ages and stages mean? And how did people think of their bodies, their aches and pains, when they fell sick? The body is the primary communications system, but historians have paid little attention to its codes and keys (anthropologists may have much to teach us here).[78]

4   *Body, Mind and Soul* I have alluded above to the fact that the territories of mind and body are not fixed – least of all fixed by biology – but possess boundaries subject to negotiation within particular systems of values, judgements and duties. This sense of the self, a totality divided into distinct faculties and offices, a mindful body and an embodied mind, often mutually at odds, has obviously been central to ethical theories, codes of jurisprudence, pedagogic programmes, and more generally, to notions of man's place in nature. Indeed, mind/body relations, and even more so, body/soul relations may be said not just to constitute a problem *within* ethics and theology, but to *generate* the very impetus for, the mystery behind, their profound speculations. The links and divides between mind and body, experience and lesions, are clearly no less central to the history of illness and medicines, as 'psychosomatic' conditions such as hysteria[79] and hypochondria[80] bear witness. We must remember that philosophies and world-views of man and his nature are commonly predicated upon an often unstated metaphysic of the human body.[81]

5   *Sex and Gender* Thanks to feminist scholarship, the constitution and reconstitution of sex and gender forms one of the very few areas of analysis of the body – specifically the female body, at once attractive yet polluted, desirable yet dangerous – which have received detailed

scrutiny. It is utterly impossible to discuss here the range of topics covered in this scholarship, or even to list it in the references.[82] One important conclusion which seems to be emerging is worth noting; the fact that no one single, uniform attitude towards the politics of the female body *vis-à-vis* existing or a reformed society was adopted by feminist opinion. Writers differed. For example many women campaigners sought sexual emancipation; others thought the way forward lay in emancipation from sex. Many feminists argued for the essential identity between men and women, united by the common attribute of reason; others built upon the unique features of the female body (e.g., its capacity for child-bearing). The notion of a single, progressive feminist 'movement' needs to be finally discarded.

What remains pitiably ignored is the history of maleness and masculinity (all too typically taken as normal and therefore normative and unproblematic). There are some signs that this is at last changing.[83]

6 *The Body and the Body Politic* Historians of political thought and literature have long investigated the metaphor of the body politic, and its associated and derivative concepts, such as the 'King's Two Bodies' – although they have often done so somewhat impatiently, eager to see these long obsolescent metaphors driven off the stage by a more philosophically rigorous language of politics from the seventeenth century onwards.[84] What has received far less attention are the ways in which political authority has actually treated the individual body. The high rhetorical goals of politics, the rights of man, are commonly expressed in abstract, intellectualist terms (free speech, freedom of conscience). Yet behind these lie assumptions about fundamental physical freedoms and immunities, not least *habeas corpus* itself. Yet we remain strikingly ignorant as to the circumstances and rationalizations under which states have possessed or regimented the body in military conscription, in time of plague,[85] indeed, in slavery. There is abundant scope for political historians and political scientists to be more sensitive to the power realities produced by the exercise of the state's authority over the bodies of its subjects.[86]

7 *The Body, Civilization and its Discontents* History is an unfinished civilizing process – a struggle, anthropologists tell us, to affirm man's distinctiveness from Nature. Yet the writing of the history of civilization has concentrated too long on the artefacts of high culture. There is a need for a different kind of history of enculturation. We come naked into the world, but we are soon adorned not just with clothes but with the metaphorical clothing of moral codes, taboos, prohibitions, and

value systems linking discipline to desires, politeness to policing. The stories of dress, of cleanliness, of eating, of cosmetics, have too long been left to specialists relatively uninterested in the larger questions of the functions served by such objects and activities in transforming individuals and societies into culture.[87]

The aim of this paper has not been to propose a new cottage industry, dedicated to weaving a gigantic tapestry of the history of the body. It has been to issue a reminder of how the body is a suppressed presence – too often ignored or forgotten – within many other, more prestigious, branches of scholarship. More alert awareness of it would undermine the enduring idealist snobberies endorsed by those whom Nietzsche characterized as the 'Despisers of the Body', and help its resurrection.

NOTES

1 Leo Steinberg, *The Sexuality of Christ in Renaissance Art and Modern Oblivion* (New York, 1983).
2 This is of course a wildly simplistic way of putting an extremely complicated situation. For the intellectual foundations of these cultural heritages see Bennett Simon, *Mind and Madness in Ancient Greece* (Ithaca, 1978); E. R. Dodds, *The Greeks and the Irrational* (Berkeley and London, 1951); and for Christianity, F. Bottomley, *Attitudes to the Body in Western Christendom* (London, 1979).
3 On Sterne, see Roy Porter, 'Against the Spleen' in Valerie Grosvenor-Myer (ed.), *Laurence Sterne: Riddles and Mysteries* (London and New York, 1984), 84–99; J. Rodgers, 'Ideas of Life in *Tristram Shandy*: Contemporary Medicine' (Ph.D. thesis, University of East Anglia, 1978).
4 For an introduction to contemporary feminist perspectives see Susan Brownmiller, *Femininity* (London, 1984).
5 A disparagement of course enhanced by traditional prudery, Bowdlerism etc. See P. Fryer, *Mrs. Grundy: Studies in English Prudery* (London, 1963); M. Jaeger, *Before Victoria* (London, 1956).
6 For critical interpretations of such processes as mere modifications within the existing system, indeed as 'repressive desublimation', see Herbert Marcuse, *One Dimensional Man* (London, 1964); C. Lasch, *The Culture of Narcissism* (New York, 1979).
7 See M. Bakhtin, *Rabelais and his World* (Cambridge, Mass., 1968); A. Schmidt, *The Concept of Nature in Marx*, tr. B. Fawkes (London, 1971).
8 See Peter Burke, 'Revolution in Popular Culture', in Roy Porter and Mikuláš Teich (eds), *Revolution in History* (Cambridge, 1986), pp. 206–25.
9 For an exemplary investigation see Peter Burke, *The Historical Anthropology*

of Early Modern Italy (Cambridge, 1987); highly useful also are Michael MacDonald, 'Anthropological Perspectives on the History of Science and Medicine', in P. Corsi and P. Weindling (eds.), *Information Sources in the History of Science and Medicine* (London, 1983), 61–80.

10 B. S. Turner, *The Body and Society: Explorations in Social Theory* (Oxford, 1984). Turner's book is the boldest attempt yet to create a sociology of the body. There is a stimulating discussion of the neglect of the body in literature in Virginia Woolf's essay, 'On being ill', in *Collected Essays*, vol. iv (London, 1967), 193–203. For Woolf's own problems with 'embodiment' see S. Trombley, *'All that Summer She Was Mad'. Virginia Woolf and her Doctors* (London, 1981).

11 The best, and most up to date, survey is Bryan S. Turner, *Medical Power and Social Knowledge* (Beverly Hills and London, 1987).

12 For a bibliographical entry see the essay by Joan Scott in this volume.

13 Arthur Imhof has been to the fore in attempting to relate technical historical demography to wider questions of social existence. See for instance his 'Methodological Problems in Modern Urban Geography: Graphic Representations of Urban Mortality 1750–1850', in Roy Porter and Andrew Wear (eds), *Problems and Methods in the History of Medicine* (London, 1987), pp. 101–32.

14 The psycho-physiological interpretation of the body is of course important in its own right. See Jonathan Miller, *The Body in Question* (London, 1978). Debate continues as to whether sociobiological perspectives can illuminate historical research.

15 W. I. Watson, 'Why Isn't the Mind-Body Problem Ancient?', in Paul K. Feyerabend and Grover Maxwell (eds), *Mind, Matter and Method* (Minneapolis, 1966), 92–102; L. J. Rather, *Mind and Body in Eighteenth Century Medicine* (London, 1965).

16 See R. Barthes, *Le Plaisir du Texte* (Paris, 1973); J. Derrida, *Writing and Difference* (London, 1978).

17 F. Barker, *The Tremulous Private Body* (London, 1984).

18 Barker's scholarship is gloriously demolished in J. R. R. Christie, 'Bad News for the Body', *Art History* 9 (1986), pp. 263–70.

19 S. R. Suleiman (ed.), *The Female Body in Western Culture* (Cambridge, Mass., 1986), 2 (editor's introduction).

20 Margaret Higonnet, 'Speaking Silences: Women's Suicide', in Suleiman (ed.), *The Female Body*, pp. 68–83; many of the assertions made there about female suicides being abandoned by men run counter to the careful empirical analysis in Olive Anderson, *Suicide in Victorian and Edwardian England* (Oxford, 1987).

21 Elaine Scarry, *The Body in Pain. The Making and Unmaking of the World* (New York and London, 1985).

22 Barbara Duden, *Geschichte unter der Haut* (Stuttgart, 1987). Duden also shows how her group of women espoused a vision of their own bodies as dynamic and powerful, the great centres of life-creation.

23 See the discussion in the introduction to G. S. Rousseau and Roy Porter (eds), *Sexual Underworlds of the Enlightenment* (Manchester, 1987).

24 For an introduction to such sources, see R. Maccubbin (ed.), *Unauthorized Sexual Behavior during the Enlightenment* (special issue of *Eighteenth Century Life*, May 1985).

25 See G. Risse, 'Hysteria at the Edinburgh Infirmary', *Medical History* 32 (1988), pp. 1–22.

26 See classically E. A. Wrigley and R. S. Schofield, *The Population History of England 1541–1870* (London, 1982).

27 Roderick Floud, Kenneth Wachter and Annabell Gregory, *Height, Health and History* (Cambridge, 1990).

28 For the problems of interpreting such evidence see D. M. Fox and C. Lawrence, *Photographing Medicine: Images and Power in Britain and America since 1840* (Springfield, Conn., 1988). For valuable interpretations see David Piper, *The English Face* (London, 1957) and *Personality and the Portrait* (London, 1972).

29 See E. Goffman, *Stigma, Notes on the Management of Spoiled Identity* (Harmondsworth, 1968); *idem, The Presentation of Self in Everyday Life* (London, 1959); *idem, Strategic Interaction* (Oxford, 1970); *idem, Interaction Ritual* (London, 1972).

30 For the construction of the self see P. M. Spacks, *Imagining a Self* (Cambridge, Mass., 1976), especially chapter 5; J. N. Morris, *Versions of the Self* (New York, 1966); S. D. Cox, 'The Stranger Within Thee': The Concept of Self in Late Eighteenth Century Literature* (Pittsburgh, 1980); J. O. Lyons, *The Invention of the Self* (Carbondale, 1978).

31 See Lloyd DeMause, *The New Psychohistory* ([New York, 1975). David E. Stannard, *Shrinking History: On Freud and the Failure of Psychohistory* (New York and Oxford, 1980) has argued that psychohistory is bunk.

32 See for instance Rhys Isaac, *The Transformation of Virginia 1700–1800* (Chapel Hill, 1981).

33 Thus all forms of materialism produce dilemmas about personal responsibility. For the Enlightenment, see Lester Crocker, *An Age of Crisis: Man and World in Eighteenth Century French Thought* (Baltimore, 1959).

34 Roger Smith, *Trial by Medicine: Insanity and Responsibility in Victorian Trials* (Edinburgh, 1981).

35 D. P. Walker, *Spiritual and Demonic Magic from Ficino to Campanella* (London, 1958); Keith Thomas, *Religion and the Decline of Magic* (Harmondsworth, 1978).

36 For the intellectual and cultural contexts of these notions of madness see Michel Foucault, *Madness and Civilization: a History of Insanity in the Age of Reason*. Translated by Richard Howard (New York, 1965); Michael Macdonald, *Mystical Bedlam: Madness, Anxiety and Healing in Seventeenth Century England* (Cambridge, 1981); fundamental here is G. S. Rousseau, 'Psychology', in G. S. Rousseau and Roy Porter (eds), *The Ferment of Knowledge* (Cambridge, 1980).

37 On Freud, see H. F. Ellenberger, *The Discovery of the Unconscious: the*

History and Evolution of Dynamic Psychiatry (New York, 1971); R. W. Clark, *Freud: The Man and the Cause* (London, 1982), Frank J. Sulloway, *Freud: Biologist of the Mind* (New York, 1979) and J. M. Masson, *The Assault on Truth: Freud's Suppression of the Seduction Theory* (New York, 1983).

38 Arthur Kleinman, *Social Origins of Distress and Disease. Depression, Neurasthenia and Pain in Modern China* (New Haven, 1986). See also Carney Landis and Fred Mettler, *Varieties of Psychopathological Experience* (New York, 1964). For broader discussion of the 'sick role' see D. Mechanic, 'The Concept of Illness Behaviour', *Journal of Chronic Disease* 15 (1962), 189–94.

39 See M. Foucault, *Discipline and Punish: The Birth of the Prison* (Harmondsworth, 1979); M. Ignatieff, *A Just Measure of Pain* (London, 1978).

40 W. M. Frazer, *History of English Public Health 1834–1939* (London, 1950), pp. 70–72, 106–112; P. McHugh, *Prostitution and Victorian Social Reform* (London, 1981) and J. Walkowitz, *Prostitution and Victorian Society* (Cambridge, 1980).

41 Public and private dimensions are explored in R. Sennett, *The Fall of Public Man* (Cambridge, 1976).

42 M. Bakhtin, *Rabelais and his World* (Cambridge, Mass., 1968).

43 See M. Foucault, *A History of Sexuality*. Vol. 1. *Introduction* (London, 1978); J.-L. Flandrin, *Un Temps pour embrasser* (Paris, 1983).

44 See generally N. Elias, *The Civilizing Process* (Oxford, 1983), and more specifically S. Schama, 'The Unruly Realm: Appetite and Restraint in Seventeenth-Century Holland', *Daedalus* 108 (1979), 103–23.

45 For early Georgian opinion see Fenella Childs 'Prescriptions for Manners in Eighteenth Century Courtesy Literature' (D.Phil. thesis, Oxford, 1984).

46 Jacques Donzelot, *The Policing of Families*, trans. Robert Hurley (New York, 1979); Jean-Louis Flandrin, 'Amour et marriage', *Dix-huitième Siècle*, 12 (1980), 163–76. See also M. Bakhtin, *Rabelais and His World*, tr. H. Iswolsky (Cambridge, Mass., 1968); and J. Starobinski, 'The Body's Moment' in *Montaigne: Essays in Reading* (Yale French studies no. 64, 1983), pp. 273–305.

47 K. Wrightson, *English Society 1580–1680* (London, 1982); E. J. Bristow, *Vice and Vigilance: Purity Movements in Britain since 1700* (Dublin, 1977).

48 P. Laslett (ed.), *Bastardy and its Comparative History* (London, 1980).

49 R. Malcolmson, *Popular Recreations in English Society 1700–1850* (Cambridge, 1973).

50 Foucault's main relevant works are *Madness and Civilization: a History of Insanity in the Age of Reason* (London, 1967); *The Order of Things: an Archaeology of the Human Sciences* (London, 1970); *The Archaeology of Knowledge* (London, 1972); *The Birth of the Clinic: an Archaeology of Medical Perception* (London, 1973); *Discipline and Punish: the Birth of the Prison* (Harmondsworth, 1979); *The History of Sexuality*. Vol. I. *Introduction* (London, 1978). See also C. Gordon (ed.), *M. Foucault: Power/Knowledge* (Brighton, 1980), especially the essay 'Body/Power', pp. 55–62.

51 M. Featherstone, 'The Body in Consumer Culture', *Theory, Culture & Society* 1 (1982), pp. 18–33.

52 For discussion of Malthus's wider concerns see Patricia James, *Population Malthus: His Life and Times* (London, 1979), chapter 2, part 4; and R. M. Young, 'Malthus and the Evolutionists: The Common Context of Biological and Social Theory', *Past and Present* 43 (1969), pp. 109–45.

53 E.P. Thompson, 'Time, Work-Discipline and Industrial Capitalism', *Past and Present* 37 (1967), pp. 56–97.

54 On the wider dimensions of education see B. Haley, *The Healthy Body and Victorian Culture* (Cambridge, Mass., 1978).

55 Virginia Smith, 'Physical Puritanism and Sanitary Science: Material and Immaterial Beliefs in Popular Physiology 1650–1840', in W. F. Bynum and Roy Porter (eds), *Medical Fringe and Medical Orthodoxy 1750–1850* (London, 1986), pp. 174–97.

56 See R. L. Engle and B. J. Davis, 'Medical Diagnosis, Present, Past and Future', *Archives of Internal Medicine* 112 (1963), pp. 512–43.

57 For such divisions see P. Burke, *Popular Culture in Early Modern Europe* (London, 1978); H. C. Payne, 'Elite versus Popular Mentality in the Eighteenth Century', *Studies in Eighteenth Century Culture* 8 (1979), pp. 201–37.

58 The best and most recent introduction is in Frank Mort, *Dangerous Sexualities: Medico-Politics in England since 1830* (London, 1987).

59 E. Shorter, *The Making of the Modern Family* (London, 1976).

60 J. Morsink, *Aristotle on the Generation of Animals* (Washington, 1982).

61 T. Laqueur, 'Orgasm, Generation and the Politics of Reproductive Biology', in C. Gallagher and T. Laqueur (eds), *The Making of the Modern Body* (Berkeley and Los Angeles, 1987), pp. 1–41. Compare Pierre Darmon, *Le Mythe de la procréation a l'age baroque* (Paris, 1977).

62 P. Gay, *The Bourgeois Experience, Victoria to Freud*. Vol. 1. *A Sentimental Education*, vol. 2. *The Tender Passion* (New York, 1984, 1986).

63 Leonore Davidoff and Catherine Hall, *Family Fortunes. Men and Women of the English Middle Class 1780–1850* (London, 1987).

64 M. Foucault, *The History of Sexuality*. Vol. 1. *Introduction* (London,1978).

65 For the Enlightenment's claim that the erotic is the healthy see J. Hagstrum, *Sex and Sensibility: Erotic Ideal and Erotic Love from Milton to Mozart* (London, 1980); Roy Porter, 'Mixed Feelings: the Enlightenment and sexuality in Britain', in P. G. Boucé (ed.), *Sexuality in Eighteenth Century Britain* (Manchester, 1982), pp. 1–27.

66 Roy Porter, 'Spreading Carnal Knowledge or Selling Dirt Cheap? Nicolas Venette's *Tableau De L'Amour Conjugal* in Eighteenth Century England', *Journal of European Studies*, 14 (1984), pp. 233–55; P. G. Boucé, 'Aspects of sexual tolerance and intolerance in eighteenth-century England', *British Journal for Eighteenth-Century Studies* 3 (1980), 180.

67 For one dimension of this new sexual psychiatry, see E. H. Hare, 'Masturbatory Insanity: The History of an Idea', *Journal of Mental Science*, 108 (1962), pp. 1–25.

68 Elaine Showalter, *The Female Malady* (New York, 1985).

69 An attempt to marry psychoanalysis with feminism is made in Juliet Mitchell, *Psychoanalysis and Feminism* (New York, 1974). For a much more sceptical set of views see Charles Bernheimer and Claire Kahane (eds), *In Dora's Case: Freud, Hysteria, Feminism* (New York, 1985).

70 For helpful general perspectives on the historiography of sex, see Jeffrey Weaks, *Sex, Politics and Society* (London, 1981); Michael Ignatieff, 'Homo Sexualis', *London Review of Books* (March 4–17, 1982), pp. 8–9.

71 For attitudes towards death see J. McManners, *Death and the Enlightenment* (Oxford, 1981). P. Ariès, *The Hour of our Death* (Harmondsworth, 1981); and W. F. Bynum 'Health, Disease and Medical Care', in G. S. Rousseau and Roy Porter, *The Ferment of Knowledge* (Cambridge, 1980), 211–54.

72 See the discussion in J. Broadbent, 'The Image of God, or Two Yards of Skin', in J. Benthall and T. Polhemus (eds), *The Body as a Medium of Expression* (London, 1975), pp. 305–26.

73 P. Camporesi, *The Incorruptible Flesh: Bodily Mutation and Mortification in Religion and Folklore*, tr. T. Croft-Murray (Cambridge, 1988).

74 For proverbs see F. Loux, *Sagesses du corps* (Paris, 1978).

75 On the important field of physiognomy see G. Tyler, *Physiognomy in the European Novel* (Princeton, 1982); M. Shortland, 'The Body in Question. Some Perceptions, Problems and Perspectives of the Body in Relation to Character *c.*1750–1850' (Ph.D. thesis, Leeds University, 1985).

76 See note 30.

77 Richard M. Titmuss, *The Gift Relationship: From Human Blood to Social Policy* (New York, 1971); and more generally on the metaphorical resonance of the body C. G. Helman, 'Feed a Cold, Starve a Fever': Folk Models of Infection in an English Suburban Community, and their Relation to Medical Treatment', *Culture, Medicine and Psychiatry* II (1978), pp. 107–37; *idem, Culture, Health and Illness* (Bristol, 1984); J. B. Loudon (ed.), *Social Anthropology and Medicine* (London, 1976).

78 J. Lane, 'The Doctor Scolds Me: The Diaries and Correspondence of Patients in Eighteenth-Century England', in Roy Porter (ed.), *Patients and practitioners*, pp. 207–47.

79 For hysteria see I. Veith, *Hysteria, the History of a Disease* (Chicago, 1963).

80 For hypochondria see C. Moore, *Backgrounds of English Literature 1700–1760* (Minneapolis, 1953); O. Doughty, 'The English Malady of the Eighteenth Century', *Review of English Studies* 2 (1926), pp. 257–69; E. Fischer-Homberger, 'Hypochondriasis of the Eighteenth Century – Neurosis of the present Century', *Bulletin of the History of Medicine* 46 (1972), pp. 391–401; Roy Porter, 'The Rage of Party: a Glorious Revolution in English Psychiatry?', *Medical History* 27 (1983), pp. 35–50.

81 L. J. Rather, *Mind and Body in Eighteenth Century Medicine* (London, 1965); W. I. Matson, 'Why Isn't the Mind-Body Problem Ancient?' in P. K. Feyerabend and G. Maxwell (eds), *Mind, Matter, and Method* (Minneapolis, 1966).

82 See Carroll Smith-Rosenberg and Charles Rosenberg, 'The Female

Animal: Medical and Biological Views of Woman and Her Role in Nineteenth-Century America', in Judith W. Leavitt (ed.), *Women and Health in America* (Madison, 1984), pp. 12–27; Nancy F. Cott, 'Passionlessness: an Interpretation of Victorian Sexual Ideology, 1790–1850', ibid., 57–89; Carl N. Degler, 'What Ought to Be and What Was: Women's Sexuality in the Nineteenth Century', ibid., 40–56; L. J. Jordanova, 'Natural Facts: a Historical Perspective on Science and Sexuality', in *Nature, Culture and Gender*, ed. Caroline MacCormack and Marilyn Strathern (Cambridge 1980), pp. 42–69.

83 See Brian Easlea, *Science and Sexual Oppression* (London, 1981); Jeffrey Weeks, *Sex, Politics and Society* (London, 1981); Lesley Hall, '"Somehow Very Distasteful": Doctors, Men and Sexual Problems Between the Wars', *Journey of Contemporary History* 20 (1985), pp. 553–74; idem, 'From *Self Preservation* to *Love Without Fear*: Medical and Lay Writers of Sex Advice from William Acton to Eustace Chesser', *Society for the Social History of Medicine Bulletin* 39 (1986), pp. 20–3.

84 W.Greenleaf, *Order, Empiricism and Politics* (Oxford, 1964); Otto Gierke, *Political Theories of the Middle Age*, trans, with introduction by F. W. Maitland (Cambridge, 1958); Paul Archambault, 'The Analogy of the "Body" in Renaissance Political Literature', *Bibliothèque d'Humanisme et Renaissance* 29 (1967), pp. 21–63; Ernst Kantorowicz, *The King's Two Bodies* (Princeton, 1957); G. J. Schochet, *Patriarchalism in Political Thought* (Oxford, 1975).

85 On medical policing see R. Palmer, 'The Church, Leprosy and Plague in Medieval and Early Modern Europe', in Shiels, *Church and Healing*, pp. 79–100; A. W. Russell (ed.), *The Town and State Physician in Europe from the Middle Ages to the Enlightenment* (Wolfenbüttel, 1981); D. Armstrong, *Political Anatomy of the Body: Medical Knowledge in Britain in the Twentieth Century* (Cambridge, 1983).

86 On women and medical power see Roy Porter, 'A Touch of Danger: The Man-midwife as Sexual Predator', in G. S. Rousseau and Roy Porter (eds.), *Sexual Underworlds of the Enlightenment* (Manchester, 1987); J. N. Clarke, 'Sexism, Feminism and Medicalism: A Decade Review of Literature on Gender and Illness', *Sociology of Health and Illness* 5 (1983), pp. 62–82; I. K. Zola, 'Medicine as an Institution of Social Control', *Sociological Review* 20 (1972), pp. 487–504; B. B. Schnorrenberg, 'Is Childbirth any Place for a Woman? The Decline of Midwifery in Eighteenth Century England', *Studies in Eighteenth Century Culture* 10 (1981), pp. 393–408.

87 For some broader perspectives on eating see P. Pullar, *Consuming Passions: Being an Historic Inquiry into Certain English Appetites* (Boston, Mass., 1970); B. S. Turner, 'The Government of the Body: Medical Regimens and the Rationalization of Diet', *British Journal of Sociology* 33 (1982), pp. 254–69; idem, 'The Discourse of Diet', *Theory, Culture and Society* 1 (1982), 23–32. On body decoration see R. Brain, *The Decorated Body* (London, 1979). There are illuminating comments in John O'Neill, *Five Bodies: the Human Shape of Modern Society* (Ithaca, 1985).

11

History of Events and the Revival of Narrative

Peter Burke

Narrative versus Structure

Like history, historiography seems to repeat itself – with variations.[1] Long before our own time, in the age of the Enlightenment, the assumption that written history should be a narrative of events was under already attack. The attackers included Voltaire and the Scottish social theorist John Millar, who wrote of the 'surface of events which engages the attention of the vulgar historian'. From this point of view, the so-called 'Copernican Revolution' in historiography led by Leopold von Ranke in the early nineteenth century looks rather more like a counter-revolution, in the sense that it brought events back to the centre of the stage.[2]

A second attack on the history of events was launched in the early twentieth century. In Britain, Lewis Namier and R. H. Tawney, who agreed on little else, suggested at much the same time that the historian should analyse structures rather than narrate events. In France, the rejection of what was pejoratively called 'event history' (*histoire événementielle*) in favour of the history of structures was a major plank in the platform of the so-called '*Annales* school', from Lucien Febvre to Fernand Braudel, who regarded events, like Millar, as the surface of the ocean of history, significant only for what they might reveal of the deeper currents.[3] If popular history remained faithful to the narrative tradition, academic history became increasingly concerned with problems and with structures. The French philosopher Paul Ricoeur is surely right to speak of the 'eclipse' of historical narrative in our time.[4]

Ricoeur goes on to argue that all written history, including the so-called 'structural' history associated with Braudel, necessarily takes some kind of narrative form. In a similar way, Jean-François Lyotard has described certain interpretations of history, notably that of the Marxists, as 'grand narratives'.[5] The problem with such characterizations, to my mind at least, is that they dilute the concept of narrative until it is in danger of becoming indistinguishable from description and analysis.

I shall not pursue this argument here, however, preferring to concentrate on the more concrete question of the differences in what one might call the degree of narrativity between some contemporary works of history and others. For some years now there have been signs that historical narrative in a fairly strict sense is making another come-back. Even some of the historians associated with *Annales* have been moving in this direction – Georges Duby, for example, who has published a study of the battle of Bouvines, and Emmanuel Le Roy Ladurie, whose *Carnival* deals with the events which took place in the small town of Romans during 1579 and 1580.[6] The explicit attitude of these two historians is not very far from Braudel's. Duby and Le Roy Ladurie focus on particular events not for their own sake but for what they reveal about the culture in which they took place. All the same, the fact that they devote whole books to particular events suggests a certain distance from Braudel's position, and in any case Le Roy Ladurie has discussed elsewhere the importance of what he calls the 'creative event' (*événement matrice*) which destroys traditional structures and replaces them with new ones.[7]

The new trend, which has begun to affect other disciplines, notably social anthropology, was discussed by the British historian Lawrence Stone in an article on 'The Revival of Narrative' which has attracted much attention.[8] Stone claimed to be doing no more than 'trying to chart observed changes in historical fashion' rather than making value judgements. In this respect, some of the best-known historical works which appeared in the 1980s confirmed his observations. Simon Schama's *Citizens*, for example, a study of the French Revolution published in 1989 and describing itself as a return 'to the form of the nineteenth-century chronicles'.[9]

All the same it is difficult not to sense Stone's regret at what he calls 'the shift . . . from the analytical to the descriptive mode' of historical writing. The title of his article as well as its arguments has been influential. It has contributed to making historical narrative a matter for debate.[10]

More exactly, historical narrative has become a matter for at least two debates, which have been taking place independently, despite the relevance of each to the other. To link the two is a major aim of this chapter.[11] In the first place, there is the well-known and long-standing campaign opposing those who assert, like Braudel, that historians should take structures more seriously than events, and those who continue to believe that the historian's job is to tell a story. In this campaign, both sides are now entrenched in their positions, but each has made some important points at the expense of the other.[12]

On one side, the structural historians have shown that traditional narrative passes over important aspects of the past which it is simply unable to accommodate, from the economic and social framework to the experience and modes of thought of ordinary people.[13] In other words, narrative is no more innocent in historiography than it is in fiction. In the case of a narrative of political events, it is difficult to avoid emphasizing the deeds and decisions of the leaders, which furnish a clear story line, at the expense of the factors which escaped their control. As for collective entities – Germany, the Church, the Conservative Party, the People, and so on – the narrative historian is forced to choose between omitting them altogether or personifying them, and I would agree with Huizinga that personification is a figure of speech which historians should try to avoid.[14] It blurs distinctions between leaders and followers, and encourages literal-minded readers to assume the consensus of groups who were often in conflict.

In the case of military history in particular, John Keegan has pointed out that the traditional battle narrative is misleading in its 'high focus on leadership' and its 'reduction of soldiers to pawns', and needs to be abandoned.[15] The difficulty of doing so may be illustrated by the case of Cornelius Ryan's well-known study of D-Day.[16] Ryan set out to write about the soldier's war rather than that of the general's. His history is an extension of his work as a war correspondent: its sources are mainly oral. His book conveys very well the 'feel' of battle on both sides. It is vivid and dramatic – indeed, like a classical drama, it is organized around the three 'unities' of place (Normandy), time (6 June 1944) and action. On the other hand, the book is fragmented into discrete episodes. The experiences of the different participants do not cohere. The only way to make them cohere seems to be to impose a schema derived from 'above' and thus to return to the war of the generals from which the author was trying to escape. Ryan's book illustrates the problem more clearly than most, but the problem is not his alone. This kind of bias may be inherent in narrative organization.

The supporters of narrative, on the other hand, have pointed out that the analysis of structures is static and so in a sense unhistorical. To take the most famous example of structural history in our time, although Braudel's *Mediterranean* (1949) finds room for events as well as structures, it has often been noted that the author does little to suggest what links there might be between the three time-scales with which he is concerned; the long, the medium and the short term. In any case, Braudel's *Mediterranean* is not an extreme example of structural history.[17] Despite his remarks in the preface about the superficiality of events, he went on to devote several hundred pages to them in the third part of his study. Braudel's followers, however, have tended to shrink his project (and not only in the geographical sense) in the course of imitating it. The now classic format of a regional study in the *Annales* manner includes a division into two parts, *structure* and *conjoncture* (in other words, general trends), with little space for events in the strict sense.

Historians in these two camps, structural and narrative, differ not only in the choice of what they consider significant in the past, but also in their preferred modes of historical explanation. Traditional narrative historians tend – and this is not exactly contingent – to couch their explanations in terms of individual character and intention; explanations of the type 'orders arrived late from Madrid because Philip II could not make up his mind what to do,' in other words, as philosophers would say, 'the window broke because Brown threw a stone at it.' Structural historians, on the other hand, prefer explanations which take the form 'the window broke because the glass was brittle,' or (to quote Braudel's famous example) 'orders arrived late from Madrid because sixteenth-century ships took several weeks to cross the Mediterranean.' As Stone points out, the so-called revival of narrative has a great deal to do with an increasing distrust of the second mode of historical explanation, often criticised as reductionist and determinist. Once again, Schama's recent book makes a good example of the trend. The author explains that he has 'chosen to present these arguments in the form of a narrative' on the grounds that the French Revolution was 'much more the product of human agency than structural conditioning'.[18]

This protracted trench warfare between narrative and structural historians has gone on far too long. Some sense of the price of the conflict, the loss of potential historical understanding which it involves, may be felt by comparing two studies of nineteenth-century India which appeared in 1978 and focus on what used to be called the 'Indian Mutiny' of 1857, and is now known as the 'Great Rebellion'.[19] Christopher Hibbert produced a traditional narrative, set-piece history in the grand manner, with chapters entitled 'Mutiny at Meerut', 'The Mutiny Spreads', 'The Siege of Lucknow', 'The Assault', and so on. His book is colourful, indeed gripping, but it is also superficial in the sense of failing to give the reader much idea of why the events took place (perhaps because it is written from the point of view of the British, who were themselves taken by surprise). On the other hand, Eric Stokes offers a careful analysis of the geography and sociology of the revolt, its regional variations and its local contexts, but draws back from a final synthesis. If one reads the two books one immediately after each other, one may be haunted, as I was, by the ghost of a potential third book, which might integrate narrative and analysis and relate local events more closely to structural changes in society.

It is time to investigate the possibility of a way of escaping this confrontation between narrators and analysts. One might begin by criticizing both sides for a false assumption which they have in common, the assumption that distinguishing events from structures is a simple matter. We tend to use the term 'event' rather loosely to refer not only to happenings which take a few hours, like the battle of Waterloo, but also to occurrences like the French Revolution, a process spread over a number of years. It may be useful to employ the terms 'event' and 'structure' to refer to the two extremes of a whole spectrum of possibilities, but we should not forget the existence of the middle of the spectrum. The reasons for the late arrival of orders from Madrid need not be limited to the structure of communications in the Mediterranean or Philip II's failure to make up his mind on a particular occasion. The king may have been chronically indecisive, and the structure of government by council may have slowed down the decision-making process still further.

It follows from this vagueness of definition that we should do as Mark Phillips has suggested and 'think of the varieties of narrative and non-narrative modes as existing along a continuum'.[20] Nor should we forget to ask about the relation between events and structures. Working in this central area, it may be possible to go beyond the two opposing positions, to reach a synthesis.

Traditional Narrative versus Modern Narrative

To this synthesis, the opinions expressed in the second debate may well have a useful contribution to make. This second debate began in the United States in the 1960s, and it has not yet been taken as seriously as it deserves by historians in other parts of the world, perhaps because it seems 'merely' literary. It is not concerned with the question, whether or not to write narrative, but with the problem of what kind of narrative to write. The film historian Siegfried Kracauer seems to have been the first to suggest that modern fiction, more especially the 'decomposition of temporal continuity' in Joyce, Proust and Virginia Woolf, offers a challenge and an opportunity to historical narrators.[21] A still more clear-cut example of this decomposition, incidentally, is Aldous Huxley's *Eyeless in Gaza* (1936), a novel composed of short dated entries over the period 1902–34 in an order which, whatever its logic, is determinedly non-chronological.

Hayden White attracted more attention than Kracauer did when he accused the historical profession of neglecting the literary insights of its own age (including a sense of discontinuity between events in the outside world and their representation in narrative form) and of continuing to live in the nineteenth century, the great age of literary 'realism'.[22] In similar vein, Lionel Gossman has complained that 'it is not easy for us today to see who is, as a writer, the Joyce or the Kafka of modern historiography.'[23] Perhaps. All the same, the historian Golo Mann seems to have learned something from the narrative practice of his novelist father. It is not entirely fanciful to compare Golo Mann's account of the thoughts of the ageing Wallenstein with the celebrated chapter in *Lotte in Weimar* evoking Goethe's stream of consciousness, apparently an attempt to go one better than Joyce. In his study, which he calls 'an all too true novel', Golo Mann follows the rules of historical evidence and makes it clear that he is presenting a hypothetical reconstruction. Unlike most novelists, he does not claim to read his hero's mind, only his letters.[24]

In contrast to White and Gossman, I am not arguing that historians are obliged to engage in literary experiments simply because they live in the twentieth century, or to imitate particular writers because their techniques are revolutionary. The point of looking for new literary forms is surely the awareness that the old forms are inadequate for one's purposes.

Some innovations are probably best avoided by historians. In this group I would include the invention of someone's stream of consciousness, useful as it might be, for the same reasons that have led historians to reject the famous classical device of the invented speech. Other experiments, however, inspired by a wider range of modern writers than have yet been mentioned, may offer solutions to problems with which historians has long been wrestling, three problems in particular.

In the first place, it might be possible to make civil wars and other conflicts more intelligible by following the model of the novelists who tell their stories from more than one viewpoint. It is odd that this device, so effective in the hands of Huxley, William Faulkner, in *The Sound and the Fury* (1931), and Lawrence Durrell, in *The Alexandria Quartet* (1957–60) – not to mention the epistolary novels of the eighteenth century – has not been taken more seriously by historians, though it might be useful to modify it to deal with collective viewpoints as well as individual ones. Such a device would allow an interpretation of conflict in terms of a conflict of interpretations. To allow the 'varied and opposing voices' of the dead to be heard again, the historian needs, like the novelist, to practice heteroglossia (see above, p. 6).[25]

Curiously enough, just as this essay was going to press, a historical work of this kind made its appearance. Richard Price presents his study of eighteenth-century Surinam in the form of a narrative with four 'voices' (symbolized by four typefaces); that of the black slaves (as transmitted by their descendants, the Saramaka); that of the Dutch administrators; that of the Moravian missionaries; and finally that of the historian himself.[26] The object of the exercise is precisely to show as well as to state the differences in viewpoint between past and present, church and state, black and white, the misunderstandings and the struggle to impose particular definitions of the situation. It will be hard to imitate this *tour de force* of historical reconstruction, but Price deserves to inspire a whole shelf of studies.

In the second place, more and more historians are coming to realize that their work does not reproduce 'what actually happened' so much as represent it from a particular point of view. To communicate this awareness to readers of history, traditional forms of narrative are inadequate. Historical narrators need to find a way of making themselves visible in their narrative, not out of self-indulgence but as a warning to the reader that they are not omniscient or impartial and that other interpretations besides theirs are possible.[27] In a remarkable piece of self-criticism, Golo Mann has argued that a historian needs 'to try to do two different things simultaneously', to 'swim with the stream of events' and to 'analyse these events from the position of a later, better-informed observer', combining the two methods 'so as to yield a semblance of homogeneity without the narrative falling apart'.[28]

Here again Price's new book offers a possible solution to the problem by labelling his own contribution that of one 'voice' among others. Alternative solutions are also worth considering. Literary theorists have lately been discussing the fictional device of 'the unreliable first-person narrator'.[29] Such a device may be of some use to historians too, provided that the unreliability is made manifest. Again, Hayden White has suggested that historical narratives follow four basic plots: comedy, tragedy, satire and romance. Ranke, for example, chose (consciously or unconsciously) to write history 'emplotted as comedy', in other words, following a 'ternary movement . . . from a condition of apparent peace, through the revelation of conflict, to the resolution of the conflict in the establishment of a genuinely peaceful social order'.[30] If the way in which a narrative ends helps determine the reader's interpretation, then it might be worth following the example of certain novelists, such as John Fowles, and providing alternative endings. A narrative history of the First World War, for example, will give one impression if the story ends at Versailles in 1919, another if the narrative is extended to 1933 or 1939. Alternative closures thus make the work more 'open', in the sense of encouraging readers to reach their own conclusions.[31]

In the third place – and this is the main theme of this chapter – a new kind of narrative might cope better than the old with the demands of the structural historians, while giving a better sense of the flow of time than their analyses generally do.

Thickening Narratives

A few years ago, the anthropologist Clifford Geertz coined the term 'thick description' for a technique which interprets an alien culture through the precise and concrete description of particular practices or events, in his case, the description of cock-fights in Bali (cf. chapter 5).[32] Like description, narrative might be characterized as more or less 'thin' or 'thick'. At the thin end of the spectrum we have the bare remark in a volume of annals like the Anglo-Saxon Chronicle that 'In this year Ceolwulf was deprived of his kingdom.' At the other end we find stories (all too rare so far), which have been deliberately constructed to bear a heavy weight of interpretation.

The problem I should like to discuss here is that of making a narrative thick enough to deal not only with the sequence of events and the conscious intentions of the actors in these events, but also with structures – institutions, modes of thought, and so on – whether these structures act as a brake on events or as an accelerator. What would such a narrative be like?

These questions, though concerned with rhetoric, are not themselves rhetorical. It is possible to discuss them on the basis of texts, narratives produced either by novelists or by historians. It is not difficult to find historical novels which grapple with these problems. One might start with *War and Peace*, since Tolstoy may be said to have shared Braudel's view of the futility of events, but in fact many famous novels are concerned with major structural changes in a particular society, viewing them in terms of their impact on the lives of a few individuals. A distinguished example from outside western culture is Shimazaki Toson's *Before the Dawn* (1932–6).[33] The 'dawn' of the title is the modernization (industrialization, westernization) of Japan, and the book deals with the years immediately before and after the imperial restoration of 1868, when it was far from clear which path the country was going to follow. The novel shows in vivid detail how 'The effects of the opening of Japan to the world were making themselves felt in the lives of each individual'.[34] To do this the author chooses an individual, Aoyama Hanzo, who is the keeper of a post-house in a village on the main road between Kyoto and Tokyo. His job keeps Hanzo in touch with events, but he does not merely observe them. He is a member of the National Learning movement, committed to an authentically Japanese solution to Japan's problems. The plot of the novel is to a large extent the story of the impact of social change on an individual and his family, a point emphasized by Toson's interruption of his story from time to time to narrate the main events in Japanese history from 1853 to 1886.

It is likely that historians can learn something from the narrative techniques of such novelists as Tolstoy or Shimazaki Toson, but not enough to solve all their literary problems. Since historians are not free to invent their characters or even the words and thoughts of their characters, they are unlikely to be able to condense the problems of an epoch into a story about a family, as novelists have often done. One might have hoped that the so-called 'non-fiction novel', might have had something to offer historians, from Truman Capote's *In Cold Blood* (1965) to Thomas Keneally's *Schindler's Ark* (1982), which claims 'to use the texture and devices of a novel to tell a true story'. However, these authors do not grapple with the problem of structures. It looks as if historians have to develop their own 'fictional techniques' for their 'factual works'.[35]

Fortunately, the authors of a few recent works of history have also reflected on problems like these and their studies sketch an answer, or more exactly several answers, of which it may be useful to distinguish four. One model is well on the way to becoming fashionable, while the other three are represented by little more than one book each.

The first answer might be described as 'micronarrative' (along the lines of the new term 'microhistory'). It is the telling of a story about ordinary people in their local setting. There is a sense in which this technique is commonplace among historical novelists, and has been since the age of Scott and Manzoni, whose *Betrothed* (1827) was attacked at the time (in the way that history from below and microhistory have been attacked more recently), for choosing as his subject 'the miserable chronicle of an obscure village'.[36]

It was only quite recently, however, that historians adopted the micronarrative. Well-known recent examples include Carlo Cipolla's story of the impact of the plague of 1630 on the city of Prato in Tuscany, and Natalie Davis's tale of Martin Guerre, a sixteenth-century prodigal son who returned to his home in the south of France to find that his place at the farm – and in his wife's bed as well – had been taken by an intruder claiming to be Martin himself.[37]

The reduction in scale does not thicken a narrative by itself. The point is that social historians have turned to narrative as a means of illuminating structures – attitudes to the plague and institutions for fighting it in the case of Carlo Cipolla, the structure of the southern French peasant family in the case of Natalie Davis, and so on. More exactly, what Natalie Davis wanted to do was to describe not so much the structures themselves as 'the peasants' hopes and feelings; the ways in which they experienced the relation between husband and wife, parent and child; the ways in which they experienced the constraints and possibilities in their lives'.[38] The book can be read simply as a good story, and a vivid evocation of a few individuals from the past, but the author does make deliberate and repeated references to the values of the society. Discussing, for example, why Martin's wife Bertrande recognized the intruder as her husband, Davis comments on the status of women in French rural society and on their sense of honour, reconstructing the constraints within which they manoeuvred.

On the other hand, the comments are deliberately unobtrusive. As the author explains, 'I . . . chose to advance my arguments . . . . as much by the ordering of narrative, choice of detail, literary voice and metaphor as by topical analysis.' The goal was that of 'embedding this story in the values and habits of sixteenth-century French village life and law, to use them to help understand central elements in the story and to use the story to comment back on them'.[39] The story of Martin may be regarded as a 'social drama' in the sense in which anthropologists use the term; an event which reveals latent conflicts and thus illuminates social structures.[40]

Micronarrative seems to be here to stay; more and more historians are turning to this form. All the same, it would be a mistake to regard it as a panacea. It does not provide a solution to all the problems outlined earlier, and it generates problems of its own, notably that of linking microhistory to macrohistory, local details to general trends. It is because it tackles this major problem directly that I regard Spence's *Gate of Heavenly Peace* as an exemplary book.

Jonathan Spence is a historian of China who has long been interested in experiments in literary form. One of his first books was a biography of the emperor K'ang-Hsi, or rather a portrait of the emperor – indeed, a kind of self-portrait, an attempt to explore K'ang-Hsi's mind by making a sort of mosaic or montage out of the personal remarks to be found scattered among official documents, arranging them under headings such as 'sons', 'ruling', or 'growing old'. The effect is not unlike a Chinese *Memoirs of Hadrian*. It is difficult to think of a study which better deserves the description 'history from above' than the self-portrait of an emperor, but Spence followed it with a moving essay in history from below. *The Death of Woman Wang* is a piece of microhistory in the manner of Cipolla or Davis, with four stories told, or images depicted, to reveal conditions in Shantung province in the troubled years of the later seventeenth century. More recently, in *The Memory Palace of Matteo Ricci*, Spence organised his account of the famous Jesuit missionary to China around a number of visual images, at the expense of chronological sequence, producing an effect reminiscent of Huxley's *Eyeless in Gaza*.

The Gate of Heavenly Peace, on the other hand, looks more like a piece of conventional history, an account of the origins and development of the Chinese Revolution from 1895 to 1980.[41] Once more, however, the author's interest in biography and in historical snapshots asserts itself and his book is built round a small number of individuals, notably the scholar Kang Youwei, the soldier-academic Shen Congwen and the writers Lu Xun and Ding Ling. These individuals did not play a leading part in the events of the revolution. From this point of view they may be compared with what the Hungarian critic Georg Lukács has called the 'mediocre hero' in the novels of Sir Walter Scott; a hero whose ordinariness allows the reader to see the life and the social conflicts of the time more clearly.[42] In Spence's case the protagonists were selected because, as the author suggests, they 'described their hopes and sorrows with particular sensitivity' and also because their personal experiences 'help to define the nature of the times through which they lived'. They are viewed as passive rather than active. Indeed, the author speaks of 'the intrusions of outside events' on his characters.[43] His concern with different individuals implies an interest in multiple viewpoints or multivocality, but – in contrast to Price's book, discussed above – this multivocality remains below the surface of the story.

Presenting the history of China in this way does raise problems. The cross-cutting from one individual to another risks confusing the reader, and so does the shift back and forth between what might be called 'public' time, the time of events like the Long March or the 1949 Revolution, and the 'private' time of the main characters. On the other hand, Spence does communicate in a vivid and moving way the experience of living (or indeed of failing to live) through these turbulent years. Among his most memorable passages are his account of a child's-eye view of the 1911 revolution, as remembered by Shen Congwen; Lu

Xun's reaction to the massacre of student demonstrators in Beijing in
1926; and the official attacks on Ding Ling in 1957, following the
suppression of the 'Hundred Flowers' Movement.

There may be other ways of relating structure to events more closely
than historians generally do. A possible method is to write history
backwards, as B. H. Sumner did in his *Survey of Russian History*
(organized by topics) or Norman Davies in his recent history of Poland,
Heart of Europe (1984), a narrative which focuses on what the author
calls 'the past in Poland's present'.[44] It begins with 'The Legacy of
Humiliation: Poland since the Second World War' and moves back
through 'The Legacy of Defeat', 'The Legacy of Disenchantment'
(1914–39), 'The Legacy of Spiritual Mastery' (1795–1918), and so on.
On each occasion the author implies that it is impossible to make sense
of the events narrated in one chapter without knowing what preceded
them.

This form of organization has its difficulties, most obviously the
problem that even though the chapters are arranged in reverse order,
each chapter has to be read forwards. The great advantage of the
experiment, on the other hand, is to allow, or even force the reader to
feel the pressure of the past on individuals and groups (the pressure of
structures, or of events which have congealed, or as Ricoeur would say,
'sedimented' into structures). Davies does not exploit this advantage as
much as he might. He does not make any serious effort to relate each
chapter to the one which comes 'after' it. It is difficult to imagine his
backward-walking approach becoming fashionable in the manner of
microhistory. All the same, this is a form of narrative well worth taking
seriously.

A fourth kind of analysis of the relation between structures and
events can be found in the work of an American social anthropologist,
yet it will complete the circle by bringing us back to *Annales*. The
anthropologist is Marshall Sahlins, who works on Hawaii and Fiji, is
extremely interested in modern French thought (from Saussure to
Braudel, from Bourdieu to Lévi-Strauss), but takes the event more
seriously than any of these thinkers do.[45] In his studies of encounters
between cultures in the Pacific, Sahlins makes two different but
complementary points.

In the first place, he suggests that events (notably Cook's arrival in
Hawaii in 1778) 'bear distinctive cultural signatures', that they are
'ordered by culture', in the sense that the concepts and categories of a
particular culture shape the ways in which its members perceive and
interpret whatever happens in their time. The Hawaiians, for example,
perceived Captain Cook as a manifestation of their god Lono because

he was obviously powerful and because he arrived at the time of year associated with appearances of the god. The event can therefore be studied (as Braudel suggested) as a kind of litmus paper which reveals the structures of the culture.

However, Sahlins also argues (contrary to Braudel) that there is a dialectical relationship between events and structures. Categories are put at risk every time they are used to interpret the changing world. In the process of incorporating events, 'the culture is reordered.' The end of the *tabu* system, for example, was one of the structural consequences of contact with the British. So was the rise of intercontinental trade. It is true in more than one sense that Cook did not leave Hawaii as he had found it. Sahlins has told a story with a moral, or perhaps with two morals. The moral for 'structuralists' is that they should recognize the power of events', their place in the process of 'structuration'. Supporters of narrative, on the other hand, are encouraged to examine the relation between events and the culture in which they occur. Sahlins has gone beyond Braudel's famous juxtaposition of events and structures. Indeed, he has virtually resolved, or dissolved, the binary opposition between these two categories.

To sum up. I have tried to argue that historians such as Tawney and Namier, Febvre and Braudel were justified in their rebellion against a traditional form of historical narrative which was ill-suited to the structural history which they considered important. Historical writing was enormously enriched by the expansion of its subject-matter, and by the ideal of 'total history'. However, many scholars now think that historical writing has also been impoverished by the abandonment of narrative, and a search is under way for new forms of narrative which will be appropriate to the new stories historians would like to tell. These new forms include micro-narrative, backward narrative, and stories which move back and forth between public and private worlds or present the same events from multiple points of view.

If they are looking for models of narratives which juxtapose the structures of ordinary life to extraordinary events, and the view from below to the view from above, historians might be well advised to turn to twentieth-century fiction, including the cinema (the films of Kurosawa, for example, or Pontecorvo, or Jancsó). It may be significant that one of the most interesting discussions of historical narrative is the work of a historian of the cinema (the piece by Kracauer, already cited). The device of multiple viewpoints is central to Kurosawa's *Rashomon*.[46] It is implicit in Jancsó's *The Red and the White*, a narrative of the Russian civil war in which the two sides take turns to capture the same village.

As for Pontecorvo, it might be said that he has made the historical process itself the subject of his films, rather than merely telling a story about individuals in historical costume.[47] It is interesting to see that Jonathan Spence uses the language of 'montage', and that *The Return of Martin Guerre* appeared more or less simultaneously as history and as film, after Natalie Davis and Daniel Vigne worked together on the subject.[48] Flashbacks, cross-cutting, and the alternation of scene and story; these are cinematic (or indeed literary) techniques which may be used in a superficial way, to dazzle rather than to illuminate, but they may also help historians in their difficult task of revealing the relationship between events and structures and presenting multiple viewpoints. Developments of this kind, if they continue, may have a claim to be regarded as no mere 'revival' of narrative, as Stone called it, but as a form of regeneration.

NOTES

1 This paper originated as a lecture and the present version owes a great deal to the comments of various listeners, from Cambridge to Campinas and from Tel Aviv to Tokyo. My particular thanks to Carlo Ginzburg, Michael Holly, Ian Kershaw, Dominick LaCapra and Mark Phillips.

2 I try to support this argument in 'Ranke the Reactionary', *Syracuse Scholar* 9 (1988), pp. 25–30.

3 F. Braudel, *The Mediterranean*, 2nd ed. rev., tr. S. Reynolds (London, 1972–3), preface.

4 P. Ricoeur, *Time and Narrative*, tr. K. McLaughlin and D. Dellauer (3 vols, Chicago, 1984–8) 1, pp. 138ff.

5 J.-F. Lyotard, *La condition post-moderne* (Paris, 1979); *The Post-Modern Condition*, tr. C. Bennington and B. Macrumi (Manchester, 1984).

6 G. Duby, *The Legend of Bouvines*, tr. C. Tihanyi (Cambridge, 1990); E. Le Roy Ladurie, *Carnival*, tr. M. Fenney (London, 1980).

7 E. Le Roy Ladurie, 'Event and Long-Term in Social History' tr. B. and S. Reynolds in his *Territory of the Historian* (Hassocks, 1979), pp. 111–32.

8 L. Stone, 'The Revival of Narrative', *Past and Present* 85 (1979), pp. 3–24; cf. E. J. Hobsbawm, 'Some Comments', *Past and Present* 86 (1980), pp. 3–8. Cf. J. Boon, *The Anthropological Romance of Bali* (Cambridge, 1977) and E. M. Bruner, 'Ethnography as Narrative' in *The Anthropology of Experience*, ed. V. Turner and E. Bruner (Urbana and Chicago 1986), chapter 6.

9 S. Schama, *Citizens* (New York, 1989), p. xv.

10 Cf. B. Bailyn, 'The Challenge of Modern Historiography', *American Historical Review* 87 (1982), pp. 1–24.

11 Cf. Ricoeur; M. Phillips, 'On Historiography and Narrative', *University of*

Toronto Quarterly 53 (1983–4), pp. 149–65; and H. Kellner, *Language and Historical Representation* (Madison, 1989), esp. chapter 12.

12 For a discussion from different points of view see *Theorie und Erzählung in der Geschichte*, ed. J. Kocka and T. Nipperdey (Munich, 1979).

13 The last point is well made in E. Auerbach, *Mimesis*, tr. W. R. Trask (Princeton, 1953), chapters 2 and 3 (discussing Tacitus and Ammianus Marcellinus).

14 J. Huizinga, 'Two Wrestlers with the Angel' in his *Men and Ideas*, tr. J. S. Holmes and H. van Marle (London, 1960). Contrast the defence of personification in Kellner (esp. chapter 5 on Michelet).

15 J. Keegan, *The Face of Battle* (1976: Harmondsworth, 1978 ed.) pp. 61ff.

16 C. Ryan, *The Longest Day* (London, 1959).

17 Ricoeur (1983) goes so far as to claim that it is a historical narrative with a 'quasi-plot' (pp. 298ff).

18 Schama (1989), p. xv.

19 C. Hibbert, *The Great Mutiny* (London, 1978); E. Stokes, *The Peasant and the Raj* (Cambridge, 1978).

20 Phillips, 'On Historiography' (1983–4), p. 157.

21 S. Kracauer, *History: the Last Things before the Last* (New York, 1969), pp. 178ff.

22 H. V. White, 'The Burden of History', *History and Theory* 5 (1966), reprinted in his *Tropics of Discourse* (Baltimore, 1983), pp. 27–50. For a philosophical defence of the continuity between narratives and the events they relate, see D. Carr, 'Narrative and the Real World: an Argument for Continuity' *History and Theory* 25 (1986), pp. 117–31.

23 L. Gossman, 'History and Literature' in *The Writing of History*, ed. R. H. Canary and H. Kozicki (Madison, 1978), pp. 3–39.

24 G. Mann, *Wallenstein* (Frankfurt, 1971), pp. 984ff.; 993ff.; T. Mann, *Lotte in Weimar* (1939), chapter 7. Cf. G. Mann, 'Plädoyer für die historische Erzählung' in Kocka and Nipperdey (1979), pp. 40–56, especially his claim that historical narrative does not exclude awareness of theory.

25 Cf. G. Wilson, 'Plots and Motives in Japan's Meiji Restoration', *Comparative Studies in Society and History* 25 (1983), pp. 407–27 which makes use of the terminology of Hayden White but is essentially concerned with the multiplicity of actors' viewpoints. N. Hampson, *The Life and Opinions of Maximilian Robespierre* (London, 1976) offers a dialogue between diverse modern interpretations of the French Revolution.

26 R. Price, *Alabi's World* (Baltimore, 1990).

27 The problem was already discussed by Thierry and Michelet. See G. Pomata, 'Overt and Covert Narrators in Nineteenth-Century Historiography', *History Workshop* 27 (1989), pp. 1–17.

28 Foreword to the English translation of his *Wallenstein* by C. Kessler (London, 1976). Mann confesses that 'the first approach preponderates' in his own book. Another good example of what Mann advocates can be found in T. H. Breen, *Imagining the Past: East Hampton Histories* (Reading, Mass., 1989).

29 W. Riggan, *Picaros, Madmen, Naifs and Clowns: the Unreliable First-Person Narrator* (Norman, 1981).

30 H. White, *Metahistory* (Baltimore, 1973), pp. 176ff.

31 Cf. M. Torgovnick, *Closure in the Novel* (Princeton, 1981), and U. Eco, 'The Poetics of the Open Work' in his *The Role of the Reader* (London, 1981), chapter 1. A move in the direction of a more open historical narrative is predicted by Phillips, 'On Historiography' (p. 153).

32 C. Geertz, 'Thick Description: Towards an Interpretative Theory of Culture', and 'Deep Play: Notes on the Balinese Cockfight' in *The Interpretation of Cultures* (New York, 1973).

33 Shimazaki Toson, *Before the Dawn* (Honolulu, 1987).

34 Ibid., p. 621.

35 W. R. Siebenschuh, *Fictional Techniques and Factional Works* (1983) discusses how this was done in the past, with special reference to Boswell's life of Johnson. Cf. R. W. Rader, 'Literary Form in Factual Narrative: the Example of Boswell's Johnson' in *Essays in Eighteenth-Century Biography*, ed. P. B. Daghlian (Bloomington, 1968), pp. 3–42.

36 Quoted in *Letteratura Italiana*, ed. A. Asor Rosa 5 (Turin, 1986), p. 224.

37 C. Cipolla, *Cristofano and the Plague* (London, 1973); N. Z. Davis, *The Return of Martin Guerre* (Cambridge, Mass., 1973).

38 Davis, *Martin Guerre* p. 1.

39 N. Z. Davis, 'On the Lame', *American Historical Review* 93 (1988), pp. 575, 573.

40 On this concept, V. Turner, *Dramas, Fields and Metaphors* (Ithaca, 1974), chapter 1.

41 J. Spence, *Emperor of China* (London, 1974); *The Death of Woman Wang* (London, 1978); *The Gate of Heavenly Peace* (London, 1982); *The Memory Palace of Matteo Ricci* (London, 1985).

42 G. Lukács, *The Historical Novel*, tr. H. and S. Mitchell (London, 1962), pp. 30ff.

43 Spence (1982), p. xiii.

44 N. Davies, *Heart of Europe: a Short History of Poland* (Oxford, 1984).

45 M. Sahlins, *Historical Metaphors and Mythical Realities* (Ann Arbor, 1981) and *Islands of History* (Chicago, 1985). Cf. P. Burke, 'Les îles anthropologiques et le territoire de l'historien', in *Philosophie et histoire*, ed. C. Descamps (Paris, 1987), pp. 49–66.

46 The original story, by Akutagawa, did not adopt this device.

47 G. Pontecorvo, *La battaglia di Algeri* (1966); *Queimada* (1969).

48 N. Z. Davis, J.-C. Carrière, D. Vigne, *Le retour de Martin Guerre* (Paris, 1982).

Index